San Diego
LEGENDS

FOR WAYNE~

ENJOY!!

San Diego LEGENDS

Second Edition

Written by
Jack Scheffler Innis

Sunbelt Publications
San Diego, California

San Diego Legends, 2nd Edition
Sunbelt Publications, Inc. Copyright © 2004 by the author
All rights reserved. Second edition 2015

Edited by Francine Phillips
Cover and book design by Leah Cooper
Project management by Deborah Young
Printed in the United States of America

No part of this book may be reproduced in any form without permission from
the publisher. Please direct comments and inquiries to:

Sunbelt Publications, Inc. P.O. Box 191126
San Diego, CA 92159-1126
(619) 258-4911, fax: (619) 258-4916
www.sunbeltpub.com

18 17 16 15   4 3 2 1

"Adventures in the Natural History and Cultural Heritage of the Californias" A
Series Edited by Lowell Lindsay

Library of Congress Cataloging-in-Publications Data

Innis, Jack Scheffler, 1951-
  San Diego legends : the events, people, and places that made history /
written by Jack Scheffler Innis. – Second edition.
     pages cm.
  Includes bibliographical references and index.
  ISBN 978-1-941384-01-5 (pbk. : alk. paper) 1. Legends–California–San
Diego. 2. San Diego (Calif.)–History. I. Title.
  F869.S22I56 2014
  979.4'985–dc23
                              2014015195

Cover illustration: "The Landing of Juan Rodriguez Cabrillo's Expedition at
San Miguel" courtesy of National Park Service. Artist Richard Schlect.

Cover photos (left to right): Villa Montezuma, Library of Congress; Wyatt
Earp, Gaslamp Books/Museum; Saint Didicus, author; San Diego skyline,
Rowell Design/San Diego Harbor Excursions.

All photos by Jack Innis unless otherwise credited

Table of Contents

vi

Acknowledgments

So many people influenced this second edition of *San Diego Legends* that it would be impossible to mention them all. But I must pay special tribute to a resource unavailable to me when I first began hunting legends for this book's first edition in 2004. This resource comprises all of the wonderful individuals who, over the course of the past 10 years, have taken the time to share with me their stories and legends of San Diego's past.

Whether contacted during public appearances (more than 100, thank you San Diego!), via letter, e-mail, or through my website www.JackInnis.com, I never tire of hearing the words, "Say Jack, have you heard about the...?"

I thank San Diego's city and county libraries for acting as repositories for our region's history. I would be remiss to not express gratitude to generations of writers who previously chronicled San Diego history in newspapers, magazines, books, and personal writings. Much of San Diego's history would have been lost to antiquity without their work and it is impossible for me to conduct any research whatsoever without feeling that I am figuratively standing on their shoulders.

Special thanks also go to Sunbelt publisher Diana Lindsay for her help and encouragement in shaping *San Diego Legends, Second Edition*. A tip of the hat also goes to good friends Karen Clark and Mike Rivkin for their contributions.

Last but not least, I thank my wonderful wife Michelle for her support and understanding. It's not always easy being married to a writer!

Preface

$\sim$

My first opportunity to act as a San Diego's Legend Hunter came in 1999 when a local newspaper asked me to write the conventional history of Point Loma for a magazine-like feature.

Scant space was allotted in which to condense hundreds of years of history, so with the blessings of my editor and publisher, I covered the "nuts and bolts" of Point Loma's past in a timeline and used the remaining space to tell some of the legends from that community's past. Readers responded very positively and I vowed to someday write a book of legends that would encompass all of San Diego County, from early times to near-present. These stories found a home with Sunbelt Publications and the very first edition of *San Diego Legends* was born in 2004.

Over the past 10 years, thanks in a large part to those who have personally shared with me colorful stories of events, people, and places that made history, I have amassed even more San Diego legends. These have been added to the original collection to bring to you three new sections containing dozens of new stories. So along with stalwarts such as *The Nudist Invasion of 1935* at Balboa Park during the California Pacific Exposition, you'll find the story of *The Torrey Pines Hermit*, a religious artist who lived secretly in a hand-dug cave in the state park between 1971 and 1990. In addition to the 1888 *Subterranean Cavern Hoax* that had San Diegans believing an ancient alien cavern existed beneath the bed of San Diego Bay, you'll read the true story, *Abalonia: Island/Nation Sinks off San Diego*, about a group of men who tried to grow an island and start a new nation one hundred miles off the San Diego coast.

San Diego Legends, Second Edition (now more than 100 stories!) offers more than mere entertainment. The stories within these pages serve as strong threads to the weave of our society. They provide us with unique insight into our cultural heritage and — since these pages contain factual accounts of San Diego's past — help make mainstream history more accessible.

So find a comfortable chair, kick off your shoes, and prepare yourself for hours of entertainment. I guarantee you'll smile — and come away with a better understanding of our great city.

SECTION I

Remarkable Characters in San Diego's Past

Before completion of the Transcontinental Railroad in 1869, crossing the continent to San Diego took months: either on foot, on horseback, riding in a wagon train, or by sailing around Cape Horn. Whether travelling by land or sea, danger was ever present and the risks were high. So it follows that the first pioneers to arrive in San Diego were rugged, hearty, self-reliant, and often a bit unusual in character.

Although a century of transportation gains has bridged the gap between then and now, San Diego still attracts characters who seem "slightly out of the ordinary."

Father Junípero Serra
San Diego's First Radical

Father Junípero Serra is widely recognized as having founded the city of San Diego in 1769 during a ceremony at Mission San Diego de Alcalá. But few know the fervor with which the 5-foot, 2-inch, 110-pound friar approached his duties as clergyman and mission founder. By present-day standards many would consider Father Serra a radical.

Serra was born to peasant parents on the island of Majorca in 1730. At an early age, he was sent to live with a religious hermit and entered the Franciscan order as a lay friar at 16. The day he took his final vows at age 18, he set aside his given name, Michael Joseph, and took the name Junípero, the name of a companion of Saint Francis. The saint once said about his companion, "Would that I had a whole forest of such Junipers!" Serra worked hard to become worthy of that name.

While the young lay friar excelled at nearly any task set before him, desire burned within him to travel as a missionary to "New Spain" (Mexico as we now know it) to baptize, convert, and save as many Indians souls as he could. For years Serra petitioned for such duty in vain.

In 1749 Serra succeeded in securing a berth aboard a ship bound for the New World with fellow monks Juan Crespí and Francisco Palóu. Although the three-month voyage across the Atlantic and around the oft-deadly Cape Horn was terrifying, Serra never succumbed to the fears of starvation, sickness, and shipwreck, "remembering the end for which they had come," he said, according to his biography *The Life and Times of Junípero Serra.*

For the next 19 years, Serra labored in Mexico, but held onto his dream to save "heathen" Indians in the wilderness of the New World's western shores.

After Spain's 1767 suppression of the Jesuit Order, Franciscan Serra finally received orders to create and oversee a string of missions in Alta California (now California).

According to the biography, the 56-year-old friar was so taken with news of his appointment he was, "unable to speak a single word for tears."

Serra's first task was to establish at least two missions: one each at the ports of San Diego and Monterey. A third would likely be constructed geographically between the first two. Others would be built as Serra saw fit.

The initial expedition was divided into groups comprising two ships and two overland expeditions. For navigation, all groups had copies of charts from Sebastián Vizcaíno's 1602 exploration of the West Coast of North America — the most up-to-date chart then available.

Despite severe inflammation to one of his legs reportedly caused by numerous insect bites, Serra stubbornly decided to travel overland and set out on March 28, 1769, from Loreto, Baja California, with a few soldiers and scant provisions. His was the last group to begin the journey. The first overland group had left a few weeks earlier from Velicatá, Baja California, and the ships *San Carlos* and *San Antonio* had sailed from the port of La Paz on January 9 and February 15, respectively.

The overland march was tough. There were no roads or well-defined trails: just miles of rock-strewn, cactus-covered desert. Indian guides hired in Mexico abandoned the expedition. Without guides, the entire party often waited for days while scouts went ahead to find the way.

At one point, Serra's leg became so inflamed that he could not stand, sit, or sleep. Yet he refused to be carried in a litter. Members of his party thought he would not survive. In exasperation, Serra summoned the mule driver. The conversation was journalized:

"Son, do you not know some remedy for this sore on my leg?"

"Father," replied the mule driver, "what remedy can I know? I have only cured beasts."

"Then consider me a beast…and give me the same treatment you would apply to a beast."

The mule driver mixed a concoction of herbs in hot tallow and applied it to Serra's wound. The ointment so reduced the inflammation that Serra slept through the night, awoke before dawn to say mass, and was able to continue his journey in relative comfort.

On July 1, 1769, from a bluff several miles southeast of San Diego Bay, Serra and his party finally spotted the harbor. Both of the expedition's ships lay at anchor. When they arrived hours later, the first overland party rushed to greet them.

Any elation they felt was short-lived.

The sea voyage had been horrible. More than a third of the 300 soldiers and ship's crew had died due to scurvy, dysentery, hunger, or eating unhealthy food. With many men dying, Serra had to immediately contend with triage rather than establish the mission. To make matters worse, a large contingent of soldiers soon left in search of Monterey Bay, leaving only a skeleton crew to provide security for the missionaries.

Finally on July 16, a cross was erected facing the harbor. Next to it, the monks constructed a crude booth of branches and reeds. The first mass was celebrated and, according to an old manuscript, the pilgrims "supplied the want of an organ by discharging firearms, (and substituting) smoke of muskets for incense."

San Diego was officially founded.

With a semblance of a mission in place, Father Serra could at last fulfill his burning, lifelong desire to begin baptizing Indians, or so it seemed.

Soon after the mission's founding, Serra prevailed upon the Indians to allow him to baptize a baby. The ceremony went smoothly, according to *The Life and Times of Junípero Serra.* But when Serra raised his hand to sprinkle the babe's face with water, the parents panicked and snatched the child from Serra's arms and ran off.

Statues of Father Junípero Serra adorn many California public places. This monument, in San Francisco's Golden Gate Park, shows Serra seemingly reaching out to California. *Photo courtesy Golden Gate Park.*

Devastated, Serra broke into tears. This was to have been San Diego's first baptism and the missionary felt that some personal inadequacy had made him unworthy, and that he had somehow caused the baptism to fail.

It is said that until the day Serra died, he could not relate that story without tears running down his face, thinking of the soul he had lost. Such was the emotion that gripped Serra's spirit.

As a preacher, the Franciscan often seemed beside himself, bursting with emotional fervor and gesticulating wildly. It was not uncommon for him to bare his chest and beat himself with rocks and sticks to demonstrate the evils that await sinners in hell.

According to the biography, once while preaching a fiery sermon in Mexico, Serra stopped to produce a chain. He bared his chest and shoulders and began to scourge himself in such a forceful manner that the congregation began weeping aloud. One man became so overwrought that he climbed Serra's pulpit, took the chain from his hands, and began to imitate Serra saying, "I am the sinner who is ungrateful to God who ought to do penance for my many sins, and not the Father who is a saint."

The man beat himself until he collapsed. He was given the sacraments of the dying by Serra and later passed away.

After establishing San Diego's Mission de Alcalá, Serra continued northward to found more missions in California. His fervor was again evidenced while exploring near Monterey where he founded San Antonio Mission.

When he and his traveling companion crested an oak-shaded rise, they laid their eyes on a beautiful valley with a flowing river. According to the biography, Serra ordered the soldiers and mule train to stop.

He unpacked the bells, tied them to a oak limb, and began ringing with all his might crying, "Hear, hear, O ye Gentiles! Come to the Holy Church! Come to the faith of Jesus Christ!"

When someone in his traveling party mentioned that there was not a human being for miles around, Serra rang the bells even harder, saying, "Let me alone. Let me unburden my heart!"

Serra kept on ringing the bells until a curious Indian appeared. That Indian became the first to witness the founding of a mission.

Serra died at his Mission San Carlos headquarters on August 28, 1784 uttering these last words: "I feel better now, I will rest."

Vessels in port at Monterey fired a 101-gun salute and the presidio cannons answered the salvo.

It is said that soldiers could not hold back the congregation of Indians who wanted to catch one last glimpse or to touch Serra before his burial.

Pedro Fages
A Thorn in Father Serra's Side

Few men tormented San Diego's founding Father, Junípero Serra, as did Don Pedro Fages.

A military leader accompanying the Franciscans, Fages (pronounced Fah-hays) was charged with providing security for the fledgling California missions. But professional and personal friction between Fages and Serra grew so chronic that at one point the Franciscan rode a mule from San Diego to Mexico City to lodge a formal complaint.

Years later, in an ironic twist of fate, Fages was appointed governor of California.

As a young officer, Fages arrived in New Spain (now Mexico) in 1767 and quickly curried the favor of those in command. He gained the rank of captain and was placed in charge of security to help Father Serra establish a chain of missions in Alta California.

Fages sailed aboard the *San Carlos* and was among the first group to arrive in San Diego on April 11, 1769. But soon after Serra arrived on July 1, problems — attributed both to Fages' inexperience and quirky personality and Serra's zeal and stubbornness — began to develop between the two. A rift developed between the two men so severe that the San Diego Mission de Alcalá was nearly abandoned.

Friction between Fages and Father Serra most likely began shortly after their arrival in San Diego. While the expedition's written orders included specific instructions about guarding the missionaries, another more general mandate included locating Monterey Bay, a beautiful and well-protected harbor noted on the expedition's only map, an ancient chart created by Spanish explorer Sebastián Vizcaíno in 1602.

Despite specific orders to guard the missionaries, two weeks after landing in San Diego (and two days before the official founding of the chapel San Diego Mission de Alcalá), Fages and expedition leader Gaspar de Portolá set off with several dozen men to find Monterey Bay. Their journey lasted six months.

Left behind in hastily constructed sagebrush shelters with a handful of sick soldiers atop what is now Presidio Hill, Father Serra's first few months in San Diego were less than heavenly. Almost immediately, local Indians began frequenting the mission and camp, and the padres handed out small gifts as good-will gestures. Soon the Indians grew tired of trinkets and began brazenly stealing, insolently mimicking the retort of firearms meant to frighten them away.

Then, on August 15, the Indians attacked the sagebrush compound. Arrows rained in from all directions and the soldiers responded with gunfire. Father Serra knelt in his hut and prayed: a small statue of the Virgin Mary in one hand and a crucifix in the other. "I believed that with such defensive armor I was in good hands," he wrote.

Serra's servant, José Maria Vegerano, ran into Serra's hut, an arrow protruding from his neck and said, "Father, absolve me, for the Indians have killed me." He collapsed on the floor and died at Serra's feet.

Several Indians also died, and both sides suffered casualties during that and another attack. Months later, in late-January 1770, Fages and Portolá returned from their scouting expedition. They reported that they had not found Monterey (actually they had, but didn't recognized it from Vizcaíno's description), but kept pressing north until they discovered massive San Francisco Bay.

Perhaps Serra forgave the young officer for not anticipating that problems might arise when he left only a skeleton force to guard San Diego. Perhaps he understood Fages hadn't thought far enough in advance to realize that since the expedition left without helping the missionaries construct buildings, plant crops, and raise livestock, the mission would be hard pressed to provide food and housing when the travel-weary wanderers returned.

But considering the events that transpired when the man in charge of mission security left for six months, Serra should be forgiven for wryly remarking that, "Returning from such a long journey without finding Monterey was like coming from Rome without seeing the Pope!"

Another incident likely helped make the weeks following Fages' return to San Diego awkward ones. A supply ship sent from Lower California was months overdue. Supplies in San Diego had almost run out.

A decision had to be reached.

Expedition leaders informed Serra that if the supply ship did not arrive by March 20 — the day of the feast of St. Joseph, patron saint of the mission-founding expedition — the entire expedition would abandon San Diego and head back to Mexico the next morning.

The idea of abandoning San Diego, and by extension plans to establish more missions, was absolutely unacceptable to Serra. He and Father Crespí vowed to remain even without support of the troops. "If we see that the foodstuffs are running low and hope is waning, I shall remain here with (Father Crespí) alone to hold out to the very last."

Late in the afternoon of the feast of St. Joseph, lookouts spotted a set of white sails on the horizon. The relief ship had arrived.

But the arrival of the relief ship did not relieve growing tensions between Fages and Serra. The men began to squabble on a long list of subjects including division of rations between friars and soldiers, whether the friars should obey the soldiers, whether the soldiers should work for the friars, and whether the friars should discipline Indians without the soldiers' consent.

Serra complained that Fages had misappropriated 40 lanterns meant for the mission. Fages complained that the church had placed a cross, the cemetery, and one grave slightly off a prescribed mathematical line that ran through the presidio. Both men squabbled about inequitable distribution of cattle, mules, horses, saddles, men, and material arriving from Mexico City.

Although the men continued to work hand-in-hand to establish missions, at one point their interpersonal bickering grew so severe that they only communicated with one another by letter, despite that they both lived in San Diego. The situation further devolved when both men began sending letters of complaint to higher authorities.

Serra wrote complaining that Fages was holding him back from establishing missions at a quicker pace. For instance, Fages had vigorously complained that too many Indians were being baptized in San Diego and ordered the friars to hold off until the mission's crops could sustain them all. Serra complained that Fages, who had longstanding problems with deserters, coaxed a friar into helping convince some of them to return. He then broke his word regarding amnesty for the deserters.

At another point in time, Serra wrote, Fages personally chased deserters and had been absent from San Diego for more than a year. Most of Fages' time "chasing deserters" was actually spent exploring the state's uncharted inland areas.

But for some reason, Serra's complaints found their way to a governor in Lower California rather than the viceroy in Mexico City. The governor, in a position similar to and sympathetic with Fages, wrote his own letter to the viceroy blaming the missionaries for the problems.

When Serra got wind of what had happened, he decided to personally travel to Mexico City to deal with the Fages problem once and for all.

In February 1773, Serra arrived in Mexico City to meet with the viceroy. The esteemed padre had a list of 32 points in hand, first and foremost being the "removal, or recall, of the officer Don Pedro Fages from his command."

In relieving Fages of command, the viceroy noted that the "the discord between Fages and the missionaries manifests a deplorable situation and the proximate ruin of the new establishments in California."

Fages' replacement was Capt. Fernando Rivera y Moncada, leader of the first land expedition to reach San Diego in 1769.

But when Rivera attempted to assume command, a now-familiar series of problems arose over paper work including accounting, division of labor, cattle in the hands of soldiers belonging to the missionaries, and horses and cattle claimed by Fages as personal possessions.

Despite delaying tactics Fages eventually returned to Mexico City, certain that his career was in ruins. But for quasi-divine intervention, it would have been.

While the deposed soldier was making his trek south, the viceroy received a letter of support for Fages. The letter stated in part that, "if my loyal services amount to anything in the eyes of army authorities, I grant and relinquish it all, and surrender it, in its entirety, in favor, and in behalf, of Don Pedro Fages. He has no knowledge of what I am doing, nor has he prompted me to take this line of action."

Beneath the glowing review was the signature of Father Junípero Serra, who evidently felt pangs of remorse for his actions in having Fages removed from his post.

Rather than facing disciplinary measures, Fages was welcomed and told to take whatever time he needed to write up an account of his years in Alta California. A year later, the soldier presented his report.

Fages' account was the first real insight officials had into the hardships and sacrifices made by those in the Alta California garrisons. Authorities were so moved that they boosted those soldiers' pay by a few pesos a month and bestowed upon Fages a 1,500-peso bonus.

Fages spent a few months on routine assignment, then was called back to New Spain's northern border to help fight Apache Indians and other hostile tribes.

In 1781 he led a counter-assault to the Yuma Indians' destruction of Spanish settlements along the Colorado River. Unbeknownst to Fages, events were unfolding that would make him governor of California.

Officials in Mexico City had already petitioned the King of Spain to advance two other officers to two positions, one of which was governor of Alta California. Just about the time the advancements were made official, a serving governor in New Spain defied specific orders and lost a major battle with the Apache Indians. Officials quickly replaced that man with one of the officers on the short list, and named Fages temporary governor of California. The king subsequently ratified the change as permanent and Fages remained head of state from 1782 to 1791.

Today, Fages' name appears on numerous state historical markers from the Arizona/California/Mexico border to the San Francisco Bay area.

Those markers mainly chronicle Fages explorations while he was supposedly "chasing deserters."

The Legend of La Loma
Young Girl Washes Up on Beach

According to an old legend, a young girl with golden hair was found shipwrecked on a deserted beach here in the late 1700s or early 1800s. San Diego residents, likely Spanish depending on the exact date of the event, were bedazzled by her blonde locks and called her La Loma.

The tale of her discovery, subsequent upbringing, and tragic demise is probably based in fact. While it is doubtful that Point Loma was named after La Loma, as some claim, her legend almost certainly inspired Bayard Taylor's poem, "The Fight of Paso del Mar," published in Boston in 1865.

La Loma's story begins one winter night when fishermen living in crude huts along the fringe of the bay thought they heard the cries of a child across the water on Coronado, which at that time was an undeveloped sandy peninsula, home to only jackrabbits and coyotes. While most fishermen thought the cries were just eerie howls of coyotes, which sound very human-like at times, one fisherman insisted the cries were human and rowed across the channel.

After a long search, the fisherman discovered a lone human figure — a child — huddled and shivering on the beach. He quickly scooped her up and rowed her back to the fish camp at Ballast Point where his wife was able to revive her.

Word of the unusual event spread throughout the night. In the morning, a large crowd gathered around the fisherman's hut, clamoring to catch a glimpse of the young girl. They were said to be awestruck by the radiant locks of her golden-blonde hair, quite a rarity in the sleepy little pueblo of San Diego.

Attempts to find out what had happened to the girl were unsuccessful because the girl spoke no Spanish. Instead, she uttered unintelligible words in a foreign tongue. A wagon was dispatched to what is now Old Town and an officer rode back to investigate. Although the officer could not understand her, he recognized the language she was speaking: Russian. There were Russian fur traders in town.

He brought the girl back with him and, with the help of one Russian trader, found out what had happened.

The young girl had been aboard a ship with her parents when a sudden and violent storm capsized the vessel. The girl and her parents clung to the pieces of wreckage long enough to be washed ashore. When asked where her parents were, the young girl replied, "Oh, they're just sleeping on the beach."

Searchers soon found the bodies of her parents.

The blonde girl was placed in the care of the pueblo's schoolteacher, and quickly learned her new language, Spanish.

Because her hair shone so vigorously, she was called La Loma, *the light*, perhaps in reference to a long-used beacon atop the promontory.

La Loma grew up to be a beautiful girl, and when she came of age, attracted many suitors. Among her admirers were two young men of very different natures. One was said to be quite refined, most likely the son of a military officer. He was kind and gentle, but timid in his ways.

The other suitor was cut from coarser fabric. He was the son of a laborer and worked in the fields. He was possessed with a fiery temper, but when it came to expressing his love for La Loma, he was excelled by none.

One day, the field worker persuaded La Loma to accompany him on a daylong outing to the tip of the peninsula. The footpath followed the cliffs along the ocean side of the promontory. At one spot along the trail the footpath became very narrow, with high boulders on one side and a steep drop-off into the ocean on the other.

Traversing that narrow spot, called Paso del Mar, with waves crashing on the rocks below, was a very dangerous feat.

No one knows why; maybe it was because he was rebuffed for unwanted advances, perhaps it was due to a rejected marriage proposal, but on that fateful day the field worker stabbed La Loma with his knife and killed her.

As he was walking back toward town on the path, he encountered the officer's son at Paso del Mar. The officer's son had no idea what had happened, but the field worker panicked. In the ensuing struggle, both men fell to their deaths on the jagged rocks below the pass.

Very little exists today to document this fantastic story save one tantalizing tidbit. A reporter from the East Coast came through San Diego in the mid-1800s and heard about the story. He is said to have collected early written accounts of the event and promised that immediately upon his return to the East Coast he would write an article about La Loma. That article was never published.

Whether based in reality or fantasy, the legend of La Loma exists in San Diego lore today. It almost certainly inspired the following poem, written by Bayard Taylor and published by Ticknor & Friends in 1865 in Boston. Bayard's poem features a shepherd and a fisherman (pescador):

The Fight of Paso del Mar

Gusty and raw was the morning,
　　A fog hung over the seas,
And its gray skirts, rolling inland,
　　Were torn by the mountain trees;

No sound was heard but the dashing
　　Of waves on the sandy bar,
When Pablo of San Diego
　　Rode down to the Paso del Mar

The pescador, out in his shallop,
　　Gathering his harvest so wide
Sees the dim bulk of the headland
　　Loom over the waste of the tide;
He sees, like a white thread, the pathway
　　Wind round on the terrible wall,
Where the faint, moving speck of the rider
　　Seems hovering close to its fall.

Stout Pablo of San Diego
　　Rode down from the hills behind;
With the bells on his gray mule tinkling
　　He sang through the fog and the wind.
The Fight of Paso del Mar

Under his thick, misted eyebrows
　　Twinkled his eye like a star,
And fiercer he sang as the sea-winds
　　Drove cold on the Paso del Mar.

Now Bernal, the herdsman of Chino,
　　Had traveled the shore since dawn,
Leaving the rancho behind him—
　　Good reason he had to be gone!
The blood was still red on his dagger,
　　The fury was hot in his brain,
And the chill, driving scud of the breakers
　　Beat thick on his forehead in vain.

(continued)

With his poncho wrapped gloomily round him,
    He mounted the dizzying road,
And the chasms and steeps of the headland
    Were slippery and wet, as he trod:
Wild swept the wind of the ocean,
    Rolling the fog from afar,
When near him a mule-bell came tinkling,
    Midway on the Paso del Mar.

"Back!" shouted Bernal, full fiercely,
    And "Back!" shouted Pablo, in wrath,
As his mule halted, started and shrinking,
    On the perilous line of the path.
The roar of devouring surges
    Came up from the breakers' hoarse war;
And "Back or you perish!" cried Bernal,
    "I turn not on Paso del Mar!"
The gray mule stood firm as the headland:
    He clutched at the jingling rein,
When Pablo rose up in his saddle
    And smote till he dropped it again.
The Fight of Paso del Mar.

A wild oath of passion swore Bernal,
    And he brandished his dagger, still red,
While fiercely stout Pablo leaned forward,
    And fought o'er the trusty mule's head.

They fought till the black wall below them
    Shone red through the misty blast;
Stout Pablo then struck, leaning farther,
    The broad breast of Bernal at last.
And, frenzied with pain, the swart herdsman
    Closed on him with terrible strength,
And jerked him, despite of his struggles,
    Down from the saddle at length.

They grappled with desperate madness,
    On the slippery edge of the wall;
They swayed on the brink, and together
    Reeled out to the rush of the fall.
A cry of the wildest death-anguish
    Rang faint through the mist afar,
And the riderless mule went homeward
    From the fight of Paso del Mar.

Felicita

Angel of the Battle of San Pasqual

Among San Diego County's most beautiful spots, Felicita Park in Escondido also offers a bit of romance. The park is the namesake of Felicita, daughter of Pontho, chief of the San Pasqual Indians.

A legend of romance and unrequited love surrounds Felicita and a man whom she saved, loved, lost, found, and lost again after the bloody Battle of San Pasqual.

Historians agree that the Battle of San Pasqual, fought during the Mexican/American War, was a defeat inflicted upon American troops by Andrés Pico, younger brother of Mexican Governor Pio Pico.

When war broke out with Mexico in 1846, President James Polk ordered Colonel Stephen W. Kearny and his company, the 1st Dragoons, to ride from Fort Leavenworth to help secure California. Along the way, the colonel seized Santa Fe, New Mexico, and was promoted to brigadier general.

Kearny and his 121-man force were met on the outskirts of San Diego by frontiersman Kit Carson, who was in the process of taking a message to Washington from Commodore Robert F. Stockton at San Diego that declared the struggle for California over.

Despite the news, Kearny got wind of a small band of undefeated Mexicans soldiers camped out about six miles distant. Thinking the camp was comprised of ill-trained rebels, Kearny sent out a few scouts to bring information on how he might orchestrate a surprise attack. The scouts were discovered and the element of surprise lost. Despite the fact that his mules and men were exhausted from a 1,700-mile-total march, and that it was cold and raining, Kearny rounded up 50 of his Dragoons and launched a pre-dawn attack in the rain.

In a classic blunder of underestimation rivaling that of General George Custer at the Battle of Little Big Horn, Kearny found himself attacking not a small, weak force of Mexican soldiers, but a highly trained platoon of about 200 Castilian horsemen.

Led by Andrés Pico, the horsemen first lured the soldiers into spreading out, then turned to attack them with lances. Kearny's men tried to outgun the lancers, but discovered that in haste they had not made sure their gunpowder was dry. Their guns would not fire.

Reduced to fighting sword against lance, Kearny lost half of his men and was wounded himself.

The legend of Felicita's love revolves around one wounded soldier. According to a May 1950 account in *The Southern California Rancher,* Felicita told San Pasqual teacher Mrs. Elizabeth Judson Roberts that she had been among a group of Indians who watched the battle unfold. Roberts wrote: "Felicita saw a fight between two horsemen in the brush near the river below. One was a Mexican carrying a long lance; the other an American who seemed only to have a sword for defense."

After a few thrusts and parries, the American's sword broke and the Mexican's lance pierced his side. The American fell off his horse and the Mexican watched him for a while before riding away.

Felicita hurried down the hill and found the American. At first she thought he was dead, but then his eyes opened and he spoke to her. She could not understand his words, but learned by sign language that he wanted water. She filled up his cap at a nearby stream. He drank, but then closed his eyes again.

Remembering the Indian remedy for wounds, Felicita hunted near the river and soon found some large green leaves. Carefully opening the soldier's uniform, she laid the leaves over the bleeding wound, binding them tightly to his body with strips torn from his blanket.

American soldiers defend against charging Mexican forces during the Battle of San Pasqual. *Illustration by Colonel Charles H. Waterhouse, USMCR, Ret., from the Marine Corps Art Collection.*

Felicita ran back up the hill and found her father, who sent a messenger to the American camp to show them where to find the soldier. Felicita and two men went back to the wounded American and made a litter out of willow trees. After a short while, the American soldiers arrived from camp and Felicita heard the soldier's name for the first time, Dick.

Dick smiled and waved at Felicita as the soldiers carried him away. Not long afterward, the war ended and San Diego became part of the United States.

One day, Felicita's father, Chief Pontho, announced that he had selected a husband for her: the son of a chief of a neighboring tribe. To the astonishment of her father and others in her tribes, Felicita refused to marry the man. Although she gave her father no reason for her refusal, she secretly pined for the American soldier, Dick.

Two years later, a company of soldiers arrived in San Pasqual to disinter the bodies of the American soldiers killed and buried in the battle; one of the soldiers in the party was none other than Dick, the soldier whom she had rescued.

Dick immediately recognized Felicita and thanked her profusely for saving his life. Since Felicita had learned English in the intervening years, the pair struck up a conversation. Dick returned to San Diego with his company that day, but made periodic visits to see Felicita.

They decided to marry, and Felicita agreed to live in a small Indian village near San Diego Mission de Alcalá so they could see each other every day.

For the first time since laying eyes on her soldier, Felicita was completely happy. However, a few short months after their marriage complications from Dick's old wound set in. He died, leaving Felicita with a broken heart.

As Felicita told Mrs. Roberts many years later, "Ae-e-e, those were weary days and sad. In dreams my soldier-man would stand near me with a smile in his eyes of blue. Then I would awake in the darkness and stillness. It was more than I could bear.

"I would rush outside and and look up at the stars, shining like spirit eyes from the Land of Death. Then I would search the shadows of the willows where we had walked together. I thought I might see his spirit shining in the darkness for just a moment, but I never saw it."

Felicita ultimately returned to her village at San Pasqual where she lived unmarried until much later in life, when the flames of romance flickered again and she wed an old friend.

The Angel of the Battle of San Pasqual lived to be more than 100 years old.

Joshua Bean
San Diego's First Mayor Murdered

While a little dated for *America's Most Wanted*, the 1852 murder of San Diego's first mayor, Joshua Bean, remains an unsolved mystery to this day.

Bean, brother of notorious Judge Roy Bean, served as the city's last Alcalde (similar to mayor) under Mexican rule before becoming the city's first mayor. In his brief leadership, Bean defrauded the city out of city hall, quit attending council meetings over a pay dispute, and presided over the execution of a popular Indian leader. Any of these maneuvers may have led to his murder.

Oldest of three brothers (Joshua, Roy, and Sam) from a Kentucky family, Joshua Bean enlisted in the Army in 1840 and came out West to participate in the Mexican-American War.

Like his brother Roy, Joshua was no stranger to controversy.

Bean seems to have acquired his initial post as Alcalde through his rank as Army general. But a diary entry by traveling artist H.M.T. Powell offers a glimpse into Bean's character beneath the uniform:

"Left books at the Alcalde's, Mr. Bean. Did not see him, heard he was drunk and asleep in Lt. Couts' room. Everybody gets drunk here."

Among Bean's last acts as Alcalde, prior to his June 1850 mayoral election victory, was to dole out land in the form of land grants. Included in the roster of recipients were himself and his friend Lt. Cave Couts, a mapmaker who certified the grants for Bean.

Records show that property transfers made the day before Bean became mayor included the land beneath city hall. Astute members of the City Council were astounded to find that Bean had deeded himself half the land for $2.50, the equivalent of about $56 in modern spending power. *The other half of City Hall was deeded to Couts. Please see Chapter 7.*

After a brief legal battle, the land and property were returned to the city.

But Bean's character had already lost much of its sheen. After finagling a then-hefty $1,200 a year salary out of the City Council, Bean in a surprise move vetoed the salary ordinance as too low, stating it was in the "best interest of our growing city" to do so.

When the council later declined to consider Bean's request for an even higher salary, he quit attending city functions altogether and resigned in early 1851. He eventually moved to San Gabriel where he opened a grog shop.

Appointed major general in the state militia's southern section by Gov. Peter Burnett, Bean was instructed to round up 60 men and ride to Yuma to retake the Colorado River ferry from 500 angry Yuma Indians. The Indians were upset because outlaw John Glanton and his gang had seized the ferry and attacked them. They had rallied, killed most of the gang, and refused to relinquish control of the Colorado River crossing.

Perhaps Bean didn't appreciate the 60 to 500 odds, so he stayed in his saloon and sent Joseph C. Morehead, the state's quartermaster general, to march against the Indians.

Not surprisingly, Morehead and his 60 men couldn't find the Indians, but instead reportedly beat up and robbed several Mexicans and immigrants they found along the way.

Bean chose to fight the next battle, and led a campaign to quell a San Diego-area revolt that started when bands of already displaced and disenfranchised Indians were added to the tax rolls.

With the help of Cahuilla Chief Juan Antonio, Bean accepted the surrender of revolt-leader Antonio Garra, and later the surrender of Garra's son and several other key players.

Bean headed a military tribunal in Chino that included his brother Roy Bean. The council convicted the younger Garra on Christmas Day, 1851, and executed him five days later.

The elder Garra was brought to San Diego where a trial was held. With Major General Bean presiding and brother Roy Bean sitting as part of the forum, Garra was convicted and sentenced to die before a firing squad on January 10, 1852.

According to written accounts, Garra's last words were: "Gentlemen, I ask your pardon for all my offenses, and expect yours in return."

On the night of November 7, 1852 Joshua Bean, now back in San Gabriel, was riding home alone from an evening of entertainment. Two men stopped him. One held the reins to Bean's horse while the other dragged him from the saddle and stabbed or shot him. Bean died the next day. His murderers were never found.

Joshua's brother Roy Bean later found himself in some sort of trouble in San Gabriel. He fled to San Diego, got into a duel, and shot an innocent bystander. Roy Bean was jailed but escaped by digging his way out. He fled to Texas where he nominated himself judge and became known by many as "The Law West of the Pecos."

Lt. George Horatio Derby

San Diego's First Joker

The army engineer responsible for turning the San Diego River away from San Diego Bay was probably best known in his time for his sense of humor, not his engineering mastery.

From time immemorial, the course of the San Diego River would change at random over its last mile, sometimes dumping into San Diego Bay, sometimes into False Bay (now Mission Bay). *See Chapter 37 on Mission Bay.*

As the Port of San Diego grew during the mid-1800s, authorities feared that the river's mud deposits would completely silt up San Diego Bay and block ships from mooring, thus ruining the economy.

The army called upon Lieutenant George Horatio Derby to survey a site and construct a dyke to force the waters permanently into False Bay. This he did ably.

But among townsfolk, Derby was best known for his witty writings, practical jokes, and wry sense of humor.

According to local lore, the army transferred Lt. Derby to San Diego because his superiors in the Midwest couldn't stand him.

By way of example, when Derby was assigned to survey Alabama's Tombigbee River, the exact words of his instructions told him to, "find out how far up the Tombigbee River runs."

After surveying the river, Derby duly forwarded his written report. The report went into great detail about the river and its topography, but concluded by remarking, "The Tombigbee River does not run up, but down!"

Derby was immediately transferred to survey military roads in the Pacific Northwest. His next report included the following comment: "It rains incessantly twenty-six hours a day for seventeen months of the year."

Secretary of War Jefferson Davis reportedly was not amused. Derby received another quick transfer and found himself at the gates of Fort Yuma, Arizona, about 175 miles east of San Diego. The desert heat did little to cool Derby's wit.

"Fort Yuma was so hot," Derby included in a report, "that when one soldiers died he went to hell and wasn't there one day before he telegraphed for his blankets."

The wisecrack-filled report brought about yet a quick transfer. Derby's next duty station was Sonoma, California. One night at a dance in town, the lieutenant came up with the idea of switching two babies, their toys, and their blankets into each other's basket.

As planned, after the dance ended the parents took home the wrong children. (The incident was reportedly used in the television series *The Virginian.*)

The fact that Derby's higher-ups failed to see the humor in switching babies may have led to his transfer to San Diego.

Here, Derby did a superb job in shifting the San Diego River into False Bay (now called Mission Bay) and easing silting worries about San Diego Bay. He also did a superb job in easing the mood in the area.

The wag once played a practical joke on two stagecoach passengers. Derby found himself seated between two men, and whispered to each of them in turn, "By the way, the other passenger is almost stone deaf." Derby then leaned back as the men shouted back and forth to one another.

On another occasion, Derby and his friend James Sherman noticed that out-of-towner Don Julio Carillo seemed extremely interested in becoming a Freemason.

When Carillo finally came out and asked if he could join the benevolent organization, Derby asked him if he was aware that all new members must be branded with a hot branding iron. Carillo hesitated and then agreed.

Carillo met Derby and Sherman later at a blacksmith's shop, where Carillo could see a red-hot branding iron glowing in the forge. Undeterred, Carillo allowed the duo to blindfold him in preparation for the branding.

Just as Sherman noisily removed the branding iron from the forge, Derby tossed a small piece of cowhide in the flames.

The timing was perfect. The moment the branding iron pressed Carillo's skin — with a wet piece of paper underneath — the aroma of burning flesh wafted from the forge. The blindfolded Carillo felt heat, but no pain.

With the ritual completed, Carillo lifted the blindfold and saw the brand had left no mark. Still not aware of the gag, the newest Freemason in San Diego fell to his knees and announced that a miracle had just taken place.

Another Derby stunt probably saved a life or two. When a pair of Derby's associates challenged one another to a duel to settle an argument, Derby loaded their pistols with bullets made out of wax, with some charcoal for color.

Both duelists were struck by these bullets, but were splattered instead of killed or wounded.

Derby also pulled a fast one on the citizens of San Diego by changing the political affiliation of the *San Diego Herald* while the publisher was out of town. J. Judson Ames, the *Herald's* publisher, was a stout Democrat and had used his newspaper to help his party carry San Diego in statewide elections. While Ames traveled to San Francisco to bask in the glory of a certain Democratic victory, he left Derby as the newspaper's editor. In just a few days, Derby published a series of articles under his pen name, John Phoenix, which persuaded the county to vote Whig.

Derby died in New York in 1861 at the age of 38. Despite that Derby spent his last few years ill and nearly

Army officer and engineer Lieutenant George Horatio Derby's keen sense of humor was both his boon and bane. *San Diego Historical Society Photograph Collection.*

blind, a friend told the media his sense of humor never flagged: "What other men would sacrifice for ambition, for love, for the attainment of fortune or personal aggrandizement, he would sacrifice for fun. His best friend would have no more chance of escape than his worst enemy."

San Diego's Squibob Chapter of E Clampus Vitus is named for Derby. See Chapter 16.

Cave Couts
Rancher, Politician, and Cold-blooded Murderer

Few characters in early San Diego history have gotten away with cold-blooded murder. Cave Johnson Couts did on one occasion, and used his political connections to save his brother from the hangman's noose on another.

Couts was born in Tennessee in 1821. As the nephew of Cave Johnson, Secretary of the Treasury under President Polk, Couts was a shoo-in for appointment to West Point. Couts graduated from the military academy in 1843 and served on the frontier until the Mexican War ended. He arrived in San Diego in 1848.

Here, Couts developed friendships with the Bean brothers: Roy, who would later become known as Judge Roy Bean, "The Law West of the Pecos," but more importantly Joshua Bean, who would become San Diego's first mayor. His friendship with Joshua Bean became the vehicle by which he got into, and out of, trouble.

As an Army cartographer, Couts was responsible for mapping much of San Diego as it was parceled out after the Mexican War. But immediately before Joshua Bean was elected mayor, Couts was granted half the land beneath San Diego City Hall for a sum of $2.50 (Worth about $56 in today's dollars, ludicrous even back then). After a brief legal battle, the duo returned the land to the city. *Bean also deeded himself the other half of City Hall. Please see Chapter 5.*

In 1851, Couts married into the wealthy Bandini family, resigned his Army commission, and became an aid-de-camp to the state governor. He sat on the tribunal that voted to hang Antonio Garra for his part in an Indian uprising.

A few years later, he moved to Rancho Guajome. Located near what is now Camp Pendleton, the massive cattle ranch had been a wedding gift to his wife from her brother-in-law, Abel Stearns.

As a duly appointed sub-agent for the San Luis Rey Indians, Couts was able to secure cheap labor for rancho operations. Rancho Guajome thrived, and became known statewide for its hospitality — mainly to the 1,000 or so whites who lived in the area. Couts even hosted Helen

Hunt Jackson while she was collecting materials for her novel *Ramona*, in which reportedly used Rancho Guajome as a setting to depict both sides of rancho life — servant and master.

Although several publications refer to him as a man of education, integrity, and manners, Couts once used his status to help acquit his brother of a murder charge.

In the 1860s, a smallpox epidemic rattled through the greater San Diego area, leaving thousands dead. According to a letter Couts penned to a friend, "Small pox is quite prevalent. Six to eight per day are being buried in S. Juan Capistrano. Indians generally. A grave cannot be dug without striking human bones ...they [Indians] were digging little holes, barely enough to cover their coffins..."

In the midst of this epidemic, Couts' brother William Blounts Couts shot and killed an unarmed man.

Smallpox had taken the life of a local cattleman, Don Ysidro María Alvarado. A deeply religious man, his survivors sought to bury him in the family plot at Mission San Luis Rey. But the property that had once belonged to the church now belonged to Couts via his wife's wedding gift.

When the cattleman's family and friends came to bury Alvarado on January 13, 1863, Couts dispatched his younger brother, William Blounts Couts, to stop the burial.

According to an account by Alvarado's son, Tomás:

> Being inside the graveyard, we lowered the coffin into the grave. We were throwing the first earth over the coffin, when William Blounts Couts arrived, suddenly, without our looking or thinking of him, and came close to the wall [of the graveyard], and said, *"Como diputado del Sherif del condado, no es permitido que este Señor se entier ra aqui."* [As deputy of the sheriff of the county, you are not permitted to bury this man here.] At the time he said this, he had in his hands a gun of two barrels.

One member of the burial party, Leon Vásquez, took umbrage at the presence of Couts and threatened him with a shovel. Couts fired his shotgun in Vásquez's direction. Vásquez jumped up on a cemetery wall. Couts fired his second barrel and struck Vásquez in the face, killing him immediately.

The unarmed burial party fled, but Couts' servant fired, wounding two men.

Three months later, William Blounts Couts was arrested on a charge of murder. But the influential Cave Couts acted as his attorney. Despite depositions from eight eyewitnesses, Cave Couts persuaded the judge to drop the charges on a variety of technicalities involving paper work. Cave Couts summed up his defense: "The fellow killed is really not worth noticing... He (Vásquez) is known as a bad character."

Two years later, Cave Couts himself shot an unarmed man. On an early winter morning in 1865, Cave Couts was standing inside George Tebbetts' butcher shop in Old Town when he noticed his former employee, Juan Mendoza, walking across the plaza.

"That man has threatened my life on sight!" Couts proclaimed. He picked up his double-barreled shotgun and marched out to confront Mendoza.

Oblivious to pleas from onlookers, Couts fired at the unarmed Mendoza. The shot missed its mark and Mendoza ran for his life. Couts fired again from nearly 100 feet away and Mendoza dropped dead.

Despite Couts' standing in the community, the citizens could not overlook the cold-blooded killing of an unarmed man in broad daylight. Couts was jailed. But a few days later, friends posted $15,000 bail and he was released.

Months later, a murder indictment came down and the trial was set for October, 1866.

One witness testified that Couts had fired Mendoza from his job at Rancho Guajome over a wage dispute. Afterward, Mendoza threatened to kill Couts. A second witness testified that Mendoza's threat was probably not an idle one. The jury returned a verdict of pre-emptive self-defense.

One newspaper account read: "General Volney E. Howard made a very eloquent appeal to the jury, and reviewed the testimony very ably. The discharge of Colonel Couts was received with much applause and the verdict of not guilty was pronounced righteous."

"Yankee Jim" Robinson
They Hang Boat Thieves, Don't They?

Few cities may lay claim to hanging a man for stealing a rowboat; but San Diego can.

Such was the fate of James "Yankee Jim" Robinson, a New Hampshire-born ne'er-do-well who was hanged in Old Town on Sept. 18, 1852, after receiving a trial that by today's standards would be deemed "criminal."

Robinson was a heavy-set man, well over six feet tall and in his late 20s when he headed west on the heels of the California gold rush. The transcontinental railroad was nearly 20 years away and crossing the continent took months; either on foot, horseback, wagon train, or by sail around Cape Horn. Yankee Jim chose to cross by land and, like a handful of others who plodded along the trail, stayed alive by any means possible.

By the time he completed the journey from the Missouri River to San Diego, Robinson had garnered a reputation as a thief and a murderer, according to what the court would later deem a reliable, but anonymous source.

However, Robinson was not a wanted criminal when he arrived in San Diego, and spent most of his time in and about the adobe gambling houses that lined the Old Town Plaza. As long as he broke no laws, authorities in the sleepy town of about 700 residents were content to leave him alone.

But on a dark August Friday the 13th night, a handful of sailors along the waterfront noticed a man drag a small boat from the beach — probably a couple of blocks south from *Star of India's* current berth — and row toward the schooner *Platus*, at anchor in the bay. The sailors thought the man seemed to be trying to row in a very quiet and cautious manner so they alerted one of the schooner's owners, Mr. Keating.

Keating raced out to the end of Barbee's Wharf and recognized his rowboat. "Whose boat is that?" he hailed. The man in the boat hailed back, "It's mine."

Keating threatened to open fire with his shotgun if the man did not turn the rowboat around. The man refused and kept rowing. Keating fired, but the unidentified man was out of range and rowed off into the night.

Early the following morning, Keating reported the theft of his rowboat (he owned it along with partners John C. Stewart and Enos Wall). Deputy Sheriff Reiner gathered a group of men to ride over to False Bay (now called Mission Bay), to search for the man and the boat. The group of men included county clerk Philip Crosthwaite and Judge Hayes.

Within a few hours the search party came upon two "suspicious looking" men whom they placed under guard. They sent out a second party on horseback to find a man in a red shirt.

The second party returned to the plaza (in the area we now call Old Town) without having found their man, but they had left word along the way to be on the lookout — and detain by any means possible — the man in the red shirt. The two suspicious looking men were taken into custody and delivered to a makeshift jail at the plaza.

Around midnight, a worker from a nearby ranch rode into the plaza leading a mule, atop which rode a big man. His hands were tied behind him and his head was bandaged with a handkerchief. He was wearing a red shirt.

News spread of the man in the red shirt's capture and the town came alive.

The ranch hand told the gathered crowd that the big man had appeared at Rose's Ranch just after dark asking for food. The ranch hand and his wife recognized the shirt by description and fed him.

After eating, the big man started to doze off, but something in the rancher's mannerisms alerted him and he bolted out the door.

The ranch hand grabbed his lariat and an old artillery sword and headed out the door in hot pursuit. For a while it was an even footrace, but eventually the ranch hand closed the gap and lassoed him around the neck.

The big man struggled, so the worker struck him with his rusty sword and knocked him unconscious. Then he bandaged the man's head, tied him up, and brought him into town.

The next morning a committee of citizens used unknown means to persuade the three men to confess. According to confessions wrested from the men, the three had ridden down from Stockton together, stealing and selling horses and committing petty crimes.

When they arrived in San Diego, they had sold their horses for $10-15 apiece and bought provisions in anticipation of stealing a boat to sail off to Mexico.

Confessions in hand, the grand jury brought charges against James W. "Yankee Jim" Robinson and William Harris, alias William Harney, for grand larceny. James Grayson Loring was charged with being an accessory before the fact.

On August 17, a jury was empanelled to hear the case. With Cave Couts as foreman, the jury included Albert B. Smith, Thomas Fox, William Conroy, Philip Hooff, Abel Watkinson, George Wasson, James Donahue, Charles C. Varney, and Charles Lloyd, plus the rowboat's owners John C. Stewart and Enos Wall.

Even in the days of early justice, it was unusual that Stewart and Wall, part owners of the stolen boat, would be allowed to act as jurors. Even more puzzling is that according to records, Robinson had challenged two other jurors and had them removed, but had allowed Stewart and Wall to remain on the panel.

During the trial held the next day, the anonymous "reliable source" furnished information to the court that Yankee Jim was a dangerous man known to have murdered and robbed miners in out-of-the-way camps in other parts of the state, robbed wagon trains, and killed a few of his partners in Arizona.

The trial was brief and the evidence scant. In addition to the coerced confessions and the anonymous source's information, the jury heard Keating testify that he recognized Yankee Jim as the man in the rowboat and identified the red shirt as having been worn by the accused that night. Although research shows the night in question was just two days past the new moon and pitch black, Keating's testimony apparently went unchallenged.

The jury returned its verdict in 30 minutes; all three men were guilty as charged.

The following morning, Yankee Jim and his partners appeared for sentencing. Both partners were sentenced to a year in prison in San Francisco. Robinson was sentenced to hang on September 18, the shortest span between sentencing and execution allowed by law.

Upon hearing the verdict, San Diego's citizens gathered together and offered to relieve the authorities of the burden of keeping Yankee Jim alive for one more month. Cooler heads prevailed.

Old newspaper accounts tell that Robinson was hanged on a crude scaffold erected on a hill south of Old Town — now the site of the Whaley House. Since there was not enough manpower or material to fashion a dead-fall, a wagon was driven underneath the scaffold and Robinson was made to stand on the back with his hands bound and head in the noose.

With the entire population of Old Town in attendance, Crosthwaite asked Yankee Jim if he had any last words.

He had none.

Upon command of county clerk Crosthwaite, the wagon driver urged the horses for ward and big Yankee Jim Robinson lurched backward and swung. The fall was by no means enough to break his neck, and the hanged man jerked and convulsed until the life was choked out of him. Thirty minutes later his body was cut down and hauled to a prepared grave nearby.

Whether Robinson had committed robbery and murder in other parts of the country will likely never be known. But what is known is that San Diego once hanged a man for stealing a rowboat, a crime hardly more serious then, than it is today.

Yankee Jim's grave lies in the tiny El Campo Santo Cemetery in Old Town, just two blocks south of the Whaley House at 2400 San Diego Ave. Both are well worth a visit.

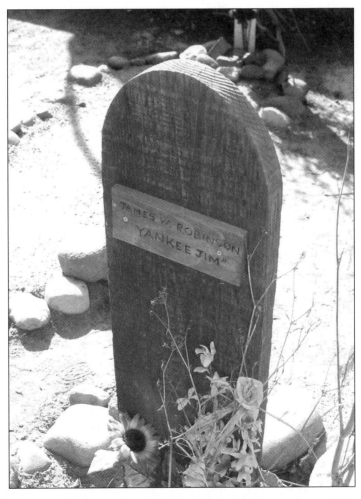

Injustice Old-West style prevailed when Yankee Jim was hanged for stealing a rowboat. Two of the jury members were part owners of the boat. *Author photo.*

Joshua Sloane Invented Political Trickery in San Diego

While San Diego has a full share of interesting characters, Joshua Sloane may be among the first to use political chicanery to gain appointment to a government post.

An Irish immigrant, Sloane came to San Diego in the early 1850's and earned a livelihood as a jack-of-all-trades. He worked as a store clerk, a deputy in Captain Pendleton's office and owned a mill near the old Mission.

By 1858 he was appointed deputy postmaster and in the following year, postmaster.

Sloane's political trickery began when his term as postmaster was about to expire.

For reasons unclear, the people of San Diego were vehemently opposed to Sloane's reappointment as postmaster, and circulated an extensive petition to the Postmaster General in Washington begging him to find someone else.

The citizens were later stunned to find that Sloane was reappointed and that their petition had been totally disregarded at the nation's capital.

Years after Sloane's left his postmaster post, he unraveled the mystery to a handful of friends. After the petition was signed and sealed, some unwitting person sent it off to the Postmaster General's office — *via U.S. Mail!*

Sloane had no doubt been aware of the petition's existence and was probably delighted to see it among the letters at the post office.

The San Diego postmaster lifted the letter, steamed it open and read the petition. Then on similar paper, he wrote a petition calling for his reappointment. He pasted the lengthy list of signatures below his own letter and slipped the altered petition back into the mail. Voila, reappointment.

Sloane's penchant for political trickery appeared again in 1861, when he was appointed collector for the Port of San Diego.

Sloane quickly hired a deputy collector, Patrick, and placed him on the port's payroll. Patrick drew a nice salary until an observant worker discovered that Patrick was none other than Sloane's dog.

Sloane died, unmarried, on January 6, 1879.

Wyatt Earp
Nasty Drinker or Kindly Neighbor?

Few characters in American history are as colorful as the legendary Wyatt Earp.

Stagecoach driver, buffalo hunter, lawman, and gambler, Earp is doubtlessly best known for his role in the gunfight at the OK Corral — a shoot-out that ended with three Clanton gang members dead, and Earp, his two brothers, and Doc Holliday still standing.

While some San Diegans are aware that Earp visited San Diego in the late 1800s, few realize he was a prominent citizen of the era. Unfortunately, his prominence was in the world of gambling, horseracing, and prostitution.

That Earp helped San Diego develop into a mecca for gamblers, prostitutes, con-artists, and crooks may help explain why these chapters in San Diego history generally remain closed.

History tells that Wyatt Berry Strapp Earp was born in Illinois in 1848 and grew up on an Iowa farm. At age 16 he moved west with his family and spent the next few years working as stagecoach driver and buffalo hunter. Earp served as a deputy marshal in the cow towns of Wichita and Dodge City, Kansas, where he became friends with Bat Masterson and Doc Holliday.

Having garnered quite a reputation as a lawman and gambler, Earp moved to Tombstone, Arizona, and bought the gambling concession at the Oriental Saloon.

It was in 1881 in Tombstone that Earp — along with his two brothers Virgil and Morgan — and Doc Holliday survived the bloody gunfight at the OK Corral.

But what is not widely known is that in the mid-1880s, Earp moved to San Diego and became one of the area's chief purveyors in depravity, operating saloons, running gambling halls, and managing prostitutes.

San Diego in the 1880s was said to be as wild and lawless as any town in the United States. The entire area, now called the Gaslamp Quarter, was known as the Stingaree District. Stingaree was virtually wall-to-wall beer joints, houses of ill-repute, gambling halls, and opium dens. It was Sin City West: a never-ending carnival.

Trainloads of high-flying weekenders would arrive from Los Angeles and beyond to the sounds of brass bands blaring a welcome on street corners. Barkers and pitch-men would be at hand, urging pedestrians into one illicit establishment after another.

Roulette, poker, and other games of chance were set up in the streets where tourists, businessmen, and con men would all rub elbows. From Tijuana to La Jolla and east to Sweetwater Grove, men and women caroused, drank, and gambled in the open.

Bull fights, bear fights, and chicken fights drew paying crowds. Prize fights were on the playbill all summer long. Fist fights and brawls in the streets were so common as to be totally ignored.

This environment is one Earp thrived in and contributed to.

The former lawman at one time or another owned four taverns in San Diego, the most famous of which was a beer parlor and gambling hall called the Oyster Bar. That establishment, in a building which still stands at 837 5th Avenue, is said to have been among the most popular in the city. Part of the popularity was doubtlessly due to a brothel above the bar called the Golden Poppy.

The Golden Poppy was unusual in that it was color coordinated. Each room was painted a different color, such as emerald green, sunflower yellow, or ruby red. Each prostitute was required to wear garments to match the room's décor.

But the colorful Earp seems to have been a gambler at heart. When not spending time in the Oyster Bar or other establishments he owned, Earp was often seen playing cards elsewhere or frequenting the horse races at tracks in Tijuana, Pacific Beach, and Escondido.

Two anecdotes attributed to Earp's San Diego years demonstrate contrasting images of the legendary peace keeper.

Thousands of men wore side arms in that era and Wyatt Earp was certainly no exception. Although there is no record of Earp ever shooting anyone — in fact there were relatively few gunfights to speak of in San Diego — the former lawman did use his pistol once.

The story told is that one night during a long gambling session, Earp's horse disappeared from a hitching post outside the saloon. Word spread of the horse's disappearance and a young boy set out on foot to see if he could find it. The boy recovered the horse and led it back to the gambling hall.

Instead of thanking him, Earp pistol-whipped the lad, apparently believing the boy had stolen the horse in the first place.

Another story shows a kinder, gentler Wyatt Earp. At the height of San Diego's land boom, Earp purchased a small vacant lot downtown with the hope of riding the value up and selling it. He had the property cleared and a five-foot lath fence installed around the perimeter. Shortly thereafter, the real-estate boom collapsed and Earp left town. The lot lay fallow.

Seeing the lot sit vacant and in need of some material to build a chicken coop, a neighbor helped himself by prying loose every second slat that made up the fence. When Earp returned to San Diego, he noticed the missing slats and eyed the neighbor's new chicken coop. The conversation went something like this:

"Quite a wind storm must have passed through here, neighbor. Half of my slats are gone," Earp said.

The neighbor gulped and said slowly, "You've never seen such a storm, Mr. Earp!"

Wyatt Earp moved to San Diego after the Gunfight at the OK Corral. Although he could be mean when he wanted to be, he never shot anyone here. *Image courtesy* "Wyatt Earp the Missing Years: San Diego in the 1880s" *by Kenneth R. Cilch.*

"I reckon I haven't," Earp smiled. "And it wouldn't surprise me if a tornado came along next and ripped the rest of the slats and all the fence posts off this worthless lot."

Earp lost a lot of money in the San Diego real estate collapse. In 1897 Earp surfaced in Nome, Alaska, where he operated a saloon during the gold rush. In 1901, he followed another gold rush to Nevada, where he operated a saloon, a gambling hall, and a mine.

Earp spent the next few years working mining claims in the Mojave Desert. Afterward, he moved to Los Angeles where he became friends with several Hollywood stars.

The man who helped shape San Diego into a Sin City West died in Los Angeles on January 13, 1929, at the age of 80.

For more information on Wyatt Earp's days in San Diego, read Wyatt Earp, the Missing Years: San Diego in the 1880s *by Kenneth R. Cilch and Kenneth R. Cilch Jr.*

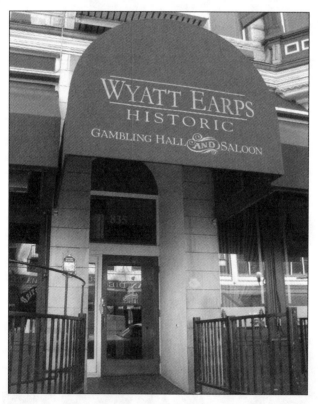

Notorious gunfighter Wyatt Earp owned or operated several saloons and gambling halls when he lived in San Diego during the 1880s. One of them, the Golden Poppy, featured a house of prostitution upstairs. The four-story Victorian building still stands at 837 5th Avenue in the Gaslamp District. *Author photo.*

Charles Hatfield, Rainmaker

Flooded San Diego

Droughts and dry spells are not unusual occurrences in San Diego, the driest county in California outside the desert-bound Imperial County.

The year was 1915 and what seemed to be a persistent drought lingered throughout San Diego County. Farmers dependent upon dam water for irrigation were faced with the prospect of another bleak year. East County's Morena Dam, completed in 1912, was still flat-out empty.

So in December 1915, the San Diego City Council voted to hire Charles M. Hatfield, rainmaker.

Hatfield had become interested in rainmaking as a child living in East San Diego County. The entrepreneur was self-taught, and did much of his research at the San Diego City Library. He conducted his first experiments on his father's ranch in 1902.

The rainmaker's technique involved building a 20 to 30-foot tower near an existing water source and placing several containers of secret chemicals atop the tower.

According to Hatfield, .12 to .15 inches rainfall per day would typically begin three to four days after his chemicals were in place. But Hatfield always made it a point to state that he would accept no money if he didn't make it rain.

Early on, Hatfield's efforts didn't amount to much. But eventually the rainmaker collected on his first $50 contract. That success led him to a series of increasingly richer contracts outside the San Diego area.

His first big contract was in central California, where he was promised $1,000 if he could make it rain more than 18 inches between December 15, 1904 and April 30, 1905. The actual rainfall for that period was 19.54 inches and he collected his reward (worth about $17,500 in modern dollars).

Word quickly spread about Hatfield's ability and his services were sought in Texas, Honduras, and throughout the western United States.

Then in December 1915, Hatfield received a rather desperate telegram from his home city of San Diego requesting he apply his rain-making talents to fill the barren Morena dam.

Hatfield hopped the next train into town and struck a deal with city hall. He'd fill Morena dam within one year for $10,000 (now about $175,000).

Hatfield wasted no time. Before New Year's Day, the rainmaker and his brother had constructed a tower near the dam. They laid their chemicals out and played checkers to kill time. No rain came. The second day was also dry.

Hatfield, realizing the enormity of the task of filling such a large reservoir in just a year, added even more chemicals to the mix.

It began raining the third day, continued the fourth and fifth, and did not stop until the 28th of January.

Hatfield was elated. By month's end the reservoir was not only filled, it spilled over enough to have filled it twice, by his estimation.

Hatfield and his brother dismantled the tower, buried the chemicals and broke up the equipment, as was their habit, and trekked into town to collect their riches.

It was on this journey that the brothers began seeing and hearing of the damages wreaked by the month-long rain. The dam below Morena had failed. Highway bridges were demolished; farms, ranches, and livestock had been washed away. So many railroad trestles had crumbled that regular train service hadn't run in a month. The county was a mess, and citizens' claims against the city for hiring the rainmaker already stood at $850,000 and would soon top $3 million.

The Hatfield brothers slipped out of town by steamship — the only means of transportation still operational — to San Pedro.

From Los Angeles, Hatfield pressed for payment but the city refused, reasoning that to pay Hatfield would be tantamount to admitting liability for the flood. The fear was that if the city hired a rainmaker who created a flood, the city would be accountable in court for damages. Hatfield, still in Los Angeles, lowered his demand to $4,000, then to $1,400, but the city would not budge.

To once and forever silence Hatfield, the city sent an emissary to Los Angeles to make a face-to-face offer: they would pay Hatfield the full $10,000 if he would sign a document stating that he personally caused the rain to fall that month.

With citizens' claims now in excess of $3.5 million (nearly $60 million in today's dollars), Hatfield declined to accept the gambit and never collected for his services.

Hatfield practiced the art of rainmaking until the late 1950s, but never again in San Diego County. He took his secret chemical concoction with him to the grave in 1958.

Ironically, during the five years preceding Hatfield's dam-busting experiment rainfall was about average for San Diego County: 1910, 10 inches; 1911, 12 inches; 1912, 11 inches; 1913, 6 inches; 1914, 10 inches; and 1915, 14 inches. Even in 1916, the year of Hatfield's flood, only 12 inches of rainfall was recorded, just above San Diego's long-term average. The tragedy occurred because most of the rainfall happened at the same time. (See *San Diego Hired Eight Other Rainmakers,* page 76).

Regardless whether Charles Hatfield's concoctions really produced the 1916 flood that turned San Diego into a quagmire, the chemist took his secret formula to the grave. *San Diego Historical Society Photograph Collection.*

Francis Grierson
San Diego's First Mystic

Among the most enchanting fellows to ever grace San Diego society was spiritualist Francis Grierson; a man who held considerable sway over believers in the occult, as well as those merely starved for entertainment.

Grierson — also known as Jesse Shepard — came to town in the late 1800s. San Diego, a sleepy city of less than 20,000, was desperately searching for status symbols associated with larger cities.

Tall, dark, mustachioed, and dapper, Grierson fit the bill.

His very arrival was heralded with a great deal of fanfare, bringing many of the town's inner circle to the train station. What a sight he must have been.

According to written accounts he stepped off the train wearing a Russian squirrel-skin coat draped over one shoulder. His jewelry included a tremendous diamond ring given to him by an Austrian duchess. His golden pocket watch was a gift from the Prince of Wales.

In short order, Grierson became the most sought-after entertainer in San Diego. Working from the homes of well-heeled San Diegans, the performer charged a fee to those wishing to hear his eerie piano and voice recitals.

Accomplished musicians would marvel at his keyboard work, calling it "strangely brilliant" even though he played solely by ear. One writer of the era pronounced him "San Diego's earliest genius."

His recitals mainly comprised odd-sounding Egyptian and religious hymns. The spiritualist claimed that all of his compositions were mystically revealed to him as he played. No piece — be it a march, a dance, an etude, or a concerto — had ever been played before. Nor could it ever be played again, he claimed.

Grierson's exquisite playing was made even better by his proportionately long fingers. According to accounts, he was able to stretch his fingers an octave and a half across the ivories.

The mystic would often complain that pianos did not contain enough keys on either end of the keyboard, and if they did, then and only then would he be able to demonstrate his true ability.

More breathtaking than his piano playing was his rich voice, which is said to have carried perfectly over four octaves. One critic who had heard him perform in a cathedral in San Francisco said it was difficult to believe his singing was but one voice, not an entire choir. "There is this peculiarity about Francis Grierson's singing. It thrills as a voice not of this earth."

Even the most recalcitrant skeptics were won over at Grierson's spiritual gatherings, in which he dazzled audiences (for $2 a person) by simultaneously singing in two voices.

One was a spirit named Sontag and the other an Egyptian who steadfastly refused to divulge his name.

Grierson changed his name to Benjamin Jesse Francis Shepard in 1899 and — while calling San Diego home — began travelling abroad, winning enthusiastic acclaim throughout Europe. It was not unusual for nobility to attend his performances and to contribute generously to his wealth.

By way of example, a letter published in 1892 tells of a reception in his honor, given by the Duke and Duchess of Cumberland, at their palace in Gmunden, Austria. The occasion was a royal family reunion. In attendance were the queens of Denmark and Hanover, the Duke of Saxe-Altenburg, and generals and members of several courts.

According to the letter: "Mr. Grierson played and sang and evidently made a tremendous hit. One nobleman spoke for all when he remarked, 'I never heard music so peculiarly grand in effect, so rich in harmony, so exuberant in power, and so exquisite in delicacy.'"

Several days later, the Duchess of Cumberland sent him a gracefully worded letter of appreciation. Along with the letter came a ring, a large sapphire surrounded by diamonds, specially made by the court jeweler at Vienna.

Grierson apparently learned his trade while traveling cross-country in his youth. Although he always referred to himself as being, "of London" in his press releases, he was said to have lived most of his childhood in the United States under very humble conditions. In fact, he was likened to a street urchin by one chronicler of the era.

Street urchin or posh Londoner, most agree Grierson achieved the highest pinnacle of sophistication without the benefit of education or training.

With such a following, it remains a wonder why Grierson chose to settle in the sleepy town of San Diego. Though once here, his followers did everything possible to keep him.

Foremost among their efforts were those of William High, who paid for a mansion for Grierson. The mansion, called *Villa Montezuma*, cost

$20,000 (today about $200,000 adjusted for inflation) to construct and ultimately covered a whole city block at 1925 K Street.

Said to be designed by spirits who guided Grierson's pencil, Villa Montezuma is an ornate, colorful, and highly decorated Queen Anne revival graced with stained glass, mosaics, and carved walnut. The mansion's windows, fireplaces, and architectural decorations were brought in from Europe.

While remarkable in every way, Villa Montezuma was outdone by the events Grierson performed there.

According to one written account: "Mother went to a séance he gave, and she said he played continuously all through the demonstration. At the same time, drums, tambourines, and trumpets were sounding all over the room, and the ceiling, and floor. Voices came from the trumpets.

San Diego's social elite entered the realm of seances and mysterious emanations when Francis Grierson, aka Jesse Shepard, rolled into town. *San Diego Historical Society Photograph Collection.*

(Grierson) stood with his back to the piano, then far off voices, like a choir coming down the street. They came nearer till they seemed to be in the same room. They died out gradually, till only the piano was heard.

"Then the piano stopped, the lights came on, and there was (Grierson) standing and bowing to the audience. He was a peculiar genius. I never understood how he worked it. I guess no one else did either."

By the late 1920s, much of Grierson's career was behind him. He moved to Los Angeles, fell into dire straits, and became an eccentric. He often wore white theatrical makeup, a very long scarlet wig, and dyed his mustache the same color.

He wrote a book in which he claimed to communicate with a number of important historical figures by a device he called "Psycho Phone."

As his internal clock moved inexorably to the last tick, he pawned a watch — purportedly given him by King Edward — to buy food.

On his final day on earth, Grierson invited several dozen followers to his house and took up the usual collection. He played a number of his inspired improvisations and gave a talk on his travels in Europe. Then he announced that his final piece would be an ancient Egyptian religious hymn.

It was said to have been a rather long piece, and when he finished, he remained perfectly motionless: dead at the age of 78.

Grierson's 1887-built Villa Montezuma (also known as the Jesse Shepard House) stands today as a leading example of Queen Anne Victorian Architecture. *Photo courtesy Historic American Buildings Survey, Library of Congress, H.G. Hanekamp.*

John Sehon

Climbed Building to Become Mayor

Perhaps wanting to distance themselves from past political chicanery, modern-day public officials are tight lipped about a mayoral race near the turn of the century, and how one candidate literally climbed to San Diego's top office.

San Diego resident and retired army officer John L. Sehon ran for mayor in the 1905 and secured a majority of the votes. Case closed? Not by a long shot.

Sehon's opponents in the race had a contingency plan. They figured that since Sehon was a retired Army officer drawing a pension, he was already on the government's payroll. By their interpretation of the law, they felt the incumbent should be ineligible to hold any paying government office: especially that of San Diego's mayor.

So they filed suit.

One legal responsibility of those filing a lawsuit is to inform the person being sued that there is a court action in the works. The most common way to do so is serve the person being sued. Often, a sheriff's deputy or other official will hand deliver notice of lawsuit.

This is where a cat and mouse game began.

Perhaps it was his Army training, but Sehon soon demonstrated that he was very adept at disappearing anytime anyone with a handful of paper came near.

In fact, Sehon kept up his disappearing act so long that soon only one week remained until inauguration. His opponents hastily hatched "Plan B."

Their plan was to ambush Sehon on inauguration day. The idea was to serve the mayor elect with the notice of lawsuit while walked from his car to the public swearing-in ceremony on the front steps of the mayor's office. The move would not only drag the mayor elect into court, it would embarrass him. Serving Sehon those papers on inauguration day would be the ultimate public relations coup!

Before dawn on the morning of the swearing in, the opponents had their paperwork server in place outside the mayor's office. Word of the lawsuit spread throughout the city and a crowd of onlookers, city officials, and opponents gathered for the swearing in ceremony.

All faces turned toward the street for any sign of Sehon's approach. Just as the clock struck noon, Sehon suddenly appeared behind the crowd. Rather than coming from the street, he had emerged from the front door of the mayor's office. As he walked toward the podium, a deputy thrust a handful of papers at him.

Then Sehon dropped a bomb of his own; he was no longer mayor-elect, he was mayor.

Sehon told the crowd that the night before, he and a city official had used a ladder to climb into the mayor's second-story office. After breaking a window to get in, the city official had sworn Sehon into office a few moments past midnight.

The surprised and outmaneuvered opponents served Sehon with the documents anyway. But when the case finally came to court months later, the judge sided with Mayor Sehon, citing the old proverb that possession — even that of political office — is nine-tenths of the law.

While others ran for office, mayor-elect John Sehon actually climbed a ladder, broke a window, and snuck in city hall to secure his place as San Diego's top elected official. *Photo courtesy City of San Diego.*

C. Arnholt Smith

From Penthouse to Doghouse

At the height of his empire building in 1968, C. Arnholt Smith had amassed an estimated personal fortune of $20 million. By far San Diego's grandest tycoon of the era, Smith controlled the 21-branch U.S. National Bank, National Steel and Shipbuilding Co., the San Diego Padres baseball team, Yellow Cab, Air California, Golden West Airlines, and had begun peppering the city skyline with skyscrapers. Smith dominated many facets of the San Diego social, business, and political scenes. He reportedly was a million-dollar contributor — including $250,000 from his own pocket — to President Richard M. Nixon's various campaigns and was a close acquaintance of then-mayor Frank Curran.

But at the time of his death at age 97, C. Arnholt Smith's empire was undone. He had lost everything and was rooming with his daughter in Murietta Hot Springs, about an hour north of the city.

In a story old as time itself, the drive that seemed to fuel Smith's greatness also seemed to bring about his undoing. Smith moved to San Diego from Walla Walla, Washington, in 1907 when he was about eight years old. After grammar school, Smith attended San Diego High School for a while before dropping out to work at a Heller's Grocery Store downtown.

A few years later he became a clerk at Merchants National Bank. There, he climbed the corporate ladder and eventually oversaw the consolidation of several banks that would later become Bank of America.

During the depression, in 1933, Smith borrowed $50,000 and took control of San Diego's U.S. National Bank, a one-branch operation. Through hard work and an impressive roster of business and city leader contacts, Smith grew the bank and ultimately branched out into the publicly held conglomerate Westgate-California.

In 1969 "Mr. San Diego" (so named by the Grant Club in 1960) was featured on the front-page story of the *Wall Street Journal*. But instead of fawning over Smith's empire building, the newspaper took him to task under the headline "Self-Dealing Tycoon — How a Californian Uses Publicly Owned Firms to Aid Private Ventures."

In the first of many attacks on Smith's methods, the Journal chronicled a 1956 deal in which Smith owned a small Arizona insurance firm, transferred the firm to a subsidiary owned by him and his family, and then sold the firm in 1963 to another subsidiary owned by a family member for $610,000. A few months later the subsidiary sold the insurance agency to the Smith's publicly held Westgate-California Corporation for $1,260,000.

It took years for the government to develop that case, but other cracks began to appear in the financial foundation of "Mr. San Diego."

Westgate-California Corporation's 1970 financial report, conducted by a national accounting firm to replace one fired by Smith, contained 17 pages of footnotes questioning profits and figures provided to them by Westgate.

In addition, the new auditors insisted that about $60 million in transactions recorded on the last day of 1970 did not benefit the publicly held corporation. Westgate was forced to rescind them.

Smith fired that firm too, but in 1971 the FBI and the Securities and Exchange Commission began a broad probe of Smith's business deals.

That same year, the Westgate-California Corporation posted a $2,621,000 net loss. Smith fired yet another accounting firm. Then in 1973, the SEC filed a lawsuit alleging that Smith and his lieutenants had engaged in massive fraud by manipulating the assets of Westgate-California Corporation and U.S. National Bank. Later that year, the U.S. Comptroller of the Currency declared the $1.3 billion U.S. National Bank insolvent. This left the Federal Deposit Insurance Corporation with $420 million in "questionable" loans made to associates and companies either owned or controlled by Smith. A month later, the Internal Revenue Service filed the then-largest-ever income tax assessment against a citizen, seeking $22.8 million from Smith.

Criminal proceedings against the tycoon dragged on. In the end, Smith was sent to a white-collar, minimum-security work furlough center for less than eight months.

Smith ultimately gave up the San Diego Padres baseball team. The former tycoon lived in his Rancho Santa Fe mansion until he was evicted in 1993.

"Mr. San Diego" roomed with his daughter until his 1996 death at age 97.

SECTION II

Legendary Groups from San Diego's Past

San Diego lore is replete with groups that range from heroic to heretical to extraordinary. While some groups simply sought to create a better life, others sought to manifest a new world vision. A common thread among them (and San Diegans in general) is that none seemed to lack faith in their convictions.

Mormons March 2,000 Miles for Naught

A lesser known saga in the history of San Diego occurred during the 1846-48 War with Mexico, when a group of 500 Mormon civilians in Iowa were recruited to reinforce General Stephen Kearny's "Army of the West" and help wrest San Diego from Mexican forces.

The battalion was formed after U.S. Army Capt. James Allen came to Brigham Young, leader of the Church of Jesus Christ of the Latter-Day Saints, seeking to enlist four or five companies of infantry to help fight the War with Mexico, which began in May, 1846.

Young directed Allen toward a destitute, temporary settlement on Indian land in Council Bluffs, Iowa, called "Winter Quarters." There, Young and Allen somehow convinced 496 men and 84 women and children to volunteer for a 2,000-mile march to San Diego to "seize the Mexican territory in the name of the United States."

After Young directed the mustering in, he gave a farewell speech in which he guaranteed the well-being of any family left behind and shared his vision that no member of the battalion would die at the hands of America's enemies.

The battalion took only a scant amount of flour and whatever small possessions they could carry and marched out of Council Bluffs July 16, 1846, to the tune of "The Girl I Left Behind Me." The column covered eight miles the first day and camped peacefully on the bank of the Missouri River.

But the remainder of the 200-mile first leg of the journey to Fort Leavenworth, Kansas, was a severe trial, and was to foretell even more severe tests to come on their march. Knowing nothing about military duties and having little equipment, the battalion was ill-equipped for what lay ahead. The route was through insect-infested, muddy lowlands that literally steamed due to heat and humidity. Swarms of mosquitoes plagued the battalion night and day and nocturnal thunderstorms deluged their campsites. Few in the battalion had tents, since they had given virtually anything of value to their families back in Winter Quarters. The scant provisions they brought were consumed the first day and many went hungry on the second night.

Malaria became widespread, and the group staggered into Fort Leavenworth on August 1, after averaging a little more than 10 miles per day. They were immediately given food and shelter. Their first paymaster was amazed that everyone could sign their own name on the payroll. The soldiers received $42 for a one-time uniform allowance and pay at the rate of $8 per month. Twenty of the women were paid as "laundresses" at $7 per month, and the rest were regarded as family and were not paid. Instead of buying uniforms and preparing themselves for the rugged journey ahead, most of the uniform allowance and pay was sent back to Winter Quarters. The battalion would march to Santa Fe, now in New Mexico, in rags.

With newly issued muskets in hand, the group prepared to journey on. Captain Allen died of malaria at Fort Leavenworth and the second segment of the journey commenced August 12 under the command of Lieutenant A.J. Smith. Smith had but one desire; to march the battalion over the 900-mile Santa Fe Trail in as little time as possible. With heat as an enemy and rapid pace an unfriendly ally, Smith pushed the group hard and fast. The company doctor treated all maladies — fatigue, sickness, blistered feet and heat exhaustion — with doses of calomel and arsenic, which were force-fed if necessary. Upon reaching the Arkansas River, Smith sent a number of women and children upstream to the city of Pueblo, now in Colorado, and pressed the debilitated battalion onward.

Lieutenant Smith delivered the weary and threadbare battalion to Santa Fe on October 12, averaging about 15 miles per day for 61 days.

Upon gazing at his charges, the battalion's new leader, Lt. Col. Phillip St. George Cooke wrote: "Everything conspired to discourage the extraordinary undertaking of marching this battalion 1,100 miles, for much the greater part through an unknown wilderness without road or trail, and with a wagon train."

There were too many families in the battalion, Cooke stated. There were too many elderly, too many feeble, and too many young. The group was undisciplined. It was "embarrassed" by too many women. It was completely worn out by traveling on foot.

"Their clothing was very scant," Cooke wrote. "There was no money to pay them or clothing to issue. Their mules were scarce, utterly broken down...and deteriorating every hour for lack of forage or grazing."

After carefully screening the battalion, Cooke sent to Pueblo all but five women, all the children, and nearly 150 of the weakest and sickest men. The men were to remain available to come to San Diego (if called for) the following spring.

On October 19, with 25 wagons and a six-wheeled cannon, 350 men and five women of the Mormon Battalion set out to cross 1,100 miles of Mexican-held territory upon which no wagon had ever rolled. Short on rations and led by guides who themselves had never traversed the route, the battalion marched westward in a large southern loop toward the Mexican village of Tucson. Their marching orders were to build a road as they traveled.

On December 11, while in another wise peaceful river valley, the battalion was repeatedly attacked by scores of wild "Texas longhorn bulls." Several men were injured and wagons damaged, but the battalion shot about 20 bulls and had a hefty supply of fresh meat in the days to come.

When the battalion arrived at the outskirts of Tucson, they learned it was being defended by 200 seasoned Mexican troops with a cannon. Somehow, Cooke managed to convince the Mexican commander that the Mormon Battalion also was highly seasoned in battle and vastly superior in numbers to the defending forces. The Mexican commander fled and the Mormon Battalion peaceably entered the village without firing a shot. Rather than sacking and looting Tucson, as was to be expected by a conquering army, the Mormons bought food, supplies, wheat for the mules and marched on, leaving behind friends rather than enemies.

In a few days, the battalion was back to leaner rations and labored constantly to keep the wagon wheels turning. To lighten the load, caches of road-building tools, mule shoes, and tent stakes were left behind. Several mules died and a wagon was lost in the mud while crossing the Colorado River, but the hardest segment of the journey was yet to come.

As they marched across the desert west of the Colorado River, their shoes and clothing in tatters, and experienced the hottest days and coldest nights imaginable. In places, the sand was so deep that the battalion split into two columns and marched ahead of the wagons to help pack the sand so the wheels could roll. At other times, the men would tug for hours to help the starving mules pull the wagons along.

At one point the battalion marched for three days without water, save for small sips they could find from wells they would dig. Mules collapsed and died. They were eaten. Broken wagons were abandoned and soon the desert claimed all but five of the original 25. When men collapsed from thirst and hunger, they were rolled underneath bushes or under the shade of rocks so the battalion could march on.

On January 14, 1847, the remaining men found Carrizo Creek and staggered down its banks to feast on its cool water. Almost immediately, the men selected the strongest among them to lead a water-laden wagon back into the searing desert to look for any collapsed men who might still be alive. To a man, the stragglers were found, revived, and brought to the lush meadow of Carrizo Creek.

The following day the battalion marched westward through heavy sand and camped between two mountains. There they slaughtered their last few scrawny sheep and ate the last of their flour. They spent the next day resting, cleaning their guns and cannon, and preparing to battle the Mexican army in San Diego.

After leading the battalion up a steep hill, Cooke's guide informed him that they could not make it to the summit. "We were penned up," the guide said. Cooke rallied his men and led an enormous two-hour, marathon effort to crest the hill.

A musician with Company E composed a song, "The Desert Route," to commemorate the feat:

> Our hardships reach their wrought extremes,
>
> When valiant men are roped with teams,
>
> Hour after hour and day by day,
>
> To wear our strength and lives away. . .
>
> How hard to starve and wear us out,
>
> Upon this sandy, desert route.

After cresting that desert hill, Cooke realized that the canyon was so narrow that the wagons could not fit through. Cooke personally led an advance detail that hammered, chiseled, and carved away at the canyon walls so the wagons could fit through. After two more day of rugged travel the battalion finally reached Warner's Rancho, near Warner's Hot Springs, on January 21 and their first real meal in months. Records show that the meat ration was increased from virtually nothing to four pounds of beef per day per man.

On January 29, 1847, the Mormon Battalion, looking more like survivors than soldiers, marched into San Diego to find the American flag already flying.

The battalion had arrived too late. Their arduous journey was for naught.

Unbeknownst to them, the *USS Cayne* had taken San Diego without force on July 29, 1846, less than two weeks after the start of the Mormon Battalion's six-month, 2,000-mile journey.

On January 30, 1847, Col. Cooke issued the following proclamation: "History may be searched in vain for an equal march of infantry."

The battalion camped at the Mission de Alcalá and set about working part-time on various community development projects. Diaries indicate the battalion "whitewashed nearly every house in town," dug 15 or more wells, fired tens of thousands of bricks, and dug a small coal mine on Point Loma.

When their one-year enlistment was completed in July 1847, the Mormon Battalion was discharged. Eighty-one members re-enlisted and the others journeyed to rendezvous with the families they had left behind, in what is now Salt Lake City.

A hearty group of Mormons, such as the one depicted in this Presidio Park statue, defied considerable odds by marching from Iowa to San Diego to act as reinforcements in the Mexican-American War. San Diego was in American hands when they finally arrived. *Author photo.*

What the Heck is the Squibob Chapter of E Clampus Vitus?

Most often it's tourists, rather than natives, who first notice the peculiar wording at the bottom of brass historical landmark plaques in the San Diego area. But the words "Squibob Chapter, E Clampus Vitus" cause locals and visitors alike to scratch their collective heads in wonder.

E Clampus Vitus is an irreverent group as ever existed. Founded more than 150 years ago, it is a loose conglomeration of amateur historians dedicated to identifying historical sites in California and erecting and preserving historical landmarks to commemorate those sites.

E Clampus Vitus also helps preserve the state's history through amateur research and writing. San Diego members call themselves the Squibob Chapter, in reference to the pseudonym Squibob used by Lieutenant George Derby, San Diego's first humorist and practical joker. *(See Chapter 6.)*

Although the group's modern-day mission has a certain amount of reverence attached to it, E Clampus Vitus was founded by miners in northern California in the mid-1800s — more as an outlet to relieve the stress of mining in the Sierra Nevada Mountains than to preserve heritage in the Golden State.

As such, a loose, jocular camaraderie has passed down to this group of armchair historians. Calling themselves Clampers, the group's irreverence is best summed up by their brief constitution:

Article One: All members are Officers.

Article Two: All Officers are of equal dignity.

Outsiders attempting to penetrate E Clampus Vitus' mystique are often stymied by the group's nonsense, whimsy, lack of organization or structure, and scarcity of written materials.

The few surviving historic written accounts paint a rather confusing picture of the aims and deeds of the group. One account proclaims that the order's watchword was, "For the benefit of widows and orphans, but more especially of good-looking widows!"

Another account boasts that gold miners who went broke could turn to E Clampus Vitus for a handout: "And when a brother, worn by toil and broken in the search for gold could no longer carry on, brethren would come to his assistance."

Rules for obtaining handouts were few but strict: "A man shall come in person to receive his dole." And, "Repayments shall commence two years after death."

The reason behind this lack of written history may be divined from the following response in a letter to a group of men seeking to rekindle a disbanded E Clampus Vitus chapter in the 1920s. "During those days, no Clamper in attendance at a stated meeting was ever in any condition to take minutes of the ceremonies."

Various bits and pieces of information about E Clampus Vitus occasionally trickle down to researchers, but not enough to do any good.

Among tidbits: "Let no benighted individual place a period after that fateful E (in E Clampus Vitus), nor let any person of whatever race, color or previous condition succumb to the heretical placing of an 's' after the 'p' in Clampus."

CABRILLO LANDING

SEEKING THE MYTHICAL STRAIT OF ANIAN (THE NORTHWEST PASSAGE) FOR SPAIN, ON SEPTEMBER 28, 1542, IBERIAN NAVIGATOR JUAN RODRIGUEZ CABRILLO BROUGHT HIS THREE SHIPS TO BALLAST POINT, THE FIRST EUROPEAN LANDING ON THE COAST OF ALTA CALIFORNIA.

CALIFORNIA REGISTERED HISTORICAL LANDMARK NO. 56

FIRST REGISTERED DECEMBER 6, 1932. PLAQUE PLACED BY THE STATE DEPARTMENT OF PARKS AND RECREATION IN COOPERATION WITH THE U.S. DEPARTMENT OF THE NAVY AND SQUIBOB CHAPTER, E CLAMPUS VITUS, SEPTEMBER 26, 1992.

While many residents and visitors notice the strange inscriptions on San Diego-area historical markers, few know the story behind the 150-year-old organization. *Author photo.*

When Wobblies Attacked

Riots broke out on San Diego city streets during a period of civil unrest caused by an invasion of "Wobblies" in 1912.

The term Wobblies refers to members of the International Workers of the World (IWW), a now-low-profile worker's liberation group that maintains headquarters in Philadelphia, Pennsylvania.

But back in 1912, a radical and much-larger IWW was exerting a stranglehold on businesses and industries worldwide. Their workers were striking and picketing railroads, mines, large farming concerns, and many other forms of commerce.

Sensing an opportunity to gain a toehold in San Diego, the IWW began ferrying striking workers from various picket lines into San Diego.

Once the Wobblies set foot in San Diego, riots and clashes on the streets began and continued with alarming frequency. When the police upped their response to the uprisings, the IWW sent more Wobblies. Soon, clashes were an everyday occurrence, and the city jail was filled to capacity. Yet more Wobblies arrived.

The crisis escalated until two police officers were severely injured in a melee.

Chief of Police J. "Keno" Wilson ordered officers on foot and horseback to patrol the train station to intercept the Wobblies as they stepped off of the train from Los Angeles.

Wobblies and suspected Wobblies were unceremoniously beaten, forced to kiss the ground, and made to sing the National Anthem before being put back on the train.

Yet more Wobblies arrived.

All San Diego officers were forced to work 18-hour shifts. The fire department was called in to use high-pressure fire hoses to scatter rioters. Nearly 25 percent of the police force resigned due to the stress of dealing with the riots. Vigilantes began roaming the city to hand out "street justice" to anyone causing a disturbance.

The invasion of Wobblies lasted until 1914, when — possibly due to its radical stance — the IWW movement began to lose steam. Evidence of extremist views is found in the preamble to the IWW constitution:

The working class and the employing class have nothing in common. There can be no peace so long as hunger and want are found among millions of the working people and the few, who make up the employing class, have all the good things of life.

Between these two classes a struggle must go on until the workers of the world organize as a class, take possession of the means of production, abolish the wage system, and live in harmony with the Earth.

An interesting side note to the invasion is how the term Wobblie came to be applied to members of the IWW. According to a document attributed to an IWW officer, it stemmed from mispronunciation that began in Canada: "In Vancouver, in 1911, we had a number of Chinese members. One restaurant keeper could not pronounce the letter 'w' in IWW. So when anyone asked for a handout, he would ask, 'you Eye Wobble Wobble?' The nickname Wobblie spread from there."

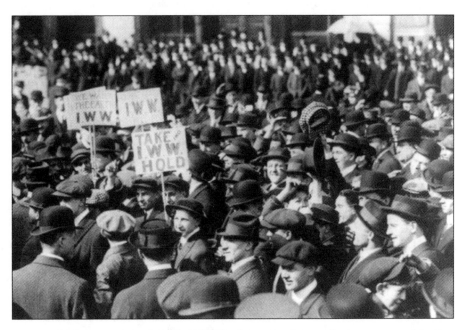

Industrial Workers of the World (I.W.W.) demonstrations and riots occurred in San Diego and elsewhere across the country. This demonstration took place in New York City in 1914. *Photo courtesy U.S. Library of Congress.*

The Nudist Invasion of 1935

Although it sounds too fantastic to be real, the legend that nudists invaded the 1935-36 California Pacific Exposition at Balboa Park is true.

Rumors started flying a few weeks before the scheduled start of the exposition when an old man named Adolph, wearing nothing but a beard, was seen building a stage in one of Balboa Park's remote canyons. Rumor turned to full-frontal fact when nudists began arriving from camps in Indiana, New York, Germany, and elsewhere in Europe.

These jaybirds quickly established a clothing-free colony in a remote park canyon and called it Zoro Gardens, after a make-believe sun god.

Their leader, "Zorine, Queen of the Nudists," met with San Diego District Attorney Thomas Whalen. After securing Queen Zorine's pledge that nudists would not wear burlesque clothing or perform indecent acts, Whalen okayed Zoro Gardens as a legitimate part of the exposition.

Nudists rejoiced and crowned old Adolph the bearded carpenter, "King of the Nudists."

Zoro Gardens opened for spectator viewing along with the rest of the exposition on May 29, 1935. Three weeks later, *Time Magazine* reported spectators were paying 25 cents to enter the gardens to "stare at the nudists." Thrifty peeping Toms looked through knotholes in the perimeter fences, *Time* reported.

When Mae West visited the Expo, the nudist's cause began to gain steam. As the movie star toured a gold-mining display adjacent to Zoro Gardens, she observed young men crowding around the fence. "I'm sorry, I didn't know the fleet was coming in," she purred to reporters. "I certainly would have come down there — I am very patriotic that way."

A few days later, a young woman imitated Lady Godiva by riding a burro through the nearby mining display. Calamity befell the exposition and "Gold Gulch Gertie" was arrested. Gertie was acquitted and later rode nude through the mining display with a police escort.

But by now, tensions between the nudists and the more staid citizens were boiling. To cool things off, Queen Zorine penned an invitation to evangelist Aimee McPherson for tea, but left it unclear as to the appropriate level of dress. The city was abuzz at the prospect of the meeting until the evangelist declined the invitation.

After summer, cracks began to form in the nudist colony's leadership. Queen Zorine announced she was leaving on a nationwide tour to promote nudism.

Ruth Cubitt was appointed interim queen. Her reign lasted about a month before the two-year exposition closed for the winter.

But wintertime was a busy time for civic leaders. In January 1936, several citizen groups and prominent church officials protested to the City Council that nudism should not be allowed during the exposition's second year. The city manager promised he would make certain there were no indecent shows, but said he couldn't stop Zoro Gardens from reopening. City Council declined to tackle the nudist issue, stating that such violations were police matters. Completing the circle, a police spokesman stated that, since there were no laws against nudity on the books, they couldn't arrest the nudists unless they were being indecent.

When the exposition reopened in February 1936, the nudist colony was not only active, but was holding a highly publicized election for queen. Competition was fierce.

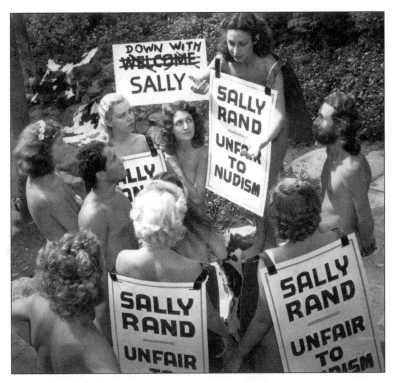

Nudists, here seen protesting the arrest of one of their members, exploited loopholes in civil codes to bring an au naturel living exhibit to the 1935-36 California Pacific Exposition at Balboa Park. *San Diego Historical Society Photograph Collection.*

Ruth Cubitt announced she was seeking re-election and her younger sister Tanya tossed her hat in the ring. Ruth's campaign centered on her incumbency. Tanya's campaign might be summed up with the slogan, "I love to sit in the nude and knit, but I always forget my knitting."

After a campaign that included a tree-sitting competition between three finalists, Tanya Cubitt was declared Queen of the Nudists.

In the summer, another queen arrived in the person of world-renowned fan and bubble-dancer, Sally Rand. Although Rand is said to have performed at the exposition, she declined an invitation to meet with Queen Tanya in the nude. "The nude is my business suit. I never appear socially in it."

A few weeks before the scheduled end of the exposition, financial difficulties beset Zoro Gardens and it closed as an exhibit. Shortly thereafter a fire swept through the canyon, leaving out in the cold nudists such as George Barr, a muscular physical fitness instructor; Prince Arlo, an archery expert; and female twins known only as Jay and Fay.

About that time, former Queen Zorine was arrested in New York. One report states that a judge turned down an offer to have her troupe perform in the courtroom to show it lacked requisite obscenity.

Back in San Diego, the California Pacific Exposition closed on schedule on September 9, 1936.

Nature Lovers Still Flock to Zoro Gardens

Soon after the California Pacific International Exposition closed, the city tore down all structures related to the nudist colony and turned Zoro Gardens into an open air butterfly sanctuary. The original walkways were preserved and butterfly friendly plants and flowers were added. Workers even chiseled small dimples into the tops of rock walls to collect rainwater for thirsty butterflies. Open every day, the modern-day Zoro Garden at Balboa Park is free to the public. Clothing is not optional!

Lemurians Believe Sin Sank Continent

Followers of the Lemurian Fellowship, founded in San Diego in the 1930s (and still active today) believe that a vast continent called Mukulia existed 76,000 years ago over what is now the Pacific Ocean. The capitol of Mukulia (or Mu) was Hamakulia. Its ruler, Emperor Meichizedec, was actually Jesus Christ. And sin caused the continent to sink about 26,000 years ago.

Lemurians, some of whom live cloistered within a secluded retreat in Ramona today, believe the Mukulian world was so highly advanced that people had no need for work or possessions. Crime was so rare that no thefts were reported between 40,000 and 28,000 BC. Freed from the banalities of life as we know it, robed Mukulians spent most waking hours engaged in highly advanced spiritual thinking.

But decadence crept into society and somehow coupled itself with geophysical forces. Mu submerged into the Pacific Ocean.

About 12,000 years later, another Lemurian Empire, commonly called Atlantis, arose from the bottom of the Atlantic Ocean. Jesus Christ ruled this continent as well, but called himself Emperor Poseidonis. Over time, this civilization also lustfully decayed and sank to the abyss.

But the mere sinking of two super-continents did not end the Lemurian way. Rather than perishing, spirits from Mu and Atlantis moved into the "other world" and formed the Lemurian Brotherhood, which actively channels its highly advanced spiritual thinking through one selectively chosen human being.

That human being happened to be cult founder Dr. Robert Stelle.

Stelle claimed that one night in 1936 a mysterious airplane landed at San Diego's Chula Vista Airport containing an emissary from Mu. After being whisked away to his D Street home in a black limousine, Stelle received special instructions from "astral spheres."

Those instructions told Stelle to immediately establish the Lemurian Brotherhood on a mountaintop. Stelle, a former osteopath and correspondence book salesman, began gathering disciples and selling correspondence courses outlining the Lemurian way in a 12-lesson, 35,000-word set.

A Lemurian brochure of the era read: "The Lemurian Fellowship was organized under the supervision of the Elder Brothers. The Lemurian Fellowship is merely the channel through which the brotherhood chooses to release its training, and is the only possible contact with it.

"To the Lemurian Fellowship has been entrusted the responsibility of carrying out this part of the Great Plan, which will result in the establishment of the New Order."

The gist of the Lemurian beliefs, as set out in the coursework, was that Christ was not God, but an individual who dwelled in an archangelic plane directly below that of God. Likewise, mankind dwells in a plane beneath that of Christ, and animals dwell beneath the plane of mankind, and so on. Death is not the end of life, but a step in a long procession of reincarnations, ending in immortality — with freedom from pain and oppression — for those trained in highly advanced spiritual thinking.

Stelle seemingly had no trouble finding followers. He capitalized on their eagerness by putting them to work in the Lemurian wood shop, churning out products for the commercial markets such as cigar and cigarette boxes, mahogany trays, dinner ware, napkin rings, nesting tables, sewing machine cabinets, lamps, and book cases.

But in 1947, several people who had earlier aspired to become one of the few, select, deserving individuals apparently became concerned less about the afterlife and more about the condition of their present livelihoods. They sued Stelle.

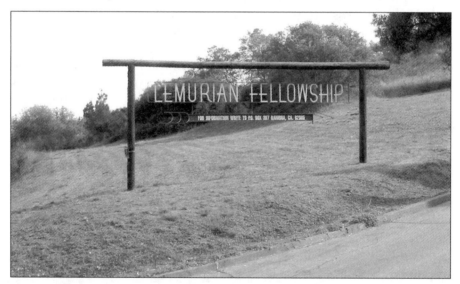

The Lemurian Fellowship, founded in San Diego in the 1930s and still active today, believes that a civilization of advanced thinkers inhabited Mukulia, a vast continent that existed for about 50,000 years until it sank into what is now the Pacific Ocean. *Author photo.*

Court records show that the Lemurian Fellowship began the action by filing an unlawful detainer in municipal court against John Zitko and his wife Dorothea to evict them from the fellowship's grounds.

The Zitkos in turn filed suit against Stelle and the fellowship, demanding an accounting of funds and an injunction to bar the sale of any fellowship property.

Zitko claimed that prior to meeting Stelle, he had been an early student of the occult and had written a book setting forth his revelations about the existence of Mu, Atlantis, and the Elder Brothers, and that this book had been used in Lemurian teachings.

According to accounts of his petition: "Richard D. Stelle approached the plaintiff (Zitko) in conversation about his intention to establish a religious school of philosophy based on the writings of Zitko."

In return for his book and a $5,800 donation to the fellowship, Zitko and his wife would be given permanent quarters on the Lemurian Fellowship grounds, "for their lifetimes and for their heirs after death," and receive a $250 monthly salary, the suit claims. Others in similar circumstances joined the Zitko suit.

The final disposition of the lawsuits, which totaled $13,000, is unknown.

Newspaper accounts of the early 1970s describe the Lemurian Fellowship as somewhat active, but there seems little written reference to the cult after that time.

The theological/metaphysical retreat exists to this day, near Ramona on Highway 67.

Rosicrucians Leave Bodies
to Heal Others

In Oceanside, on the north side of Mission Avenue overlooking the municipal airport, stands the world headquarters of the Rosicrucian Fellowship. Those who follow the Rosicrucian way believe in occult revelation, astrology, a sixth sense, and a way of healing which makes use of fellow Rosicrucians who leave their bodies during sleep to help heal others.

But although the Rosicrucian philosophy is mystical, it is founded upon Christian principles and is not really a religion, its leaders are quick to point out.

The Rosicrucian philosophy teaches that life is but a series of school-like reincarnations. On each new existence on earth, we achieve greater perfection. The grades achieved during each reincarnation account for the differences in each person's fortunes.

Scattered about the facility's 52 acres are three dozen buildings, most of them of unusual and varying design. Among buildings are bungalows, dormitories, learning centers, a chapel, a library, a Red Cross lodge for visitors and a Temple of Healing for followers of the Rosicrucian way.

The fellowship draws income through the sale of books, donations, and legacies. To that end there is a print shop which produces books such as *Occult Principles of Death and Healing, Astro Diagnosis, Simplified Scientific Astrology,* and *Gleanings of a Mystic.*

Followers pass through three levels of membership: Students who have passed a 12-unit Cosmo Course, Probationers who have been regular students for at least two years, and Disciples who have gained special instruction after being Probationers for at least five years.

Those who attain the higher levels of "evolution" become Invisible Helpers, those who leave their bodies during sleep and help cure patients with "effluvia," a sort of anti-matter to the physical body (which in itself is a vital force). Effluvia is obtained by having the patient write letters. The effluvia is said to escape from the pen onto the paper and afford the Invisible Helpers pathways to the patients' systems.

Standard medicine may bear the brunt of criticism. One popular joke among Rosicrucians pokes fun at the medical profession: An intern is following a doctor down the corridor and asks, "What did you operate for?" The doctor replied "$2,000." The intern said, "No, I meant what did the patient *have?*" The doctor replied, "$2,000."

The Rosicrucian Fellowship sprang from the writings and efforts of founder Max Heindel, an engineer who sought wisdom at a European school for mystics in the early 1900s. Heindel became disillusioned and returned to America. He soon received a visit from an Elder Brother of the Rosicrucian Order who suggested Heindel located in Oceanside.

Heindel died in 1919 at the Oceanside headquarters.

The group rarely prods outsiders to join, and many lifelong Oceanside residents haven't a clue as to the nature of the activities behind the gated fellowship.

This allegorical diagram representing the second degree of the Rosicrucian Order came from a manuscript published in Germany in 1785. *Image courtesy Library of Congress Rare Book Division.*

Unarius (Outer) Space Academy

Arguably, the world's most famous UFO organization is the San Diego-based Unarius Academy of Science. The Unarian belief blends reincarnation, extraterrestrial life, channeling with dead earthmen, and using a 10,000-year-old crystal skull named Max to enhance psychic powers.

To its credit, the El Cajon's group has published more than 100 books detailing their sci-fi beliefs and has been featured on *Current Affairs*, *Real People*, and *The Daily Show* segments.

Unarius was founded in 1954 when Ernest Norman met his wife-to-be, Ruth Nields, at a psychic convention in Los Angeles. They were a perfect match. Ernest claimed he was the reincarnation of Jesus Christ. Ruth was convinced that in her 54 previous incarnations she had been Buddha, Charlemagne, King Arthur, Peter the Great, and Socrates.

Together they founded Unarius. After her husband's death in 1971, Ruth moved to El Cajon and opened the Unarius Academy on Magnolia Avenue. Literature claims that Unarians have 300,000 followers worldwide in 60 countries. Nearly 500 followers live in San Diego County. They pay $5 apiece to attend weekly meetings.

According to reports, students who live at the academy contribute more than $450 per month. Private donors often mail substantial monthly contributions.

Unarius (an acronym for UNiversal, ARticulate, Interdimensional Understanding of Science) leaders dispute assertions that their organization is a cult. They claim it to be a science, based on the highest precepts of logic and reason.

But understanding Unarianism is not quite as easy as untangling its acronym. According to academy literature:

> Based upon information previously gained during contact with extraterrestrial beings on earth-like planets not visible to the five senses, Unarians believe that the earth will soon join a confederation of 32 neighboring planets that was broken apart 300,000 years ago. When Earth joins these planets, all inhabitants will work together to stabilize life in the universe.

The cult espouses that Tyrantus of the Orion Empire, who later became Satan, is alive and well but is being kept under control by certain Unarians. They also believe that Ruth, who calls herself the Archangel Uriel (for Universal, Radiant, Infinite, Eternal Light), also led past lives as: Cryston, bringer of love to the Orion Empire; Dalos, leader of the Pleiadean people; Poseid, founder of Atlantis; Yuda, leader of the Yu civilization; Skott, light bringer to the Scarpathians; Ra Mu, spiritual leader of Lemuria; Isis; Queen Elizabeth I; Dalai Lama; Akbar, Emperor of India, and countless others, sometimes simultaneously.

Members of the group claim to gain strength in their psychic powers when they meditate with "Max," a crystal skull purported to be 10,000 years old.

For years they preached that a cluster of spaceships from the Interplanetary Confederation would land in 2001 at a 67-acre site Unarius-owned site in east San Diego. The 22 spaceships, some a mile wide, were to have linked-up to one another to form the earth's first interplanetary college, a model of which is kept within the Star Center at the El Cajon site. The 2001 prediction failed to materialize.

The organization still maintains a Cadillac with a miniature space ship bolted to the roof. Signs painted on the gas guzzler's doors proclaim, "Welcome Your Space Brothers!"

Uriel, co-founder of the Unarius Academy of Science in El Cajon, was born Ruth Norman. In past lifetimes she was Socrates, Peter the Great, Charlemagne, Queen Elizabeth I, and Queen Maria Theresa. *Photo courtesy Unarius Academy of Science.*

San Diego: Area 51 West?

It was the darndest thing I've ever seen. It was big, it was very bright, it changed colors and it was about the size of the moon....We watched it for ten minutes, but none of us could figure out what it was. One thing's for sure, I'll never make fun of people who say they've seen unidentified objects in the sky. If I become President, I'll make every piece of information this country has about UFO sightings available to the public and the scientists.

— *Presidential candidate Jimmy Carter, 1976*

Most people don't associate San Diego with UFO sightings, but the city's history is rife with flying object sightings, both unidentified and identified, either real or imagined. If reporting a UFO sighting to the international press did not prevent Jimmy Carter from becoming the 39th president (1977-81), maybe there is credence in the following reports culled from newspaper archives.

Starlet from a Nearby Planet

The earliest and perhaps most famous sighting occurred in 1952 in the desert. According to an article in *The San Diego Reader*, George Adamski had been on a mission to photograph UFOs when he was approached by a man from Venus who had landed his spacecraft on a desert landing strip.

Witnesses sketched the alien as they watched him converse with Adamski. The space visitor was a 5-foot-tall male who resembled in no small way starlet Yvette Mimieux, according to written accounts. Adamski claimed that the alien radiated a "feeling of infinite understanding and kindness with supreme humility." During the next few years Adamski met with his alien friends on numerous occasions. He wrote three books on his experiences before his death in 1965.

1973: San Diego Hosts Rash of Sightings

Five reports of UFO sightings hit the newspapers in 1973. A Mira Mesa mother and housewife, Gloria Vega, reported in the November 21, 1973, *Evening Tribune* that she saw a UFO crash on her way home from a night-school class November 12.

"I saw it for about five seconds before it fell to earth and disintegrated," she told the paper. She further described the fluttering spaceship wreckage as "beautiful flashing green with streamers about the size of a 50-cent piece."

Several more UFO reports were documented in the same Tribune story. One day later, on the evening of November 13, an 18-year-old college student saw a bullet shaped UFO, "with white lights on the side and red lights in the middle," while walking near her dormitory with a friend. Tina Hughes told reporters that the UFO appeared west of the campus and made a humming sound.

November 14 was unusual for retired Navy Capt. H.L. McGraw, who told *Tribune* reporters he watched a UFO plunge into the ocean north of Coronado. "It was 10 or 15 degrees above the horizon, a sparkling blue-white ball of flame with a tail approximately 100 times its length."

The busy week continued with yet another report on November 15 by a Clairemont man who did not wish to be identified because of what his neighbors might think. The man claimed he had spotted a UFO outside his window moving slowly from east to west. "It was shaped like an oil drum and had a cross of bright white lights," he said.

On November 16, two 11-year-old boys were walking through a backyard on Crane Street when they claim to have encountered a dark disc-shaped object about 20 feet in diameter. It was topped with a silver dome and was perched on three legs. When one of the boys tapped the craft, it levitated about 5 feet off the ground and began flashing green and red lights. The boys ran off.

UFO Lands, Cat K.O.s Self

In October 1974, a San Diego family reported that a perfectly round object had landed on a hill next to their house. Their account was chronicled in a Feb. 8, 1990, *Reader* article. According to four members of the family and a friend, the object changed color several times before streaking away. During the time on the ground, the family's horses whinnied and bucked, their goats began jumping up and down, their dog started clawing the back of his doghouse, and their cat ran headlong into the side of garage, knocking itself unconscious.

Also in 1974, a law enforcement officer allegedly called the UFO Educational Center in North County to report she had watched a flying object race around Mission Valley above Interstate 8 during rush hour.

Astronomers Fail to Spot UFOs

The same *Reader* article also detailed a 1975 incident in which two high school youths reported a UFO parked on San Pasqual Valley Road, southeast of Escondido. The lads claim they drove their car to within 15 feet of the 30-foot saucer, but when they jumped out to investigate, the oval-shaped UFO shot straight up into the air and vanished among the stars.

Numerous UFO sightings were also reported that year from Palomar Mountain. Palomar Observatory scientists have never glimpsed a UFO in the facility's 200-inch telescope.

Woman Wagers Big Bucks: Spacemen Due in 1977

A member of the alien-friendly Unarius Society wagered thousands of dollars that spacemen would land in Jamul in 1977. According to a November 12, 1977, *San Diego Evening Tribune* article, there was no such reported landing. Records do not indicate whether or not Ruth Norman made good on her bets, but there are some who say Norman mailed a $500 international money order to a London bookmaker.

Seen here aiming his telescope toward the sky, George Adamski was among the first to claim contact with aliens from distant planets when he rendezvoused with five-foot-tall spacemen in the Anza-Borrego Desert in 1952. Adamski chronicled his meetings in several books, which helped San Diego become a hub for UFO sightings. *Photo courtesy ©G.A.F. International / Adamski Foundation Box 1722 Vista, CA 92085 www.gafintl-adamski.com.*

Upside-Down Saucer Spied

At four a.m. on September 7, 1977, several residents of La Mesa were awakened by flashing colored lights and loud humming and beeping sounds. According to a story in the *Reader*, the La Mesa residents said they saw an upside-down saucer within a white cloud hovering over Grossmont Hospital for nearly an hour. A nurse at the hospital dismissed the commotion as a helicopter, but later discovered that there were no helicopter flights that morning.

Say "Green Cheese!"

On July 1, 1990, a Pacific Beach drywall installer was snapping pictures in East County with some friends. According to an article in the *Los Angeles Times*, when Michael Orrell picked up his film, he noticed some dots that appeared off in the distance near a canyon. When he had the photographs enlarged, the dots appeared as 10 triangular-shaped objects flying in formation. The objects seemed to have shiny metallic undersides.

"Oh, the Humanity (Spared)"

Dozens of startled San Diegans called police to report a UFO on November 17, 1990, the *Los Angeles Times* reported. This invasion from space turned out to be an advertising blimp on its maiden voyage. Representatives of the San Diego-based Virgin Lightships sought to soothe San Diegan's senses and sensibilities by confessing the unannounced voyage was an advertising ploy meant to create a stir.

Lumonicists Lived for Harmony

More a lifestyle than a religion or cult, Lumonics came on the scene in the Olivenhain district of North San Diego County in the 1980s. The Lumonics movement, founded in Florida in the 1970s, fashioned its namesake from the Latin word "lumen," or light.

Lumonicists believed that homes and cities should create auras of pleasant experiences for their denizens. Entering a Lumonics house was not unlike entering a spacecraft from a future world, according to accounts. Anterooms were generally quiet and bathed with the sounds of gently falling water. Inside main chambers, in which eight people lived, colored lights shifted and moved to the rhythm of piped-in music or to tones played upon brightly colored acrylic sculptures, some of which moved. There were also glass sculptures were filled with colored water made to resemble futuristic buildings and cities.

Lumonics homes were open to the public for a small fee, mostly on Friday nights and by appointment only. Once inside, the furniture, electronics, and music worked to create an active environment said to make a permanent change in those who visited. Lumonicists and guests sat on large upholstered cushions and throw pillows.

Those living in Lumonics houses kept them free of clutter by stowing all personal belongings in assigned closets. They dressed simply, eschewing traditional garb for all-white clothing, believing that a person's outer space affects his or her inner space. Lumonicists felt that if a person's outer spaces (homes and clothing) didn't nourish, give pleasure, and have meaning, their inner space (self) would be negatively affected.

Lumonics leaders, who generally eschewed characterizations altogether, were reluctant to accept being labeled as a religious group, although some members referred to it as such. Instead, leadership asserted that Lumonics adherents were merely groups of individuals who came together to offer the experience to others.

The ultimate goal of the Lumonics movement was to build more homes, larger homes, and ultimately entire cities that would become jewels of civilization. Little was chronicled of the group after the 1980s and few know what became of their dreams for an ultra-modern, enlightened environment.

Moonies Criticized for Mind Control

Several San Diegans filed complaints about how they were treated after joining the Reverend Sun Myung Moon's Unification Church in the late 1970s.

One husband and wife pair, whose names were withheld in press accounts of the incident, claimed they joined the church to help reform the world, but were brainwashed and forced to hawk candy and flowers on the streets to support the organization.

According to literature, followers believe that Adam came to the world to create the perfect family, but failed. Christ appeared on the earth not to save mankind as Christians believe, but to complete Adam's failed mission.

When Christ was rejected by God as the "second Adam," God allowed Christ to die, but says he will reappear in time as the "third Adam" or "second Messiah" to establish the perfect family for God.

The September 1976 incident involving the unidentified husband and wife occurred shortly after they joined the sect.

According to their complaint, the couple was split up immediately upon entering the organization. They could not communicate with one another, only other Unification Church members. They claimed Moonies deprived them of sleep, made them to listen to long hours of sermons and lectures, and direct them to offer all prayers to Reverend Moon, whom followers called the "second Messiah." The man and woman were also made to spend most of their spare time on the streets soliciting support for the organization.

The couple remained with the Moonies for four months before seeking help from a psychologist who specialized in extricating people from cults. He determined the Moonies had been employing "mind control" tactics on the couple.

Sun Myung Moon, the self-professed second messiah, died in 2012 at the age of 92.

The Unification Church today is perhaps best known for holding an international mass wedding ceremony called the Cosmic Blessing. In it, thousands of couples exchange vows of matrimony.

CHAPTER 25

Heaven's Gate Mass Suicide

Undoubtedly the most notorious cult to call San Diego home was Heaven's Gate, which drew worldwide attention when 39 of its members committed mass suicide at a Rancho Santa Fe mansion in 1997. Six weeks later, a 40th member of the cult joined his fellow members in death.

Authorities believe Heaven's Gate spawned from a defunct 1970s cult called Human Individual Metamorphosis, also known as the Overcomers.

Heaven's Gate preached a blend of biblical teachings, dire warnings about satanic angels, and the belief that the Hale-Bopp comet would afford "classmates" a one-time shot at immortality.

Cult leader Marshall Applewhite was convinced that evil space aliens called "Luciferians" had programmed mankind to lead meaningless lives. According to his Internet writings:

> They want you to be a perfect servant to society — to the "acceptable establishment," to humanity, and to false religious concepts." Part of that "stay blinded" formula goes like this:
>
> Above all, be married, a good parent, a reasonable churchgoer, buy a house, pay your mortgage, pay your insurance, have a good line of credit, be socially committed, and graciously accept death with the hope that "through His shed blood" you will go to Heaven after your death.

Applewhite compared himself to Jesus Christ and iterated that Luciferians, who were actually spirits of the dead, were programming human beings so that the bodies of most humans would become useless when needed in the afterlife.

The cultists believed they had been sent down to earth to inhabit human bodies and that they could achieve a higher form and rendezvous with a UFO which was hidden in the tail of Hale-Bopp, only if they shed their "containers."

The spaceship within the comet would take them to a utopian "Next Kingdom."

So it was that 38 cultists followed Applewhite's lead on March 24, 1997.

They donned matching black jogging suits and oversized shirts and new tennis shoes. They dutifully packed flight bags and suitcases and placed them at the foot of every mattress. They ate pudding laced with lethal drugs, washed it down with vodka, placed plastic bags over their heads with rubber bands tied around their necks. They lay down on their mattresses and died.

Authorities called to the scene several days later found many of the plastic bags outside in a trash can. This led them to believe that the mass suicide had been planned precisely and that several members waited for others to die first, before removing their bags and replacing them with purple cloths.

The Heaven's Gate cult left behind a video and several Internet messages explaining matter-of-factly that they had left their human bodies to "graduate" from earth into the Kingdom of Heaven. They also left behind hundreds of pages of written material explaining their suicide, but experts doubted many would understand the cult's reasoning.

In a chilling video-taped statement, one female cult member said, "Maybe they're crazy, for all I know. But I don't have any choice but to go for it, because I've been on this planet for 31 years and there is nothing here for me."

Then-Governor Pete Wilson said, "To call it bizarre, I think, is to understate it."

Six weeks later, a 20-year follower of the cult checked into a Leucadia motel room to join in the afterlife his wife and the 37 others who had killed themselves in Rancho Santa Fe. Before downing a lethal dose of poison, he wrote, "By choosing to leave in the manner of my classmates, I have eliminated my anxieties in that I have secured for now my continued relationship with the Next Level."

Followers of the Heaven's Gate cult believed they would find salvation by ending their lives and hitching a ride on the Hale-Bopp Comet's tail as it passed by earth. The comet, a mixture of ice, frozen gases, and dust passed within 120 million miles of our planet without picking up cosmic hitchhikers. *Photo courtesy European Southern Observatory (ESO).*

San Diego Hired Eight Other Rainmakers

After the destructive deluge attributed by San Diegans to Charles Hatfield in 1916 (see chapter 37), it is no small wonder that city leaders were skeptical about rainmaking. Thus it was not surprising when, in 1935, a miner by the name of John Coop did not receive a standing ovation when he pitched his idea for a machine that could turn clouds into a never empty spigot.

Coop described his method to have rain on tap: The city would erect dozens of 1,000-foot skyward-reaching tubes, either along the mountain slopes or attached to towers built on level land.

The tubes would naturally draw warm air from the bottom to the top. When the warm air hit the colder air in the strata above, rain would be produced in the area below the tops of the tubes.

In fact, after studying the idea for 23 years, Coop determined that the only way to stop the rainfall would be to install shut off valves at the bottom of the tubes to limit the natural flow of the warm air updrafts.

One of the miner's main concerns was that the tubes would cause so much bad weather they would damage themselves.

"It is a known fact that precipitation of moisture is caused by warm air currents ascending to cooler strata above, causing cloud formation and hence, rain," he stated with confidence.

One detail: to function properly the tubes would need to be about 20 feet in diameter and reach skyward 500 to 1,500 feet, quite possibly higher than that, he admitted. But the miner felt it was still possible.

"Why, they are talking now in France of building a mile-high tower. I estimate that 10 of these tubes…about 14,000 feet in elevation would irrigate about 100,000 acres."

Coop conceded that the project might be cost-prohibitive, but reminded the city that the Boulder Dam was also expensive, and he urged the City Council to consider what that dam had accomplished.

The city declined to put Coop's theories to the test.

In 1948, San Diego was into another serious dry cycle and the City Council again considered employing a rainmaker. The city paid

$750 toward a $3,000 feasibility study by noted California Institute of Technology scientist Dr. Irving P. Kirk on ways to draw rain from the moisture-laden clouds that seemed to form an eastbound train of tantalization.

But when San Diego's old friend Charles Hatfield, living in northern California, heard of the city's quest, he promptly offered to reapply his rainmaking skills. Fearing another Hatfield deluge, the City Council backed out of its deal with Kirk and decided to forgo rainmaking. One newspaper reported that the City Council, "just decided to let nature take its course."

In 1951, City Council apparently re-examined its rainmaking policy and signed a two-month contract with Rainfall Corporation of America to seed the clouds above the region. The city's water director told council that rainmaking operations were proven to be "somewhat beneficial" and that precipitation in this company's target areas was three times heavier than elsewhere due to cloud seeding.

Cloud seeding was a relatively simple operation, according to company president Ronald Bollay. Using numerous ground-based smoke generators, the company would infiltrate the clouds with microscopic particles of silver iodide. The iodide would become artificial nuclei around which water droplets form. As the water droplets super-cooled, they would become snowflakes. The snowflakes would grow larger and heavier until they fell into lower and warmer atmospheric levels and formed raindrops.

An important concern, Bollay shared, was that careful planning was necessary to calculate the drift of the cloud "seeds" so they only produced rain in the specified run-off areas.

Inability to prove the effectiveness of Rainfall Corporation of America's operations may have led to the cessation of the San Diego venture. Although at that time there were several studies which seemed to indicate at least some quantifiable results, Bollay was hesitant to cite them. "We don't claim to make rain," he said. "We can't even guarantee more rain. But we do know, from information available so far, that in a normal year we can materially increase the amount of rain which will fall in a given area."

Bad luck with rainmakers and their wacky ideas did not stop the city from hiring a rainmaking company the following year.

In 1952 the city paid W. Floyd Jones' Weather Modification Company to seed the clouds above San Diego in order to achieve higher rainfall totals. While the results were the subject of constant debate between meteorologists, politicians, and ersatz rainmakers, the weather company received a total of $17,000, about half from the city and half from the county, for its efforts.

Apparently, a great deal of those efforts were expended on convincing city hall that it was producing results. Jones at one point cited that an outlying San Diego County area had received 20 to 40 percent more rain with seeding than they had during the previous year without cloud seeding. According to Jones' math, there was only a one in 28 chance that the increase could have occurred solely from nature.

One weatherman didn't mind the Weather Modification Company's attempts to squeeze the sky. "When we miss our forecast of rain, I can always blame cloud seeders."

Records reveal no funding for cloud seeding by the city or county during the 1953-54 period.

In 1957, San Diego County entered into a $17,500, four-month contract with another company, The Weather Corporation.

The company installed 21 silver iodide generators throughout the county at private residences in Rainbow, Fallbrook, Pauma, Oceanside, Escondido, Encinitas, Del Mar, Mission Beach, Coronado, Chula Vista, San Ysidro, Lower Otay, Dulzura, Potrero, Campo, Alpine, Lakeside, Live Oak Springs, Pine Valley, Ramona, and Santa Ysabel. Company officials would wait for conditions to ripen before phoning residents to light up the iodide burners.

Rainfall Corporation of America's Ronald Bollay, now acting as engineer and vice president of The Weather Corporation, was again reluctant to brag about the results. "Last month," Bollay said at a directors' meeting, "we operated 21 silver iodide generator-burners 540 hours over an eight-day period. We don't know yet what good we did, if any, but we do believe that later when we compare our seeded areas with non-seeded areas outside the county that an increase will be noted in the seeded areas."

The City Council may be forgiven, then, for declining a January 1961 offer by Edmond Jeffery to produce 40 inches of rain in 40 days for $8,000. Not only was the offer presented to council 45 years to the month after the infamous Hatfield offer, but Jeffery told the city he had devoted all of his spare time studying chemistry and Charles M. Hatfield.

Although he did not learn Hatfield's secret formula, the former advertising man, gold prospector, bush pilot, and self-proclaimed scientist had concocted a formula of his own based on what he had learned about Hatfield's chemistry.

Jeffrey's formula consisted largely of sodium hydroxide and worked, according to his theory, like this: By exciting the sodium hydroxide, clouds would rise out of the solution. Those clouds would combine with the oxygen in the air and create water.

The city panned the idea, but Jeffrey set out for Morena Reservoir anyway with the goal to prove to himself and the world that he could create 40 inches of rain in 40 days. As a kicker, he guaranteed the first rainstorm would arrive within six days.

Jeffrey assembled his chemicals in pots and pans of various sizes and shapes on the ground near a small trailer at Morena Village. The chemicals reacted together, excited one another and bubbled but produced no rainfall.

Several dry days later, the 48-year-old Jeffrey began construction of a Hatfield-like tower and rekindled his chemical experiments. After 39 days of relentless San Diego sunshine, Jeffrey told the press, "If it's not raining cats and dogs by noon tomorrow, I'll agree everything's over."

True to his word he called it quits the following day, saying, "I'm sure someone can produce rain."

As he tore down his 25-foot tower and packed up his pans and chemicals, he reportedly mumbled to reporters, "Well, do you know of any jobs for ex-rainmakers?"

The call was "ions away" for two San Diego County water districts in 1965. Betting $4,000 of taxpayers' money on equipment, officials at the Vista Irrigation District and the Escondido Mutual Water Company sought to shoot positively charged ions aloft to produce rain. Called electrostatic emission, the goal was to string about a mile of ultra-thin stainless steel wire above Lake Henshaw. "This rain making is a simple one that merely helps nature along," officials boasted.

The system was to have worked like this: Large amounts of electricity were to be surged through the wires in a deliberate attempt to overload them. As a result of the overload, ions or electrified atoms would be released and carried aloft by air currents.

The ions in the air would combine with ions already in the clouds, causing condensation, or nucleation to occur. The moisture increase would cause droplets to form and fall to the ground. Once triggered, the rainfall would continue long after the machine was turned off, experts said.

On a brief initial test, a check of recording instruments to the east of the dam showed that electrical charges were whirling aloft. By mid-afternoon, a downpour occurred east of the dam. Officials were rubbing their hands in anticipation.

But the next day, an electrical transformer failed. After a one-month delay, a new one arrived. Officials again put the system into use, but no rainfall arrived and the Lake Henshaw Dam watershed remained dry. Quietly, the project was discontinued, the equipment dismantled, and the wires unstrung.

Overhead cloud seeding was the most recent approach to rainmaking in San Diego. In 1989, Atmospheric Inc., a Fresno company, was hired by the city and two water districts to see if the airborne approach might enhance rainfall.

Using a Piper Apache twin-engine airplane, the company's $84,000 experiment was based on seeding clouds from within, using a formula of silver iodide and liquid fuel. As the plane flew into the clouds, the solution was ignited and smoke would pour out of a 6-foot-long, 8-inch-diameter stainless steel cylinder attached to the plane's underbelly.

The formula's combustion was supposed to produce microscopic particles which would attract surrounding liquid cloud droplets, reports stated. In attracting the droplets, the silver iodide particles would grow into larger and larger ice crystals, eventually falling and melting to become rainfall.

Atmospheric Inc.'s experiments ended without success and marked the last known effort by the city to produce rainfall.

San Diego receives nearly all of its precipitation from storms marching down from the Gulf of Alaska.

Unfortunately, they deposit most of their rain between November and April, not in the summer growing season. Moreover, the county's yearly rainfall is best described as a pattern of extremes. A rainfall of 21 inches one year may be followed in consecutive years by 5 inches, 11 inches, 6 inches, 4 inches, etc.

Long-term records reveal cycles of long droughts followed by periods of heavy precipitation. San Diego's heaviest rainfall (since record keeping began in 1850) occurred in 1884 with 26 inches. The lightest rainfall was 3.5 inches in 1961.

Tree-ring studies, in which narrow bands indicate droughts and wide rings indicate maximum growth years, show a 61-year drought between 1760 and 1820, and severe droughts between 1600 and 1625, 1720 and 1730, and 1865 and 1885.

SECTION III

Famous San Diego Sites

Whether one considers San Diego a city, a county, or a frame of mind, it is helpful to bear in mind that San Diego is like an island.

Bounded by the Pacific Ocean to the west, the Mexican border to the south, Marine Corps Base Camp Pendleton to the north, and the Anza-Borrego Desert to the east, the "island" of San Diego contains an abundance of physical sites that hold secrets of days past.

To live among them, to drive past them on the way to work or play — without knowing about them — is to miss their significance entirely. As one San Diego wag said, "You don't know what you don't know."

Ballast Point Once Home to Whale Bombers

Long before recreational boats, naval ships, cruise liners, and cargo carriers made San Diego Bay a port of call, hordes of gray whales did.

From accounts in the early 1800s, whales came into the bay in such numbers at times that it was dangerous, if not impossible, to cross the harbor. Descriptions written of that era told that, "Scores were to be seen spouting and basking in the sunlight. They came in such numbers that it was dangerous to try to cross the channel to North Island to get fresh water from the springs there."

Whales were known to exhibit several behaviors that could be dangerous to small craft, and the humans within them, in the bay. Gray whales may reach a length of 49 feet and weigh up to 80,000 pounds. Even at those monstrous proportions, the whales of San Diego Bay would sometimes breach (leap out of the water) and splash down with a crash that resounded for miles.

San Diego Bay whales were also famous for lobtailing, which is the act of pointing their heads straight down and lashing their tales from side to side, sending up clouds of spray, and wreaking havoc on any small craft nearby. Sailors of the era were deathly afraid of the spray from a whale spout; it was said to have a highly corrosive effect on human skin.

Even the most seemingly sedate whale could not be ignored in the bay. Such slow-moving leviathans were known to capsize small boats by merely swimming into them or surfacing from beneath them.

More sinister were certain whales that were known to purposefully rise up underneath boats. Boaters were warned to avoid the oily slick left on top of the water after a whale submerged, for the monster below knew exactly where that slick floated and would rise up from underneath if it sensed a boat was there, sending yachtsmen, picnickers, and fishermen overboard for a swim.

It is no small wonder that early San Diegans did not do much pleasure boating during the whales' December through March migrations.

For several decades in the 1800s, San Diego was a whaling town. Whale oil was a valuable commodity as a lubricant and for burning in oil lamps.

Unlike whalers on the East Coast, San Diego-based whalers had an advantage. Whales were so thick in the bay that many whalers never left the harbor. Those who did only traveled a few miles off shore.

While San Diego whalers occasionally found sperm whales, right whales, finbacks, humpbacks, and blue whales, their main quarry was the California gray whale.

But California gray whales were not easy prey. They were said to have a natural mean streak and would often extract more from the whaler, in terms of broken boats and lost gear, than the whaler could extract from the whale in terms of oil. The whale's nasty reputations earned them such nicknames as hardheads, ripsacks or devilfish.

Written accounts indicate that one of the first whaling ships to operate in San Diego was the New England-based whaler, *Ocean*. *Ocean* was said to be the largest such vessel of her time, and first dropped anchor in San Diego Bay in 1830, beginning three decades of making the harbor a port of call.

Using Ballast Point as a staging site, *Ocean* operated as a mother ship, sending out her whaling boats, overseeing the processing of whale oil, and ferrying the barrels of oil back to New England when her holds were full.

Unlike glamorous Hollywood portrayals, whaling was a dirty, smelly occupation, especially in the rendering stages when whole whales were beached at Ballast Point. Sailors first peeled the blubber off the whales, chunked the blubber into manageable sections, and then heaved the chunks into burning cauldrons. A single whale so rendered might yield 35 to 40 barrels of oil.

When a Ballast Point crew was finished extracting the oil, the carcass was often just slipped from its lines and allowed to sink into the bay. Countless carcasses later washed up on nearby beaches or lagoons after a few changes of the tides.

The whalers were crewed mostly by New England Indians, Polynesians, and a few Quakers. Discipline was lax. The whaler *Ocean* was the scene of more than one mutiny within the otherwise sleepy confines of San Diego Bay. History tells us that under the command of Captain Clark, a mutiny erupted aboard *Ocean* in 1847 in which San Diego Sheriff Philip Crosthwaite was forced to call in the Mormon Battalion of the United States Army.

The battalion handed *Ocean* back over to her master and maintained order as Capt. Clark had the ringleaders flogged.

At another point in time, fishing for whales with bombs became popular. While either inside the bay or just offshore, men in small boats would throw bombs into the water near whales, stunning or killing them.

Although most whales killed in such fashion died and irretrievably sank, the ones that floated were lashed by the tail and towed to Ballast Point for processing.

One story tells of a group of fishermen in a small boat off of La Jolla who happened to venture close to a dead whale floating on the surface. Unbeknownst to the fishermen, the whale had been shot with a bomb-tipped harpoon a week before. Although the bomb had failed to detonate when the harpoon hit the whale, the creature ultimately died of the harpoon wound itself, and was bobbing up and down in the water when the fishermen approached.

As luck would have it, just as the fishermen neared the whale, the bomb exploded. Rancid smelling meat, blubber, and putrefied oil rained down on the men from every direction, creating a most miserable experience.

At its heyday in San Diego, whalers in 1871-72 exported 55,000 barrels of whale oil each year. But soon thereafter the nation switched from whale oil to kerosene-burning lamps, and the demand for whale oil faded.

The last documented attempt at whaling in San Diego was in 1935 and involved a showman named Ray George, a few harpoons, 6,000 gallons of embalming fluid, and who-knows-what kind of wacky idea. George reportedly killed two whales and left town in a hurry.

Today, the business of whaling in San Diego exists in a much more environmentally friendly form — ferrying passengers out to sea on whale-watching excursions.

Gray whales were known to leap out of the water and land on boats in San Diego Bay. Sailors thought whale spout spray was corrosive to human skin. *Photo courtesy Merrill Gosho, NOAA.*

CHAPTER 28

The Legendary Subterranean Cavern Hoax

January 1, 1888 — the *San Diego Union* newspaper headline screamed, "The Bowels of the Earth: Discovery of an Immense Subterranean Cavern in San Diego."

As though that were not enough to entice readers to continue, the sub-headline continued, "A Prehistoric Race Found Entombed in Coffins Chiseled Out of Solid Stone — A Cave of Crystals Under the Bed of San Diego Bay."

Thus began the most brazen, elaborate, and convincing hoax ever perpetrated upon the citizens of San Diego.

In a hotel room, late on the afternoon of December 31, 1887, a reporter by the name of Charles F. Degelman interviewed the eminent geology Professor Robert Stearns prior to the professor's departure that afternoon for the East Coast.

After extracting a solemn promise not to divulge the exact location of the cavern's entrance, Stearns related his amazing account of the discovery and exploration of a vast cavern beneath the bed of San Diego Bay. Degelman's ensuing 6,500-word story was splashed across page one and rocked the citizens like no earthquake could.

Stearns' credentials and background seemed beyond reproach. As "Paleontologist of the United States Geological Survey" and "Curator of Molloseo" of the United States National Museum in Washington, Stearns claimed to have spent decades studying San Diego geology, paying special attention to the difference in elevation between the Salton Sea area and the coastline.

It was common knowledge in that era that surveyors had (correctly) measured the elevation of the Salton Sea Basin at about 200 feet below sea level.

Playing upon bits of information available at that time, Stearns built an intriguing case that the laws of nature demanded such a cavern existed: The Salton Sea Basin is below sea level. The water there is salty. That proves that at one time the Pacific Ocean must have fed the basin. The Laguna Mountains prohibit any above ground stream from connecting the Pacific to the Salton Sea. Therefore, an underground river originating on the Pacific Coast must have brought salt water to the sea until some sort of geological upheaval closed off its entrance.

Stearns offered more "proof:" Since San Diego Bay does not have a distinctive delta, as do most such bays, "the existence of such a river is necessary to the formation of the harbor," he told Degelman. Had not the underground river once run, "the shore of San Diego would be as unbroken as the remainder of the California coast from San Francisco to the Mexican line."

Despite his little slip up in omitting several sans-delta harbors along the coastline, Stearns continued to say that after several afternoons spent digging, he and his associate had uncovered the cavern's entrance on a sandy beach in Coronado.

Equipped with coal-oil torches, ropes, and balls of twine to mark the way through the cavern's twists and turns, the professor and his assistant descended into the cavern. They passed through several tight spots before reaching an area of complete blackness. Even with the torches, the men could only see faint points of light.

"My first thought was that we had again reached the outer air with its starry sky," Stearns recounted. "But soon, I realized we were in the mouth of an immense cavern, whose tops and sides were hung with sparkling crystals."

As the pair headed onward, the cavern narrowed again and the walls grew more thickly studded with crystals. It was as though they had entered a kaleidoscope. Various colored and shaped crystals shined everywhere. Cavern walls bulged with wide veins of gold-bearing quartz. Valuable minerals lay at their feet.

The men pressed onward. They passed a small underground stream fed by water dripping from the bay above and noticed it emptied into a bowl-like basin of solid white rock that appeared to be hand-carved.

They shrugged off that find and continued more than two miles through the cavern until their general sense of direction told them they were beneath downtown San Diego.

There, they discovered a door-like opening obviously chiseled by some sort of tool.

Through the opening, the men found a small square-sided room that held roughly hewn blocks of stone, each about eight feet long, three feet wide and three feet high. Irrefutable evidence of an ancient race was at hand.

These blocks were piled on top of one another almost to the ceiling and were arranged in rows with aisles between them. Stearns tapped on the blocks and determined they were hollow. By scraping with the blade of his knife, the professor discovered that each box had a stone slab cover about six inches thick.

The men were not able to remove the heavy stone slabs, so they hoisted a small boulder to the top of one of the piles and dropped it several times onto a low-lying block. When the cover finally crumbled, "A sickening resinous odor was immediately emitted," Stearns said. "We lowered ourselves as soon as possible to continue our investigations. As I supposed, the block proved to be a stone coffin, in which the dead had been hermetically sealed after being embalmed. The coffin was full of a black, grimy, and very ill-smelling substance."

The professor used his knife blade to scrape away some of the substance to reveal a human corpse. But before he could examine the body more closely, he was overcome by a suffocating stench. On the way out, he picked up a small, triangular fragment of slate that had unusual characters chiseled on it.

He paused during the interview to show Degelman the slate and a few pieces of quartz. The reporter examined the objects and agreed the symbols on the stone resembled Egyptian glyphs.

Stearns went on to say his preliminary findings were that the ancient race was at least 5,000 years old and possibly older. It predated the Egyptian pyramids, he said, and certainly proved beyond doubt that civilization in North America was at one time more advanced than anywhere in the Near or Far East.

"After our retreat from the malodorous sarcophagus," the professor continued,

> I noticed by reference to my watch that the night had far advanced. It was certain that we must retrace our steps if we wished to emerge from the opening before dawn. We easily found our way back by following the course of the twine that we had unrolled behind us. After gaining the outer air, we bent ourselves to the task of entirely concealing the opening. This we accomplished after an hour's exertion, and I believe we did the work effectively. I have no fear that the place will be discovered, as no possible trace of an excavation is visible.

Stearns disclosed several reasons for keeping the location of the cave from the general public. Vandals would soon remove the beautiful crystal stalactites and hundreds of torches would blacken the walls and ceiling. Worse, salt water dripping from the ceiling indicated that only a thin layer of rock kept the enormous weight of water in the bay from crashing in the cave's ceiling. An enemy of the state could take a few pounds of dynamite and blow open the roof of the cave, Stearns claimed. The tremendous weight of the water would instantly enlarge the hole and the river would soon be rolling in its former full volume through its ancient underground channel. The result would be the flooding of the entire Colorado Desert to a depth of 200 feet. The middle of San Diego Bay would become a perpetual, swirling vortex. Any ship or boat venturing too close would be sucked in and engulfed in the subterranean current. San Diego Bay would become useless as a harbor.

The reporter was shown the door, and the professor vowed to continue his investigations from Washington and return with his findings. There is no account of his ever showing up in San Diego again.

The next day's page-one headlines and article gave sleepy San Diego scintillating gossip for weeks and months to come.

Over the last century, questions have been asked: Did a phony scientist put one over on a gullible reporter? Did a savvy reporter fool his editor? Did the editor and reporter dupe the newspaper's publisher? Or did the entire newspaper staff pull off an elaborate New Year's Day hoax on the city?

Decades after the legendary hoax, reporters for the *San Diego Union-Tribune* set out to answer that question. Searching the newspaper's employment records, they failed to find any mention of the reporter, Charles F. Degelman.

A search of numerous federal agencies in Washington failed to find any credentials for Professor Robert E. C. Stearns, or any other substantive information.

CHAPTER 29

Gunfight at the Gaskill Store

Few San Diegans are aware that a shootout in East County exceeded in intensity — and in fact predated — the legendary Gunfight at the OK Corral.

Brothers Luman and Silas Gaskill were among the first to settle in Campo in the spring of 1868. Sixty miles east of San Diego City and two miles north of the Mexican border, Campo was often targeted by thieves and cattle rustlers who could attack and retreat back into Mexico with ease.

But word among thieves was that the Gaskill brothers were handy with firearms and best left alone. In fact, the brothers had hunted bear for a livelihood in northern California prior to moving to the San Diego area.

In Campo, the brothers prospered. Large herds of cattle grazed on their 900-acre ranch. They raised sheep and hogs and at one point had 400 beehives that reportedly produced 30 tons of honey in one summer.

By 1875, the brothers had built and established a store, a mill, a small hotel, a blacksmith shop, and several residences.

This prosperity did not escape the attention of Pancho Lopez, a Mexican bandit and gang leader headquartered just over the border in Tecate, Mexico. Lopez' gang was the remnant of a larger force that had been broken up when several of its leaders were captured and hanged.

Lopez wanted to rebuild his gang and resume raiding in northern Mexico. He thought an attack on Campo was a good way to get money and supplies to do so.

Lopez had heard of the Gaskills' skill with firearms but conceived a plan in which six men on horseback would launch an initial attack. Once that attack began, nine additional outlaws in two wagons would join in. As far as Lopez knew, it would be just the two Gaskill brothers against 15 armed bandits. The numbers were in his favor.

Accounts of the gun battle vary, but by compiling a number of reports and several firsthand descriptions, we can imagine what it was like.

On a clear December 4th morning, nine men in two farm wagons passed through Campo eastward, down the dusty road to Tecate. The men casually nodded as they passed a half dozen riders headed in the opposite direction toward town. The riders continued. The wagoneers stopped, ready to race toward town at the first gunshot.

At about the same time, Silas Gaskill was mending a wagon wheel in the blacksmith shop across from the store when a young Mexican appeared at the door. In his words:

> A Mexican was hanging around the shop and he seemed to be pretty nervous. I was busy and paid no attention to him. He waited until he could talk to me alone. Then he slipped up and whispered in my ear. He said Pancho Lopez and his gang was coming to clean us out. I had been on good terms with the informer and fed him occasionally when he was broke. Anyhow, he put me on guard.

The Gaskills wasted no time. They hid pistols and shotguns throughout the store, the blacksmith shop, the house, the stable, and even outside. Then they went about business as usual.

It was mid-morning when Lopez and his gang rode into Campo. Trying to emulate travelers, the bandits dismounted and split up. Four bandits casually strolled over to a cantina. Alonzo Cota and Jose Alvijo headed toward the store.

After a few moments, Lopez joined Cota and Alvijo and the trio walked into the store. Lopez raised his hand and signaled the attack. As the two men reached for their guns, Lumen Gaskill yelled, "Murder!" and ducked behind the counter to grab his shotgun.

Both Cota and Alvijo jumped over the counter. Cota grabbed Lumen by the hair and held him. Alvijo stuck his pistol into Lumen's chest and fired. The bullet went through Lumen's chest and he slumped to the floor, bleeding from the mouth.

Upon hearing the cry and gunshot, Silas grabbed one of his cached shotguns and whirled just as the bandit Rafael Martinez rushed into the shop. The robber fired first and nicked Silas, who returned fire with the shotgun, wounding the robber and knocking him to the floor.

Bandits Teodoro Vásquez and Pancho Alvitro were approaching the blacksmith shop door when they saw their accomplice shot down. They quickly scurried around behind the shop, but Silas circled the shop from the opposite direction and surprised them.

Silas blasted Vásquez into the next world, and then took aim at Alvitro, who apparently didn't realize the double-barreled shotgun was empty. Alvitro ran toward the mill and took cover behind a stack of lumber. Silas began running toward his house to grab another shotgun.

At the same time Silas was engaging the bandits, a man known only as "the Frenchman" galloped into town. He leapt from the saddle and, using his horse for cover began firing his pistol at the bandits in the street.

One of his shots hit gang-leader Lopez in the neck, knocking him to the ground. But the gritty Lopez kept firing.

While Silas and the Frenchman exchanged gunfire with the bandits, Lumen lay on the floor of the store bleeding profusely. Summoning all of his energy, the grocer took his shotgun from under the counter and crawled to the door. From there, Lumen saw the man who had shot him, Alvijo, working his way toward the Frenchman's horse. Lumen fired from the prone position and dropped Alvijo.

Meanwhile, Silas bolted toward the house to get another shotgun, passed a stranger named Livingston, who had wandered into town to see what the commotion was all about.

Silas sprinted past Livingston and tossed him his empty shotgun. Silas couldn't find the gun he had hidden in the house and ran back out the front door just in time to see a bandit advancing on Livingston. It was Alvitro, who had been hiding near a woodpile. He was walking toward the stranger and aiming his pistol.

Silas grabbed the still-empty shotgun from Livingston's hands and aimed it. Alvitro, apparently still not convinced the gun was empty, raced for cover. But Alvitro's path took him directly through Lumen's line of fire. Still lying on the ground and bleeding, the storekeeper shot and dropped Alvitro.

Lumen then crawled back behind the counter and slipped through a trap door in the floor normally used to access cold water from the creek below.

Then silence fell over the Gaskill store. One bandit was dead, several were wounded, and the two wagons with nine men never showed up. Lopez and Alvitro, both wounded, managed to mount their horses and ride out of town with the uninjured Cota trailing close behind them. Alvitro was so seriously wounded he could not continue. Lopez helped him off his horse, dragged him to a clump of bushes, and shot him in the head.

Vásquez lay dead behind the blacksmith shop. Another bandit, the slightly wounded Martinez, was captured. Alvijo, who had been felled in the street by Lumen's shot from the store, crawled off into the chaparral and hid, planning to make his way back across the border after dark.

The townspeople of Campo quickly rallied and early that afternoon a posse of 10 ranchers rode out in search of the bandits. They employed a tracker to comb the hillsides. One tracking party returned midafternoon with news that they had found Alvitro's body about three miles out of town.

Fearing the bandits would regroup and launch a full-scale invasion, the ranchers returned to town and gathered enough weapons and food to outlast any siege. Lookouts were placed atop nearby hills and the townsfolk of Campo waited.

Just before dawn the next morning, a wounded and shivering Alvijo staggered into town and begged for help. He was placed under guard with the captured Martinez in a cabin.

That night, the man assigned to watch the prisoners let his guard down just long enough for the ranchers to carry off the prisoners. The two were found hanging from an oak tree near the Mexican border, swinging from a single rope.

Lopez and Cota, the two bandits who escaped, headed east toward Yuma, leaving a trail of mayhem and murder in their wake. Lopez was shot and killed a few years later while rustling sheep.

Lumen Gaskill recovered from his wound and both brothers lived normal lives. According to one account, several years after the gunfight a sheriff in El Paso, Texas, sent word to Silas Gaskill that he captured Cota and would deliver him to San Diego for $1,000. The Gaskill brothers passed on the offer.

A botched hold-up in 1875 led to a running gun battle at the Gaskill Brothers' store in Campo. The east county shootout was more deadly than the Gunfight at the OK Corral. *San Diego Historical Society Photograph Collection.*

The gunfight at the Gaskill Store never received the notoriety that the Gunfight at the OK Corral did. Nonetheless, it remains a bastion of San Diego lore.

The shootout at the OK Corral on October 26, 1881, in Tombstone, Arizona lasted less than a minute. It left three cowboys dead and three lawmen wounded. The 1868 Gaskill gunfight took hours to unfold and left four robbers dead and both Gaskill brothers wounded.

After a deadly gun battle, the townspeople of Campo quickly rallied and hired a tracker to lead a posse of ranchers to search for the outlaws. *Image of a tracker titled 'On a Hot Trail,' by artist T. De Thulstrup, courtesy* Harper's Weekly.

Buffalo Soldiers Roamed
San Diego's Border

While many are familiar with the exploits of the Buffalo Soldiers, few are aware that the legendary black cavalry troopers operated in the rugged mountains east of San Diego during World War II.

These men guarded the U.S./Mexican border against a possible Japanese invasion, fought brush fires, patrolled dams, and protected the San Diego-Arizona Railroad from sabotage.

For 18 months, they trained for the day they'd be called into combat with Army units in Europe and North Africa. That day never came.

The Buffalo Soldiers were formed when the Army organized two black cavalry regiments in 1866. During the next two decades, soldiers of the 9th and 10th regiments fought Indians in the Great Plains, Texas, New Mexico, and Arizona. It is said the troops were nicknamed Buffalo Soldiers by adversaries who thought their hair resembled buffalo fur.

The Buffalo Soldiers distinguished themselves during the Spanish-American War by fighting in Cuba alongside Theodore Roosevelt's roughriders in 1898. They also fought with General John J. (Blackjack) Pershing in the Philippines and later fought in Mexico as part of the Mexican Punitive Expedition against Pancho Villa in 1916-17.

After WWI, the two regiments were dispatched to various posts throughout America's heartland until 1942. The 10th Cavalry was then ordered to east San Diego County's Camp Lockett to form the 4th Cavalry Brigade.

Built in 1941, Camp Lockett originally housed the Army's 11th Cavalry, an all-white regiment that guarded San Diego's Presidio and patrolled the Mexican-American border. Shortly after the 11th Cavalry was called away to fight in Europe, the 10th arrived and became part of the 4th Brigade.

In February of 1943, the Army brought the 4th Brigade up to full strength by creating the 28th Cavalry Regiment. In order to create a cavalry regiment out of thin air, the Army relied on the experience of the soldiers of the 10th Cavalry. Men, many of whom had no familiarity with horses, were brought in from reception centers in the East and Midwest.

An estimated 1,200 - 1,500 horses were brought in from Texas. Intensive training began.

Machine-gun troops rode the rolling hills around Camp Lockett while service troops kept supplies coming. A medical detachment, headquarters troops and a marching band rounded out the regiment. Within four months the 28th Cavalry was adept enough to ride alongside the 10th.

On July 24, 1943, Army top brass called for a full mounted review of the troops. Campo residents who witnessed the review were treated to the unforgettable spectacle of thousands of mounted cavalrymen riding in close formation.

Black soldiers experienced segregation on and off base at Camp Lockett. Since black soldiers were prohibited from attaining any rank higher than sergeant, about 300 white officers were assigned to lead the two regiments comprising about 3,500 men. Blacks were also relegated to separate seating at the base's movie theater. The on-base hospitality house for visiting wives was off limits to blacks. Private hospital rooms were reserved for white soldiers only, regardless of rank.

Off-base treatment was largely the same. Black soldiers were prohibited from riding in all-white train cars from Campo to San Diego and back. Only when enough blacks had congregated at a depot would the conductors attach an additional car to the back of the train. In town,

The legendary Buffalo Soldiers were stationed at Camp Lockett in Campo and patrolled the United States/Mexican border prior to WWI. Several soldiers in this 1890 photograph are wearing buffalo robes. *Library of Congress photo.*

black troops were prohibited from entering the U.S.O. Most restaurants and bars outside the "Negro District" were off limits as well.

Despite their earlier successes and recent combat training, the Army never sent the Buffalo Soldiers into battle as combatants. Numerous historical sources point to the fact that despite a pressing need for American combat troops overseas, most commanders refused to accept black soldiers. Although there were some exceptions, most black soldiers overseas were assigned to support duties, rather than combat.

Failing to find a combat role for the 4th Brigade, the Army opted to convert the unit (along with its parent unit, the 2nd Cavalry Division) from a combat unit to a service unit.

Without publicizing the move, the Army gave the 10th and 28th regiments new weapons and shipped them to North Africa. Many men in the regiment thought they were headed into combat. In actuality, they arrived in North Africa only to find out that their regiments had been disbanded.

Fred Jones, a 28th Regiment veteran actively involved in the effort to turn Camp Lockett into a state park, told *Traditions Magazine* a few years before his death in January 2003:

> When we left Camp Lockett, we thought that we were being shipped overseas to fight. None of the men — maybe with the exception of the older troopers — thought we would be put into service units. We didn't know that our division had already been disbanded.

Although the Army officially denied that the breakup was racially motivated, federal Judge William H. Hastie, acting as liaison to the black community stated: "The truth of the matter is that these original combat units have been problem children of the Army for more than two years, not because they were incompetent, but because no one wanted them."

Most men from the two Camp Lockett regiments were sent to service or training battalions. Although many black men saw combat during WWII, few Buffalo Soldiers did. Jones was sent to Italy to become part of an engineering unit after the breakup. He later saw combat after he volunteered to join the black 92nd Infantry Battalion.

As World War II drew to a close, Camp Lockett briefly became a prisoner of war camp, and later converted to a military convalescent hospital. The military closed the hospital in 1946 and the federal government returned the land to San Diego County.

CHAPTER 31

Chinese Empress Started Tourmaline Craze

San Diego County mines have produced more than a billion dollars in tourmaline crystals, but few residents have heard the amazing legend surrounding their discovery and operation.

The story begins millions and millions of years ago when pressurized streams of molten magma from the earth's core extruded through cracks and fissures in granite on their way to the surface. As the lava cooled, it formed pockets and seams. Over the millennia, minerals crystallized in those seams.

Pockets of these beautiful crystals, in a wide range of colors including red, pink, green, dark blue, and black, occur in the mountains in an area that runs from northern San Diego County through Pala, Ramona, Julian, and Jacumba.

Credit for the discovery of tourmaline is somewhat clouded in history. According to some accounts, local Indians had discovered tourmaline outcroppings in the rocks centuries before the arrival of Europeans but found the gems of little value. Some stories tell of Indian youths who used tourmaline for rock throwing and trading for penny candy at the general store in Pala, about 45 miles north of San Diego City. Others say Belgian shepherds wandering throughout the hills ventured upon the crystals but kept quiet about the discovery. Still other accounts tell of a travelling salesman in the 1880s who noticed barefoot Indian children playing with bright green and red marbles. He acquired a few of the stones, had them analyzed and discovered they were chiseled from tourmaline.

Regardless how its presence was made public, the discovery of tourmaline didn't particularly excite San Diego's turn-of-the-century miners. Tourmaline was already being mined elsewhere in the world and locally, other minerals such as gold, garnet, beryl, and kunzite were being extracted more profitably.

One miner, C.R. Orcutt, began digging for tourmaline deposits in the Pala area in 1892 and discovered a large vein of pink tourmaline. News and specimens of the pink tourmaline, dubbed "Pala Pink," reached the ears of Tzu His, the Empress Dowager of China.

According to legend, the empress became so deeply entranced by the translucent gem that she declared pink tourmaline, rather than jade, China's new sacred stone. This bode well for San Diego miners, since few other areas produced the gem in its pink form.

Quickly, procurement agents from China descended upon San Diego and began shipping back hundreds and hundreds of pounds of pink tourmaline crystals. Demand was so high that for a fleeting moment tourmaline became more valuable than diamonds.

The Boxer Rebellion (1899-1901), an uprising against foreign influence in religion, politics, and trade, brought down the Ch'ing Dynasty and ended the tourmaline craze. Here, a company of Boxers marches in Tien-Tsin, China. *Photo courtesy U.S. Library of Congress.*

More than a dozen mines opened during the peak of activity as prospectors sought — and sometimes fought — to unearth tourmaline pockets. One claim jumping dispute led to a four-year court battle that culminated in 1902 with a $40,000 settlement (about $850,000 in today's currency), ordered to be paid to the rightful owner of the San Diego mine.

Even the famous Tiffany family of New York got into the act by acquiring, some say through devious means, the Mesa Grande mine.

Hundreds of tons of tourmaline crystals were shipped to China's Forbidden City until the Boxer Rebellion of the early 1900s destroyed the power of the Ch'ing Dynasty. By 1912, exports to China all but stopped and many tourmaline mine owners went bankrupt.

In the decades that followed, many mines closed while others worked only sporadically. Among mines yielding the gemstones throughout the years were the Himalaya, Stewart Lithia, Pala Chief, and Tourmaline Queen.

In 1972, a magnificent specimen was extracted from the Tourmaline Queen by mine-owner Bill Larson. The stunning "Candelabra Tourmaline" comprises three large, candle-shaped, red tourmaline crystals growing straight up from a bed of orange quartz. More than 12 inches overall, the specimen at the time was dubbed, "The find of the century," by the American Museum of Natural History.

The Candelabra Tourmaline is praiseworthy in part because the three crystal "candles" are three inches long and more than two inches in diameter. The average tourmaline crystal is about the size of a stubby pencil.

The Smithsonian Institution purchased and now displays the specimen. Its present-day worth is said to exceed $1 million.

Until a few years ago, a handful of Pala-area mines were worked for profit or operated as tourist attractions. From the 1960s to the early 1990s, the mines shipped about $1 million of tourmaline per year, making San Diego the world's third largest source behind Brazil and Sri Lanka, according to a February 1990 *Fedco Reporter* article.

Ultimately, legal issues, insurance costs, and environmental concerns forced the mine owners to cease all significant operations. Mines were closed and securely padlocked. Tours were halted. On-site gem stores were boarded up. And San Diego's tourmaline industry lost its luster.

CHAPTER 32

A Lighthouse Too Tall

In general terms, taller lighthouses are better than shorter lighthouses. It stands to reason that due to the curvature of the earth's surface, light beamed from atop a tall structure can be seen from a greater distance than light from a shorter structure.

It may stand to reason, but it didn't work in San Diego. A lighthouse, built at the summit of the Point Loma Peninsula in 1854, became the source of complaints from ship captains.

Point Loma actually may have served as a beacon site long before the first Europeans arrived in 1542. Native Americans used such promontories and other prominent places to set fires to relay signals over vast distances.

According to one early written account, "Indians were spectators at every event. Never a ship that came up from the south, but notice flew from hill to hill."

What happens to a lighthouse built so tall (462 feet above sea level) that it doesn't aid mariners? It becomes the centerpiece of the Cabrillo National Monument, one of the most visited national parks in the United States. *Author photo.*

After the Mexican-American War ended in 1848, officials began construction plans for a lighthouse atop Point Loma. The lighthouse would tower high above the ocean so that its beam could reach as far as possible without being blocked by the curvature of the earth.

In 1854, United States Army engineers completed such a structure. Called the Spanish Lighthouse, it towered 462 feet above sea level.

The lantern was state of the art for its era. Barrel-shaped, about six feet in diameter and eight feet tall, the glass light was a beautiful example of French glass cutting art. Called a Fresnel lens (pronounced frenel), its glass surface was divided into 12 panels. Each panel focused the light into a bull's eye prism. This focusing multiplied a single kerosene burner 400 times so that the lens produced 60,000 candle power.

The newly completed lighthouse was taller and more brilliant that any other similar structure. Officials beamed with pride until complaints started rolling in.

The Point Loma light couldn't be seen at all during foggy periods, ship captains grumbled. San Diego has a thin but persistent layer of clouds, called a marine layer that hangs over the water. The newly built lighthouse beam was so high that instead of lighting the way for mariners in low visibility situations, the beam bounced off the top of the marine layer. Unable to penetrate the mist, the grand lighthouse was practically useless to boats at sea.

Engineers immediately realized their mistake and began plans for a new lighthouse to be built farther down the hillside nearer the ocean. The new lighthouse was opened and the Spanish Lighthouse shut down in 1891 after serving a mere 37 years — a drop in the bucket for lighthouse service.

Although the new lighthouse's 88-foot elevation limits its beam to about 17 miles compared to the 462-footer's 33-mile range, the light is visible in a far greater range of weather conditions.

The new lighthouse utilized Spanish Lighthouse's Fresnel lens more than 100 years, until gradual settling of the structure caused a failure in its support mechanisms.

When the Point Loma lighthouse's replacement lens arrived in January, 1999, boaters were amazed to learn that the new unit was roughly the size of a five gallon bucket. But this little lens packed a big punch. It produced about 200,000 candlepower, far more than the old Fresnel lens even after conversion from kerosene to electricity in the early 1900s.

Today, the old Spanish Lighthouse is the crown jewel of the Cabrillo National Monument, the second most-visited national park in the United States. Only the Statue of Liberty draws more visitors.

San Diego: Harlem of the West

Few reminders exist of San Diego's Harlem of the West, a black community that flourished from the mid-1890s through the 1950s near the city's present-day Gaslamp Quarter.

Centered around the Douglas Hotel and the Creole Palace, Harlem West hosted music, dance, and show venues rivaling any found in San Diego today. Jazz and blues superstars Louis Armstrong, Cab Calloway, Nat King Cole, Ella Fitzgerald, Billie Holiday, Jelly Roll Morton, and Charlie "Bird" Parker performed in hotels and nightclubs throughout the district.

Frequent music and dance festivals beckoned amateurs and professionals from across the United States.

But perhaps the biggest draws were the cakewalk contests. The cakewalk traces its roots to African American slaves. Couples form a square, bend back at the waist and high step and strut to lively music. This grand promenade is actually a parody on formal ballroom dancing and includes exaggerated bowing, waving canes, and doffing hats. The cakewalk became a national phenomenon through the 1920s and was often performed on stage in Harlem West. Although professional dancers entertained audiences with it, amateur contests were the most exciting.

In contests, couples danced until eliminated by judges. The last dancers won a lavishly decorated cake — thus the name cakewalk.

Many Harlem West hotels appealed to blacks in the area because they were mixed-use facilities that included kitchenettes, restaurants, barbershops, billiard rooms, and laundries, according to Gaslamp Black Historical Society president Barbara Huff. At one time, more than 20 hotels in the area were black owned or operated.

But the area's centerpiece was the Douglas Hotel. Built as a luxury hotel in 1924, the Douglas provided upscale accommodations for musicians such as Billie Holiday and Cab Calloway who performed in the adjacent Creole Palace.

It also welcomed black screen stars such as Lena Horne and Dorothy Dandridge, the first black woman nominated for an Oscar for best actress in "Carmen Jones" in 1954.

Remnants of the era were evident well into the 1980s, Huff says. Though blacks continue to own businesses in the district today, most had moved to Logan Heights by the 1960s. The Douglas Hotel and Creole Palace were demolished in 1985.

Not much remains of San Diego's Harlem of the West today except a few old structures that have been deemed historically significant by the city's Historical Resources Board. The buildings include dilapidated and boarded up apartments, cinder-block studios, a pink stucco house, and a few vacant lots.

Those structures are caught in a tug-of-war between those who would like to bulldoze them for a new downtown residential area and those who envision a Harlem of the West thematic district, replete with museums, shops, restaurants — and hopefully a few jazz and blues clubs. Wouldn't that take the cake?

Centered around the Douglas Hotel and Creole Palace in today's Gaslamp District, Harlem West hosted music, dance, and show venues featuring superstars such as Louis Armstrong, Cab Calloway, Nat King Cole, and Ella Fitzgerald. A dance called "The Cakewalk" was in vogue at the time. *San Diego Historical Society Photograph Collection.*

CHAPTER 34

The Salton Sea Disaster

One of the most severe and long-lasting ecological disasters in the history of the United States occurred in San Diego County in 1905 when the Colorado River burst through a series of man-made irrigation channels.

Despite efforts to regain control of the river, water flowed out into the desert for two years and created the Salton Sea, according to a *Las Vegas-Review Journal* article. The salty, shallow, 36-mile-long by 15-mile-wide desert lake has since been dubbed, "An ecosystem gone haywire" by one national magazine.

Although some San Diego boosters are quick to point out that the Salton Sea lies in Imperial County, not San Diego County, they overlook the fact that Imperial County was not created until August 1907. When the disaster actually occurred, Salton Sea was within San Diego County.

The dream of converting the arid desert into lush farmland was first acted upon in 1900 when a series of short canals were dug. In 1901, the canals were filled and water flowed. But in addition to water, silt entered the canals at an alarming rate, enough by volume to elevate one square mile of land 53 feet per year.

Two years of heavy rainfall in 1904-05 sealed the project's fate when the Colorado River burst through its containment and flooded the Imperial Valley.

From one written account:

> The immense volume of water, flowing with increased strength and velocity as it defined for itself a more distinct channel down the steeper grade of the Basin, began cutting in the soft soil a vertical fall that from the foot of the grade moved swiftly up-stream; a mighty cataract from fifty to sixty feet in height and a full quarter of a mile wide, moving at the rate of from one to three miles a day and leaving as it went a great gorge through which a new-made river flowed quietly to a new-born and ever-growing sea. The roar of the plunging waters, the crashing and booming of the falling masses of earth that were undermined by the roaring torrent were heard miles away.

When the wall of water ultimately subsided, it had carved immense channels across the desert and ultimately began to pool up in a bowl left behind by ancient Lake Cahuilla, which lies about 228 feet below sea level.

In little more than two years, with nowhere else to go, the Colorado River had formed the Salton Sea; a sea with no outlet.

At first, news of a new lake in the middle of the desert created a buzz for San Diego and Los Angeles residents. The newly formed desert lake gave coastal dwellers a new place to frolic in the winter. Desert climates seem inviting when air temperatures along the seashore hover in the low 60s and the ocean water falls to the high 50s.

For a while, the Salton Sea drew more visitors per year than Yosemite. Vacationers frolicked along the shore. Trout and other freshwater fish were introduced. Marinas and motels sprang up, housing lots were sold, and streets were paved and posted with names such as Mecca, Sea View, and Sea Garden.

But all was not well in this new Mecca. The once-stable body of freshwater was growing too salty to support several species of the imported fish. Researchers discovered the cause. The Salton Sea was being supplied somewhat salty water by the Colorado River. Since the Salton Sea had no outlet, the water had no place to go. So the water would sit under the desert sun and evaporate. Since salt does not evaporate, the water left behind becomes increasingly salty.

Today, the Salton Sea is approximately 25 percent saltier than the Pacific Ocean and the salt content keeps rising. Several species of salt-tolerant fish were introduced in the 1960s, but many scientists believe that even the hardiest species will eventually succumb to the lake's high salt levels. Even now, millions of tilapia, croaker, and other fish die off each year due to too much salt and too little oxygen. After taking a canoe trip across the sea, one journalist wrote, "The smell is rancid; not that clean smell of fresh-cut fish in a harbor, but a wafting smell of decay, windless plumes of fish-stink rising from the sea. When I land on the beach, the boat makes a harsh scraping. This beach is made from the spines of dead tilapia."

Evaporation in the Salton Sea also tends to concentrate natural- and man-made chemicals. Pesticides from nearby agricultural concerns and the heavy metal selenium have become so concentrated that health officials warn against eating more than modest amounts of fish from the sea.

The desert lake's ecologically vile soup can be deadly to other wildlife as well. The Salton Sea has become an important habitat for more than 350 species of birds, including the endangered southern bald eagle, California brown pelican, and peregrine falcon. But the sea can kill. In 1996, a botulism outbreak killed thousands of endangered California brown pelicans and other birds. Periodically other diseases will strike and millions of fish and bird carcasses will wash up on shore, making national headlines. One such event, an algae bloom, killed an estimated 7.6 million fish and countless birds in 1998.

The Salton Sea Authority currently spends millions of dollars per year on salinity control. Part of that spending supports a rapid-response program that utilizes spotter airplanes to direct boats and shore personnel to remove dead fish and birds.

To restore water quality to the Salton Sea, taxpayers would have to pony up billions of dollars and fund up to one billion in annual maintenance fees — all for a problem that began in San Diego County more than 100 years ago.

The once thriving destination resorts are now like ghost towns, with only a handful of permanent residents. Visitors to the area remark about the inescapable rotting smell in the air and stare in awe at the surreal sights of abandoned mobile homes and buildings, caked with mud and salt.

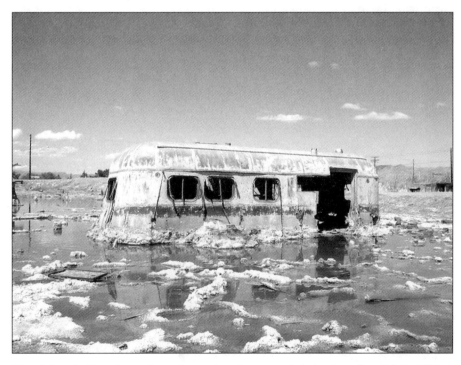

The Colorado River burst through a series of man-made irrigation channels in 1905 to create the Salton Sea, which is considered by some to be an environmental nightmare of epic proportions. The Salton Sea was part of San Diego County until 1907. *Author photo.*

Explosives and Bad Cinema
The Gunpowder Point Story

On the eastern shore of South San Diego Bay sits the 46-acre Living Coast Nature Center, a gateway for those wishing to visit now-rare California wetlands.

The Nature Center buildings are designed to look like New England boathouses. Once inside, visitors may view nature exhibits, participate in interactive displays or watch stingrays swim in a shallow tide-pool-like aquarium.

But few visitors realize the bayside site once hosted a gunpowder factory, an artillery emplacement, a cottonseed mill and warehouse, a large-scale farm, a landfill, and a cult movie set.

At the beginning of World War I, the Hercules Powder Company opened a gunpowder factory on the site. The factory's purpose was to

Today, the Living Coast Nature Center sits atop Hercules Powder Company. Decades after the powder factory burned to the ground, Gunpowder Point served as a movie set for the cult classic, *Attack of the Killer Tomatoes*. *San Diego Historical Society Photograph Collection.*

take kelp harvested from offshore Point Loma and extract acetone and potash from it. The chemicals were used to make cordite, a relatively smoke-free explosive sought after by the British.

Hercules brought in three kelp cutters, dredged a canal, and installed a railroad spur. In its heyday, Hercules employed 1,500 people around the clock. Most workers lived in Chula Vista and were brought out to the factory at Gunpowder Point by a trolley line from "Potash Junction" at E Street.

It was said that the rotting kelp stench from the factory was so bad that people living downwind could scarcely open their windows. Most workers were not allowed inside their own homes after a shift without first showering and changing their clothes. Hercules closed the gunpowder factory after four years.

With the brick buildings still standing, San Diego Oil Products Corporation next occupied the site. That operation grew quickly to become the nation's largest cottonseed warehouse, producing prodigious amounts of cottonseed oil and cottonseed meal. Even the cottonseed's oily husks were sold for cattle feed.

Disaster struck in 1929 when the cottonseed plant caught fire. Local fire departments fought valiantly for nearly 12 hours until the inferno drove them back. The oil-fed fire on Gunpowder Point burned for days and ultimately reduced the buildings to rubble. The loss was estimated at $330,000, about $3.3 million in today's dollars.

From 1930 through the mid-70s, the site hosted several large-scale farms that produced tomatoes, celery, lettuce, strawberries, and cucumbers. Growers erected four farmhouses, a bunkhouse, and a cafeteria said to have its own tortilla-making machine to serve the Hispanic workers.

Then in 1978, giant mutant killer tomatoes overran the farmland. At least, that's what the script read. Filming had begun by Four Square Productions on a low-budget, sci-fi spoof entitled *Attack of the Killer Tomatoes.*

The "it's so bad it's good" screenplay was penned by Steven Peace, who would later become state senator. The story features thousands of ordinary tomatoes turning into savage predators. The tomatoes move throughout San Diego, burning and pillaging, until it is discovered they can be killed by bad rock music.

After nearly a century of accommodating an unusual assortment of activities, the Living Coast Nature Center opened on Gunpowder Point in 1987. But even today, savvy visitors notice signs of the land's checkered past: thousands upon thousands of odd-shaped bricks from the abandoned gunpowder plant, a silted up canal, a rusty overgrown railroad spur, and on occasion a rogue tomato or two.

Imperial Beach Mystery Submarine

One local legend that surfaces with remarkable regularity, usually during periods of very low tides, is that there's a submarine wreck off of Imperial Beach.

That legend is true.

The sunken submarine *S-37* is only occasionally visible from shore, but has been a fixture off the San Diego shoreline since 1945. The wreck lies in about 30 feet of water with its bow buried in the sand. Its 219-foot hull makes a somewhat popular scuba diving destination, although those who have visited the wreck caution others to use care. The sub's hull is a mere 20 feet wide, and the interior is quite cramped.

Naval history tells us that *S-37* was constructed in 1919 by the Union Iron Works in San Francisco. The 1,000-ton vessel carried a crew of 42. Top speed was 15 knots on the surface and 12 knots when submerged. *S-37* saw action in the South Pacific in WWII, and is credited with sinking at least one Japanese destroyer off of Borneo.

According to one account, on the evening of February 8, 1942, the *S-37* spotted a Japanese convoy with destroyer escorts. According to *S-37's* logbook:

> At 6 p.m., the destroyer, allowed to pass unmolested, disappeared to the northwest. Thirteen minutes later, the mast and upper works of three destroyers in column were sighted: distance 5 miles. *S-37* went after the destroyer formation. Moving on the surface, she closed on the destroyers, all four in column, distance 8,000 yards.
>
> All torpedoes were readied; and, at 7:46, she commenced her approach. By 8:30, unable to gain an unimpaired shot at the transports, *S-37* shifted to attack the destroyers. Between 10:36 and 10:40, she fired one torpedo at each destroyer. Thirty seconds after firing the third torpedo, she observed a hit between the stacks of the third destroyer, and, as black smoke rose, the destroyer buckled in the middle and the mid-ship portion rose approximately 20 feet above the bow and stern. *Natsushio* was going down.

The two remaining destroyers attacked *S-37* with depth charges. Although the Japanese failed to sink *S-37*, damage to the propulsion system caused the sub to spew out a one-mile-long oil slick. By following this slick, the destroyers were able to concentrate their underwater barrages.

Although she escaped the depth-charge barrages, it was nearly a month before the submarine could slow the oil leak to one gallon every 20 minutes and finally head to the nearest friendly port in Australia. The weeks in transit were nothing short of hell. According to one junior officer's account:

> The bunks beyond the wardroom are filled with torrid, skivvy-clad bodies, the sweat running off the white, rash-blistered skin in small rivulets. Metal fans are whirring everywhere. I am playing cribbage with the skipper, mainly because I don't like to wallow in a sweat-soaked bunk most of the day. I have my elbows on the table near the edge and hold may cards with my arms at a slight angle so the sweat will stream down my bare arms, without soaking the cards.
>
> Overhead is a fine net of gauze to catch the wayward cockroaches, which prowl across the top of the wardroom and occasionally fall straight down. They live in the cork insulation, which lines the inside of the submarine itself. We've killed over sixteen million cockroaches in one compartment alone.

Over the course of the following two years, *S-37* conducted six war patrols in the Western Pacific. By the time *S-37* returned to the United States to be hauled out for extensive repairs in San Diego, she had earned five battle stars, including one for torpedoing the 2,776-ton Japanese merchant vessel *Tenan Maru.*

S-37 spent the remainder of the war in San Diego serving as an anti-submarine training vessel. Such vessels typically play hide-and-seek with destroyers within a few miles of San Diego Bay.

S-37's active career ended when she was decommissioned on February 6, 1945. The sub's final assignment was to serve as a target for aerial bombing. But as she was being towed toward one of the area's target ranges, a storm arose and her tow-line snapped.

Before the line could be reattached, *S-37* came to rest completely submerged in about 60 feet of water. The Navy left her there.

Over the next few years, scattered reports appeared in newspapers of a sunken submarine off San Diego, but the Navy denied such reports.

It seems the Navy had lost both the submarine and any record of the submarine.

In the late 1950s, a pair of divers confronted the Navy with hard evidence that such a submarine existed. The Navy searched its records and declared the submarine was a WWII-era submarine that had broken from its towline en route from Panama. The Navy was wrong.

The wreck was later correctly identified when divers showed the Navy one of the brass propellers they had salvaged. According to information stamped into the brass, the propeller had been reshaped in the 1920s.

Shortly thereafter, a private salvage operator attempted to re-float S-37. The sub was raised to the surface but slipped from its line and sank. It eventually floated toward the beach and buried its nose in the sand in about 30 feet of water.

Since the sub lists to port (leans to the left in landlubber terms) about 20 degrees, the conning tower is visible from shore only on those rare days when the tides are low and the surf runs high.

Imperial Beach lore describes a wrecked submarine just beyond the surf that can be seen when the surf is high and the tides are low. The wreckage is that of the American submarine S-37. *Photo courtesy California Wreck Divers.*

From False Bay to Duckville
The Mission Bay Story

The transformation of False Bay to Duckville to Mission Bay Park, the 3,900-acre crown jewel of San Diego, is the stuff of which legends are made.

Mission Bay was listed as False Bay on charts used by ancient mariners since the first European explorers in the mid-1500s.

False Bay appropriately described the large expanse of water that was little more than shallow tidelands. Any mariner who mistakenly steered his sailing ship into False Bay instead of San Diego Bay would soon discover himself stuck in the mud.

The nature of False Bay began to change in the mid-1800s when San Diego — a fledgling city recently made part of the United States — wanted to attract a greater share of maritime trade. A major problem for shippers at that time was that San Diego Bay continually filled up with silt carried downstream by the San Diego River.

The river, which runs through Mission Valley past Old Town, confounded city officials in charge of keeping silt out of San Diego Bay. That's because the river randomly changed its course. Some years it would dump into San Diego Bay. Other years it would dump into False Bay. Even though the San Diego River was almost small enough to jump across during the summer, winter storms could send enough sediment downstream to easily wipe out months of dredging. The city needed a plan to keep San Diego Bay open to sailing vessels that traded up and down the coast.

So, in 1853, authorities commissioned Lt. George Horatio Derby to construct a dike parallel to the San Diego River, on the south side, to force the river to empty into False Bay. The silting of San Diego Bay ceased. But the silt had to go somewhere and before long False Bay began silting up. Eventually, the river deposited so much silt that once-shallow marshes turned into solid land. Over the years, crude buildings began to appear. Among those buildings (where Mission Bay Yacht Club now sits) was a collection of shacks built by duck hunters in the 1920s. They called the encampment Duckville.

Ducks were so numerous around the turn of the 19th century that according to written accounts, trains would routinely stop on the tracks. "Why, the ducks were so thick that it got to be a regular stop on the old San Diego and La Jolla steam railroad," said one old timer.

"The engineer would stop about halfway up on the east side of (False Bay) and the passengers would all get out and bag themselves a mess of ducks for dinner. But for the real duck hunters, we built that Duckville."

Over the years, a ramshackle cluster of shacks grew on the site. Duckville flourished as a weekend retreat for hunters and party-loving men of the era.

It wasn't long, though, before land developers started seeing the possibilities for the area. Portions of the bay were dredged; paid for by property owners who wanted a channel from Crown Point to Mission Beach. A causeway, built by John Spreckles in 1916, connected what is now Midway Boulevard to Crown Point.

Although progress was piecemeal, Duckville became an increasingly popular destination for swimming, fishing, and boating. A master plan, drawn up in the 1930s, changed the name to Mission Bay. By the 1940s, authorities were convinced that all of the dredging done on the bay

Before being developed, Mission Bay was affectionately known as Duckville, a home for ducks and the men that hunted them. *San Diego Historical Society Photograph Collection.*

Mission Bay, seen here with the San Diego Skyline as backdrop, boasts 27 miles of meandering shoreline, waterways, inlets, and islets to explore. The bay's Fiesta Island is pet friendly too! *Author photo.*

could be undone if a major storm hit San Diego. Plans were made for a flood control project that comprised three stone jetties. Two jetties would create the entrance channel to Mission Bay and the third would extend the flood control channel beyond the Ocean Beach shoreline.

Completion of that project — and subsequent dredging throughout the years — created Mission Bay as we know it, the crown jewel of San Diego.

If Mission Bay is so popular, why isn't it ringed by expensive, high-rise hotels, tourists often ask?

The secret to the success of Mission Bay is that the city passed what's called by locals the "75-25" referendum, which limits development of the bay to 25 percent of its total area.

Although the city and developers have made numerous attempts to circumvent that referendum, the citizens of San Diego always rally to keep Mission Bay Park open and accessible to all.

Bate's Folly
The Shelter Island Story

Among the most-visited and prominent features of San Diego Bay, Shelter Island grew out of a simple sandbar and one man's vision.

Throughout recorded history, a sandbar near the shore of San Diego Bay served as a safe haven for boats at anchor. The sandbar that would become Shelter Island was first charted in 1769 by Spanish Captain Vincente Vila during a voyage to supply Father Junípero Serra's expedition. The inlet behind that sandbar served as a convenient anchorage for more than 150 years. It was so popular among boaters that by the mid-1800s, wooden piers jutted out from the sandbar and from the mainland. Since the piers never connected the sandbar with the mainland, mariners rowed to and from their boats.

In the early 1900s, the port began piling sand and other materials from harbor projects upon the sandbar. Perhaps it was while watching the sandbar grow (and the distance between it and the mainland decrease) that San Diego Harbor Department director Joe Brennan first thought of connecting the sandbar to the mainland. But Brennan abandoned his idea after receiving a blistering barrage of criticism from Point Loma residents.

The man who picked up the idea and made it happen was John Bate, a city engineer. As a boy, Bate fished and swam from the island. Later in life when he became port director, Bate wanted to make that part of the harbor more accessible to residents and visitors.

When Bate first went public with his idea, he was met with the same derision as Brennan encountered. Point Loma residents quickly labeled the new proposal, "Bate's Folly."

Undaunted, Bate took his idea door-to-door, explaining to each and every resident that Shelter Island would offer something to everyone: yachtsmen, fishermen, and tourists. "They feared a Coney Island, or worse," Bate said, recounting the initial resistance.

After assuaging residents' fears, the port developed the island between 1949 and 1954.

A causeway was built to connect the island to the mainland and a 400-foot channel entrance was dredged to create the yacht basin. The 300-foot-wide island was raised and leveled off at about 14 feet above the low water mark, leaving less than seven feet of land at the highest tides.

In homage to East Coast tourists, Bate insisted that palm trees line Shelter Island Drive. "East Coast snow birds come here to see waving palm trees and flowers, not the evergreens that grow in their back yards."

Today, Shelter Island, once known as "Bate's Folly," is home to marinas, boatyards, marine businesses, motels, yacht clubs, restaurants, commercial and sport fishing landings, a boat ramp, a small beach, and a few acres of lawn for fun and relaxation.

A narrow pier with two buildings on it sits on the future site of Shelter Island in this 1895 sketch by artist Maud McMullan. The Hotel Del Coronado is seen on Silver Strand in the background. *Image courtesy Library of Congress.*

Harmony Grove
50 Years of Séances

In the decades between 1900 and 1950, spiritualists met weekly at a 30-acre park near Escondido called Harmony Grove. Those summer sessions were chronicled by Edmund Rucker, who wrote for the *San Diego Union* and other periodicals.

The weekend meetings were presented by the Harmony Grove Spiritualists Association and were packed with mediums, mind readers, and séance holders from several nearby states. Many such occultists were card-carrying members of organizations such as the California State Spiritualist Association, the National Spiritualist Association, and the International Spiritualists General Assembly.

A roster of those who attended Harmony Grove would include Dr. H. Robert Moore, who, with the guidance of spirits, could materialize objects, produce mystical slate writings, produce drawings of spirits, and fall into a trance and speak for the dead (called trumpeting).

One rather large, woman from San Bernardino (name unknown) would pace back and forth before the podium before bending her body into an awkward position and falling into a mind-reading trance:

> I can get a vibration from this lady in the second row.
> I hear the voice of a little child. This child has long been
> on the other side. It is sending love. Now there comes a
> new light. I get a vibration from a gentleman on the aisle.
> He wants to know if it would be advisable for him to ask
> for a raise in pay. I don't think so, or at least maybe not
> in this direction — probably up or down. There comes a
> vibration from that lady with the red hat. She is expect-
> ing a visitor. I see that visitor coming from the east. It's a
> woman, a near relative. Her trip will be safe.

Also present was Reverend Phillip Brown from Long Beach who described himself as a "freelance worker" and specialized in answering questions, not from the silent audience, but from those in the spirit world.

The Reverend Ethel Fowler, pastor of New Hope Spiritualist Church on Sixth Avenue, performed as a trumpet medium. She could produce voices in several different languages while holding water in her mouth.

Another regular, Anna Eva Fay, eschewed spiritual guidance in favor of thrilling audiences with feats of mind reading.

Mark Probert, a 42-year-old ex-bellhop, would swoon into a trance-like state and have deep and meaningful conversations in different voices with the likes of Enrico Caruso, Will Rogers, Lawrence of Arabia, financier John Jacob Astor, Thomas Edison, and Lao Tzu, founder of the Chinese philosophy Taoism. The writer Rucker witnessed one such exchange and wrote down several aphorisms supposedly uttered by Lao Tzu while conversing with Probert:

"Man builds great tabernacles in the midst of poverty."

"No one owns anything — all of you are only borrowers. When you come over to this side, you must give up all earthly possessions."

"Each man must be his own church."

"Most men believe God created men — it was just the reverse."

At the end of his talk, Lao Tzu would say through his appointed bell-hop/medium, "Good evening, my friends, I have been honored."

A quick review of Lao Tzu's classic Taoist book, *Tao te Ching*, reveals no matching, or even similar, aphorisms.

Harmony Grove Spiritualists Association meetings were packed with mediums, mind readers, and séance holders. This sketch, 'The Injun Control' was rendered by Joseph C. Lincoln in 1920. *Image courtesy Cosmopolitan Magazine*

San Diego-Coronado Tunnel?

Few San Diegans are aware that the San Diego-Coronado Bay Bridge was first proposed as a tunnel.

The year was 1929 and the idea was rather advanced for its time. A one-mile-long, 35-foot diameter concrete tube would run under the bed of San Diego Bay to connect Coronado to the city. The tube, about 90 feet below sea level at its lowest point, would hold a 23-foot-wide, two-lane roadbed and a four-foot-wide sidewalk. Plans called for pre-casting 250-foot concrete segments of tunnel on land. The 7,000-ton segments would be floated into the bay and lowered into a 60-foot-deep trench carved into the bay's bed. Divers would splice the tube sections together. Dredges would then refill the trenches to cover them.

The $6.5 million project was to have taken about 2 1/2 years to complete and was to have been financed by a city bond. The bond would be repaid over 50 years by tolls collected by the tube's developer and operator, the San Francisco Bridge and Tunnel Company.

The underwater tunnel almost got built!

The city performed requisite seafloor explorations, granted an operating franchise to the bridge and tunnel company, and secured proper rights-of-way through the state. But being no stranger to contractual controversy even back then, the city neglected to file paper work necessary to get the ball rolling. A crucial 60-day "accept or reject" deadline passed. The San Francisco Bridge and Tunnel Company — possibly weary of doing business in a slipshod manner with the city —backed out of its deal with the city and did not forfeit its $25,000 surety bond.

That led to a round of finger-pointing by City Council. One councilmember (who had voted for and signed the original ordinance granting the tunnel company the right to proceed) declared, "I thought when I signed that paper that it was worthless."

Although he quickly recanted his words, the city attorney bristled. He said to local media, "I have no hesitancy in pronouncing the bond worthless, a joke in form and substance."

The idea of a trans-bay tube surfaced again in the early 1950s, when the city solicited input from interested firms. One company conducted a preliminary survey and came up with a figure of $21,836,000 for a tunnel, including ramp connections at Pacific Highway and Market Street areas (in the vicinity of present-day Seaport Village), and Fourth and Pomona Streets in Coronado. In a letter to the city manager dated April 23, 1951, the company stated, "We are pleased to advise you that we have carried out studies and investigations regarding a subaqueous tube to the point where we are of the firm opinion that financing and construction of the project are entirely feasible."

Although the Navy signed off on the tunnel proposition, it was never acted upon.

The existing San Diego Bay Coronado Bridge opened on August 3, 1969 after 2.5 years of construction at a cost of $47.6 million.

Including approaches, the bridge stretches 11,288 feet. But only 1,880 feet span the actual channel. The 90-degree turn mid-span serves to make the bridge long enough to achieve a 4.67 percent grade for automobile traffic, while at the same time achieving a vertical clearance of 200 feet from the water below. This height was designed to allow the passage of Navy aircraft carriers, some towering nearly 200 feet to the top-most mast.

The orthotropic design used in the 2.12-mile long bridge originated in Germany during World War II in the construction of battleships. The structure is said to employ the world's longest continuous box girder. The girder conceals braces, joints, and stiffeners normally visible in other bridges and provides a sleek, smooth appearance.

The 30 arch-shaped concrete towers were designed to reflect San Diego's historical mission architecture. Girders are painted blue to harmonize with the predominant color of the sky, bay, and sea.

The towers rest on 487 pre-stressed reinforced concrete piles, 54 inches in diameter. Some piles were driven 100 feet into the sand and clay beneath the bay.

Under the roadway is a steel-mesh catwalk built to facilitate bridge maintenance. The highway department conducts routine inspections to detect concrete flaking and exposed bare metal surfaces. Painting the bridge is a never-ending job. A four-person crew works year-round to keep it protected from salt-laden ocean breezes.

The roadway consists of five lanes. The center lane doubles as a safety median. With the help of a new moveable barrier system as a switch lane, the center lane provides three lanes in one direction during peak traffic periods.

The 34-inch-high barrier railings are low enough to allow an unobstructed view while crossing the bridge. The design of the railings, wide at the bottom and narrow at the top, redirects the wheels of any errant vehicles back to the roadway with little or no damage.

A toll was charged to cross the bridge. Originally $0.60 each direction, the toll was modified in 1980 to collect $1.20 collected only on the Coronado side. The toll was supposed to be terminated when the original bond was paid off. In actuality, the toll provided extra money to the city of San Diego City for 17 years. In 2001, San Diego City Council voted to halt toll collections altogether in 2002.

One urban myth surrounding the bridge is that the center section is designed to float in case an earthquake or other such catastrophe fells the bridge. The logic behind the legend is that a floating mid-section would prevent the fallen center span from blocking transit of warships berthed south of the bridge. Although a number of Navy ships berth south of the span, they are mostly auxiliary, supply, and repair vessels. The aircraft carrier piers are north of the bridge, nearer the harbor mouth.

Now an integral part of San Diego's skyline, the San Diego-Coronado Bay Bridge might never have been constructed if earlier plans to create a tunnel had been adopted. *Photo by Dale Frost/Port of San Diego.*

CHAPTER 41

San Diego's (Un)Official Nude Beach

Nude bathing at isolated Black's Beach, below towering cliffs in north La Jolla, was tolerated throughout the 1960s in much the same way as it is today. While an occasional nudist might be sighted and cited, for the most part authorities turn a blind eye toward frolicking in the buff at Black's.

But between 1974 and 1977, Black's Beach enjoyed official designation as San Diego's swimsuit optional zone. During this period sunbathers enjoyed swimming, surfing, Frisbee, and volleyball without the encumbrance of clothing.

Since nudity was banned at all other San Diego beaches (notwithstanding occasional jaybirding at some Sunset Cliffs sandy coves), people drove from miles away to experience the sun, surf, and sand. But with the crowds came cars and soon the well-heeled residents atop the cliff had had enough. By exerting political pressure, La Jolla residents were able to sway the city into painting most of the curbs red to thwart beach parking.

Although the red curbs were undone at a later date, behind-the-scenes plans were being fomented to ban nude bathing at Black's Beach. First came an innocent sounding proposal to enhance beach access by creating better trails and developing a paved road, which is closed to motor vehicles. But fresh on the heels of that development, the city council declared that Black's Beach had lost the isolation it previously enjoyed. San Diego Municipal Code 56.53C was adopted and nude sunbathing banned.

Yet to this day at the northern end of Black's Beach, nude sunbathing is alive and well. In fact, San Diego City Lifeguards often mark the clothing-optional boundaries with orange cones.

Beach access is arduous: either hike down and back up the 300-foot-tall cliff via one of the trails or walk in. From La Jolla Shores beach head north about two miles. From Torrey Pines State Natural Reserve beach head south about three miles. If you go, serious nudists ask that you follow these five rules: 1) Don't go out of established nude areas. 2) Refrain from inappropriate behavior. 3) Leave your camera at home. 4) Don't gawk. 5) Give nudists distance and recognize when you are unwelcome.

Don't forget the sunscreen!

SECTION IV

West of Eden

San Diego has long been described as a near-perfect place to live. Yet over the course of history, people have tried to improve this veritable Garden of Eden. Some searched for mythological islands of untold beauty and wealth. Some established collectives intended to bring about new social orders within our county's borders. Yet others sought to somehow grow offshore islands in dogged pursuit of life, liberty, happiness and possibly legalized gambling and offshore banking.

Efforts to establish new societies West of Eden varied in their persistence. Several thrived for years and failed only after significant elemental or leadership changes occurred. One in particular seems, in retrospect, little more than a lofty abstraction never meant to face the rigors of practical application.

Nonetheless, one wonders how San Diego might have changed if any of these groups' underlying principles took serious foothold.

Spaniards Searched for Mythical Island of Beauty and Gold

W hat exactly was Spanish explorer Juan Cabrillo searching for when he landed in San Diego in 1542?

Mainstream history teaches us the explorer sailed in search of a new trade route to the Orient. But one alternative, albeit controversial, theory stubbornly persists: Cabrillo and early Spanish explorers searched for an island of gold inhabited by a race of robust and lusty women.

The legend of the island of California and its queen Calafia dates back at least to the 1510 novel, *Las Sergas de Esplandián* by García Ordóñez de Montalvo. His novel describes in graphic and sexist terms an island that may have ignited the passions and fears of explorers and political leaders alike. It reads in part:

> Know ye that on the right hand of the Indies there is an island called California, very near the Terrestrial Paradise and inhabited by black women without a single man among them and living in the manner of the Amazons. They are of robust body, strong and passionate in heart, and of great valor. Their island is among of the most rugged in the world with bold rocks and crags. Their arms are all of gold, as is the harness of their wild beasts which, after taming, they ride. In all the island there is no other metal.
>
> Over this island of California rules a queen, Calafia, statuesque in proportions, more beautiful than all the rest, in the flower of her womanhood, eager to perform great deeds, valiant and spirited, and ambitious to excel in all those who have ruled before her.

Although the idea of an island of unimaginable riches governed by beautiful women waiting to be conquered is considered indefensibly misogynic by today's standards, had Cabrillo managed to discover California and subdue Calafia, he certainly would have had little trouble recruiting men for future expeditions to this island west of Eden. It also bears mentioning that in the years prior to Cabrillo's landing in San Diego Bay in 1542, Francisco de Coronado spent considerable time on a mission to find Cíbola, the Seven Golden Cities, based only on the verbal claims of a solitary shipwreck survivor.

So did early Spanish explorers search for a new trade route to the Orient? Undoubtedly! But did they also keep their eyes on the horizon, hoping to spot an island of gold inhabited by Amazon women? Calafia-theory adherents maintain they did. After all, the explorers ultimately named their new land California!

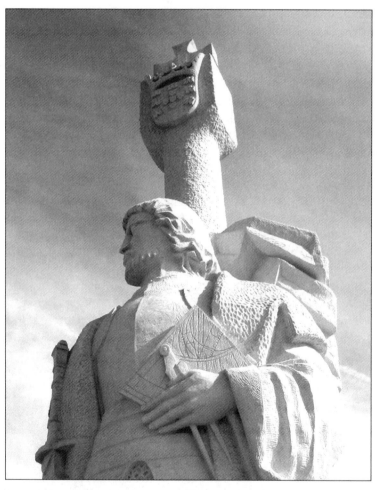

Some believe Juan Cabrillo was searching for a city of gold inhabited by robust, lusty women, when he landed in San Diego in 1542. *Author photo.*

Madame Tingley Utopia Aimed for Divine Wisdom

No effort to create a utopian society within San Diego County borders lasted as long as Madame Katherine Tingley's Theosophical Society, which occupied what is now Point Loma Nazarene University from 1897 to 1942. In its heyday, the sprawling 330-acre complex housed Tingley's Raja-Yoga School and College, the Universal Brotherhood and Theosophical Society, and the School for the Revival of the Lost Mysteries of Antiquity. Many of Tingley's followers and families lived at the complex, united by the goal of creating a utopian atmosphere that would ultimately benefit mankind in general. Among the eclectic mix of buildings still gracing Point Loma Nazarene University is the first Greek Amphitheater in America, built in 1901.

Visitors in that era entered the complex through an enormous Roman gate, then continued through an equally impressive Egyptian pillared gate. Directly ahead stood, and still stands, a beautiful, single-story building with an intriguing mixture of design elements including arches, pillars, an ornate exterior spiral staircase that leads to the roof, and an octagonal cupola topped with an onion dome. An impressive Temple of Peace was endowed with carved woodwork and painted arabesques rising to an amethyst glass dome.

Just as the society's architecture borrowed design elements from Madame Tingley's world travels, the Universal Brotherhood and Theosophical Society borrowed liberally from the world's religions, philosophies, and cultures. While rejecting organized religion and science with equal fervor, Theosophists attempted to discover "divine wisdom" through their investigations into spiritualism, deism, and the occult. (Theosophy derives its name from the Greek words *theos*, meaning God and *sophia*, meaning wisdom.)

Based largely upon Helena Blavatsky's mystic-inspired book *The Secret Doctrine*, Theosophists believed strongly in reincarnation and that life is made difficult by an evil wave of karma brought about by personal deeds and by mankind's activities in general.

Also central to elementary Theosophy belief was the recurrence of the number seven: white light was composed of seven colors. There were seven notes in the musical scale. All matter was comprised of the following seven types: *corpuscular or subatomic, atomic, gaseous, liquid, living, colloid inanimate,* and *colloid crystalline.*

They also believed the number seven imposed itself on the table of atomic elements. If all the elements known to chemistry were arranged one after another in the order of their atomic weights, beginning with the lightest; then the first, eighth, fifteenth, twenty-second would be

Madame Tingley helped bring to San Diego an odd mixture of Eastern philosophy and spiritualism. Several buildings at Point Loma Nazarene University reflect that eclecticism. *San Diego Historical Society Photograph Collection.*

found to have similar properties to the second, ninth, sixteenth, twenty-third, and so on, ad infinitum.

In addition, all facets of human nature were exhibited in seven ways, known to the Theosophists as *sthula-sarira, linga-sarira, prana, kama rupa, manas, buddhi,* and *atma.*

An important feature of life at the complex was the inclusion of music, drama, and the arts as integral parts of the daily routine. Unlike conventional schools, the system of education at Point Loma was not confined to routine classroom activities at certain hours of the day, rather in the regulation of the child's whole life. Students as young as three, talented or not, practiced playing an instrument, sang with the choir, acted in Greek and Shakespearean plays, and learned to draw and paint.

But the organization's requirement that children be segregated completely from parents raised eyebrows and ultimately brought accusations of cruelty. Newspapers began to publish accounts of séances and other occult events. Soon, public opinion shifted and many of San Diego's 17,000 residents began to regard the curious architecture and occult-like atmosphere as threatening. Local clergy started speaking out against Tingley and her Universal Brotherhood and Theosophical Society. Numerous lawsuits were filed and rifts developed within the society's leadership. The utopia began to unravel and the Theosophical Society was forced to sell off parcels of land to stem the tide of red ink.

Katherine Tingley died on July 11, 1929, at the age of 82 while on a European lecture tour. Following Tingley's death, a gradual erosion of the Theosophical Society continued. The utopia endured 13 more years, albeit on increasingly shaky financial footing, until it closed and many of its core assets sold in 1942. A few years after World War II, the final 90-acre lot was sold to Balboa University, which was subsequently renamed California Western University. In 1973, the Church of Nazarene bought the site and opened Point Loma Nazarene College, now a university.

Tingley's Theosophical Society still exists and publishes books and offers coursework from its international headquarters in Altadena, California.

Little Landers
"A Little Land and a Living"

Some may say William Ellsworth Smythe couldn't see the big picture, that San Diego already was a utopia when he founded an idyllic, agriculture-based colony in San Ysidro in 1908.

But Smythe saw things differently when he established Little Landers, a quasi-commune founded on the belief that one man should be able to support an entire family on a single acre of land. His idea, summarized in the group's motto, "A Little Land and Living," was predicated on the notion that one acre of land, correctly laid out, properly irrigated, and situated near a big city could sustain a self-supporting farm that would require very little work. Free time could then be used for self-betterment, or to just plain loaf around. Idyllic indeed!

Smythe came to San Diego in 1901 after having participated in several experimental colonies across the United States. San Diego County was in the midst of a population boom, but skyrocketing real estate prices created financial and land-use pressures on the area's independent farms and ranches. The 39-year-old former journalist with a background in irrigation engineering picked up on negative public sentiment that the Industrial Revolution was rapidly displacing traditional agrarian lifestyle, so he purchased a real estate option on a 500-acre ranch in San Ysidro about 15 miles south of San Diego.

Smythe subdivided and began promoting his back-to-the-land utopian vision during a series of Sunday lectures at San Diego's Isis Theater. He routinely quoted Abraham Lincoln from a speech given 50 years earlier, "The most valuable of all arts will be the art of deriving a comfortable subsistence from the smallest area of soil."

The promoter's passionate speeches garnered positive publicity. *The San Francisco Call* newspaper gushed, "A Little Lander is a man who, if he be not in the city, is yet of the city. He is neither a farmer nor a rancher. He is a scientist. He is an artist. He is a man with initiative. He is an independent, self-employing man. To his trees, his plants, and his vines he gives the ineffable touch of love. He is the spiritual man of the soil."

Smythe's highly idealistic Little Lander speeches hit their marks; about a dozen families became Little Landers in 1909. Twenty-six more families joined the following year. By the fourth year, 116 families called the San Ysidro commune home.

Although steeped in idealism, Smythe's ideas worked. The colony became self-supporting and soon began producing more fruits and vegetables than they could consume. As per plan, a horse-drawn wagon came to individual farms every day and took excess produce into the nearest big city, San Diego. The fruits and vegetables were sold on the streets direct to consumers to maximize profits. Soon, the collective's produce became so popular that they were forced to sell the horse and wagon and buy a truck to do the hauling. Shortly thereafter, they opened an independent market in San Diego called Little Lander's Co-operative on the corner of Sixth and B streets.

The colony had a vibrant social life that centered around a rustic clubhouse called Redwood Hall. The clubhouse served as venue for Monday-night Little Lander business meetings, worship services, and extended studies including literature and music. But doing nothing was considered time well-spent too. A plaque above one cobblestone fireplace quoted Walt Whitman: "I loaf and invite my soul."

Life at the collective was idyllic indeed. By 1916, the Little Landers movement spawned four other colonies in California. With Smythe giving presentations and selling lots, Hayward Heath in Alameda County, Runnymede near Palo Alto, and colonies in San Jose and the San Fernando Valley were created and settled with 20 to 60 families apiece.

But back in San Ysidro seeds of discontent were being sown. Those with little ken for farming found it difficult to generate levels of income sufficient to meet anything more than very basic needs. Conversely, those adept at agriculture complained they were not getting enough cash for their crops. Some withdrew from the cooperative and sold their produce independently. Several prominent and productive members quit the commune for higher paying jobs. Accusations spread that Smythe was nothing more than a slick real-estate promoter and that some lots sold were virtually worthless for farming.

One colonist accused Smythe of allowing, "Any old dear lady with five hundred dollars to settle on a stone pile and try to make a living on it."

Although dissention fostered a great deal of negative publicity, the fact remained that most could make a decent living on one acre, even if they had to supplement their income with outside work. And even those who couldn't farm at all found it possible to live on just a few dollars per month since food, housing, and basic utilities were taken care of by the commune.

So the San Ysidro utopia managed to survive, even thrive, until one fateful day when Smythe's path crossed that of another well-known fellow from San Diego's past, Charles Hatfield, a rainmaker hired by the city of San Diego to fill up Morena Reservoir.

On the morning of January 18, 1916, whether caused by Hatfield's cloud seeding activities or not, a devastating flood swept through San Ysidro. The flood (see page 35) wiped out Little Landers' crops, killed livestock, wrecked the colony's irrigation system, and left 100 colonists homeless.

Despite that they were still reeling from the flood, the citizens of San Diego came together to help Little Landers get back on their feet again. But the colony never quite regained its former luster.

In 1918, Smythe's wife died and he moved back East. Without leadership, the Little Landers colony all but ceased operations.

William Ellsworth Smythe died in New York City in 1922. Today, all that remains of his name is a street in San Ysidro named Smythe Crossing.

But it is said that to the very end, Smythe never wavered from his dream that intensive, small-scale, Little Lander farming might someday establish a permanent "utopia within a utopia" here in San Diego.

American poet Walt Whitman wrote, "I loaf and invite my soul." Those words inspired the 1908 creation of Little Landers, an idyllic, agriculture-based colony in San Ysidro that encouraged off-hours loafing. *Image courtesy Library of Congress.*

Sealab

Undersea Utopia Try Flops off San Diego Coast

There seems no limit to the amount of effort humankind will expend to find a perfect place to live. While most are content to live their lives on earth's thin skin, others dream of colonizing distant planets. Still others dream of living in specially built homes beneath the sea.

Who wouldn't enjoy watching barracuda or sea bass swim gracefully by their living room window, or waking up Saturday morning to tend a front lawn comprised of colorful sea anemones and sponges?

Although nowadays it seems like a massive step in the wrong direction, given modern society's seemingly ingrained drive to colonize the moon and distant planets, the federal government in the early 1960s put into motion a plan that, had it succeeded, would have led to the colonization of sea floors throughout the world. The three-phase, U.S. Navy-run Sealab program began in Bermuda and ended, tragically, off the coast of San Diego.

In July, 1964, the world's first four "aquanauts" entered Sealab I for a planned three-week immersion in Bermuda. Sealab I, not much more than a pair of surplus floats repurposed into a pressure-resistant vessel, was about the size of a small travel trailer. The interior featured bunks, a kitchenette, hot showers, and refrigeration. Railroad-car axles served as weights to keep the vessel pinned on the ocean floor 100 feet below the sea surface. The aquanaut's first sojourn went well until a tropical storm cut their stay short after 11 days.

Meanwhile construction was underway on Sealab II, a custom-built, 57-foot-long by 12-foot-diameter cylinder about the size of a large motor-home. It was built to withstand underwater pressures encountered on the seafloor at 200 feet and designed to accommodate three, 10-man teams that would each stay 15 days for a total of 45 days off the shore of La Jolla.

About a year after the Sealab I experiment, Sealab II was towed into place about a mile off La Jolla and slowly lowered into place. The lowering went to plan, but an error in navigation caused Sealab II to be placed so close to the sloping edge of La Jolla Canyon that its eight stubby support legs couldn't level it out. Sealab II quickly became known as the "Tiltin' Hilton."

Nevertheless, Sealab II provided a functioning test bed for underwater habitation. Astronaut Scott Carpenter took a leave of absence from NASA to lead two of the 10-man teams. Carpenter ultimately spent 30 consecutive days on the ocean floor.

Living at these depths required a precise metering of helium, nitrogen, and oxygen. But breathing helium distorts the human voice and those who inhale the gas tend to sound a bit like Donald Duck. Although the divers became accustomed to one others' high-pitched voices, a special congratulatory telephone call from the White House is said to have left President Lyndon Johnson feeling somewhat confused.

In addition to physiological testing, Sealab II divers tested new tools, new methods of salvage, and an electrically heated "dry" wetsuit. The Navy even trained a porpoise named Tuffy to shuttle supplies up and down so divers wouldn't have to spend hours decompressing to readjust to atmospheric pressures. The program was declared a complete success and it looked as though an entire new frontier for human habitation had opened up, right off the San Diego coastline.

Sealab II was brought to the surface and work began to upgrade it for the vessel's final submersion as Sealab III.

NASA astronaut Scott Carpenter readies Sealab II, a 1960s experimental structure designed to prove that humans could colonize the ocean floor. *Photo courtesy U.S. Navy.*

In February 1969, Sealab III was taken 60 miles west of San Diego off San Clemente Island, a Naval reserve, and lowered into 600 feet of water. Almost immediately, divers and others associated with the Sealab program began wondering why project planners chose 600 feet when most of the world's potential underwater habitat sites were less than 200 feet deep. Few scuba divers had ever submerged to the 600-foot level and those who had stayed only a very short while. Rumors began to circulate that the Navy had more or less high-jacked the program with the aim of secretly testing new submarine escape equipment.

On the morning of the first dive controllers noticed Sealab III was leaking gas, so the first dive team geared up to find and patch the leak. Four men were sent to the bottom in a specialized pressure travel capsule. Two remained in the capsule while 38-year-old Navy warrant officer Robert Barth and 33-year-old Berry Cannon, a civilian diver from the Navy's Mine Defense Laboratory, tried to effect repairs.

The communication system was horrible. There were no lines between the divers and the capsule, only between the capsule and the topside crew. Moreover, messages sent topside were full of static and very difficult to understand due to squeaky voices caused by the helium breathing mixture. A grainy, fixed position video camera showed the men leaving the capsule and dragging their umbilical cords toward the habitat.

Cannon managed to open a ballast valve on the outside of Sealab III, but returned to the capsule after 13 minutes, completely exhausted from working at such depths and suffering from hypothermia.

Barth had made his way underneath Sealab III to the vertical entrance hatch. The four-foot hatch was built to be opened with only moderate force, but it was stuck. After watching him struggle, Barth's backups in the capsule quickly figured out that the leak had caused a pressure buildup inside Sealab III and that, owing to the enormous water pressure outside the vessel, it would take more than six tons of force to open the hatch.

With no way to communicate that information to Barth, the capsule crew had no choice but to watch the diver work in vain. Barth struggled 20 minutes before returning to the capsule, exhausted. While the four men ascended the Navy worked on a plan of attack for the next day.

But topside, a public relations storm brewed. The Navy had billed Sealab III as a big media event, but numerous delays, including the flooding of several unmanned travel capsules, had turned the habitation into a media nightmare. Now, with local, national, and international reporters standing by, the Navy couldn't even open Sealab III's hatch!

The following morning, the same dive team returned to the ocean floor. Barth began prying the stubborn hatch with a crow bar while

Cannon swam alongside, out of camera range. Suddenly, Barth dropped his crow bar and raced off camera. Silt kicked up off the sea floor and obscured the video view but when Barth came back into view a minute later, he was towing Cannon. Barth tried in vain to get Cannon's head into a small pocket of breathable air near the hatch. Then he tried to get Cannon to breathe through his emergency regulator, but that didn't work either.

Barth struggled to tow Cannon back to the capsule but his umbilical cord snagged on Sealab III's ladder. By the time Barth untangled the cord and got the stricken diver into the capsule, Cannon was dead.

The following day, news agencies across the globe reported the deadly accident. The Navy immediately suspended Sealab III's habitation indefinitely and within a few months cancelled the project and sent Sealab III to a scrap yard.

To this day, there are those who say that had the Navy not hijacked Sealab's relatively shallow-water habitation project to work on deep-water submarine escape systems, undersea utopian living might have begun right here, off the San Diego coast.

A scientific experiment that could have led to the colonization of the ocean floor off San Diego failed when a deadly malfunction occurred aboard Sealab III. *Photo courtesy U.S. Navy.*

Abalonia

Island/Nation Sinks off San Diego

All hail the King of Abalonia!

Although it sounds like a line from an obscure Three Stooges movie, that cry may have echoed through the halls of a brand new island nation about 100 miles off the southern California coastline if the plans of two San Diegans had succeeded.

Granted it does seem like a 1950's science fiction plot, but in 1966 two businessmen believed they had discovered a way to create an off-shore island upon which they could create a new and sovereign nation. They'd call it, Abalonia!

Richard Taggart and Bruce McMahan knew about an undersea mount that lies due west of San Diego. Like an island that never grew all the way to the ocean's surface, the 35-mile long by 12-mile-wide mount lies completely underwater. At its shallowest, the undersea peak — called the Cortes Bank — reaches to within 30 feet of the surface. Fishermen and divers frequent the bank to catch fish, lobster, and abalone. Taggart and McMahan hatched a plan to literally own the bank, thereby corner-ing the abalone market.

To make their plan work the men would have to finish what nature never could: that is, to somehow create an island atop the sea mount. But first, they would have to somehow have to stake a claim to the area by declaring the Cortes Bank a new and independent nation.

"I know it sounds fantastic," Taggart said in an October 31, 1966, interview with the *Pasadena Independent*, "but we have consulted experts in international law and they say there's nothing to prevent us from starting our own country if we want to. The Cortes Bank is in interna-tional waters off the continental shelf and beyond either U.S. or Mexican jurisdiction."

Taggart and McMahan claim to have been told by experts that creat-ing sovereignty and asserting jurisdiction on the site is a simple matter of erecting a monument such as used to stake a mining claim on land. One advisor, maritime attorney and manager of the American Tuna Boat Association, August Felando, told reporters that ownership of the Cortes

Bank had surfaced as a point of discussion at the Marine Technology Society in Washington D.C. earlier that year. Some experts opined that according to the Geneva Convention the configuration of the ocean bottom at the Cortes Bank placed it beyond the continental shelf. Thus it was fair game for nation forming.

"If beyond the shelf, it is outside American or Mexican jurisdiction," Felando claimed.

Armed with that knowledge, the two men next considered how they could erect an enduring monument in the middle of the ocean. They hit upon the idea that they could scuttle a ship on the undersea mount in such a way that the upper decks protruded above the sea surface. After staking their initial claim, the duo planned to create an island about one mile in diameter by barging in old concrete, rubbish, rock, and dirt from a quarry in Ensenada, Mexico. The whole project, from scuttling the ship to topping off the undersea mount, would only take a few years to complete.

So the pair brought together a handful of investors and purchased a derelict freighter, the 7,000-ton WWII-era *Jalisco*. The 380-foot-long by 60-foot-wide concrete ship was towed to San Francisco and outfitted with machinery, a freezing plant, boilers, and living quarters to accommodate 45 divers and workers.

Meanwhile, the U.S. Department of the Interior heard about the pair's plan and issued an edict claiming ownership of the Cortes Bank. The department claimed that the Geneva Convention permitted nations to control the ocean bed adjacent to the continental shelves. Such control includes "exploitation of the natural resources of that area," which meant that the Cortes Bank was not open to undersea building. Furthermore, the government claimed, "The Interior Department's interpretation of the 1958 Geneva Convention allows that the U.S. continental shelf extends to Hawaii."

Undaunted, the group had the freighter towed to Cortes Bank on a gray morning in mid-November 1966. Their plan was to open several valves in the bottom of the ship to allow the hull to slowly fill with water. If done properly, the flat-bottomed vessel would settle in the upright position and the upper decks would be dry and stable as any on land.

Had the duo known in the late 1960s what we know today about extreme weather conditions that crop up unexpectedly at the Cortes Bank, they likely never would have planned to scuttle *Jalisco* in November. That's because even small storms that barely affect San Diego typically create fierce winds and enormously high waves 100 miles offshore.

Indeed, very large open-ocean waves have been known to crest and break upon the bank. By way of example, on January 19, 2001, a big-wave surfer rode the then-biggest wave in the world at Cortes Bank.

Mike Parsons rode a wave that measured sixty feet tall, the height of a six-story building, winning him $60,000 at the Swell/XXL Biggest Wave Surf Contest.

So it was that gargantuan waves, not maritime law, caused the undoing of the island/nation Abalonia and nearly claimed the lives of Taggart, McMahan, and several others.

On the morning of November 14, 1966, just as the 100-foot tugboat *Olson* began nudging the freighter *Jalisco* into position to sink, a violent storm suddenly arose and with it, huge waves. About that time, a radio message came through from U.S. Attorney General Edwin Miller ordering the men to stop. Sinking *Jalisco* would only create a hazard to navigation, not a sovereign nation, he said.

Undaunted, tugboat Captain Cliff Miller jockeyed *Jalisco* over the bank. Just as they were about to begin scuttling operations, a series of 40-foot waves cropped up on the horizon. When the rollers reached the undersea mount they leapt up so high that they broke over the freighter's upper decks. After a few minutes of bashing, *Jalisco* was listing at a 30-degree angle and its decks were awash. The four-man *Jalisco* crew tried to hang on but they were washed overboard by white water. Captain

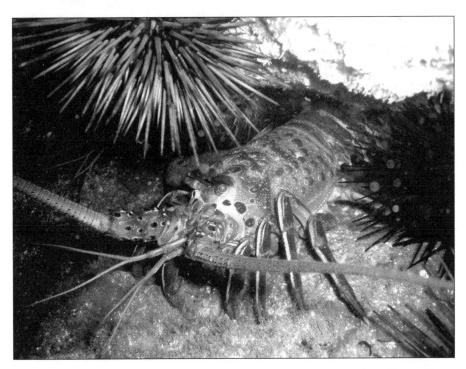

In 1966, two businessmen sought to grow their own island 100 miles off San Diego. Residents of the island/nation Abalonia would support themselves by harvesting abalone, lobsters, and fish. *Photo courtesy NOAA.*

Miller ignored personal peril and turned his efforts to rescuing the men. One of Miller's crewmen used an acetylene torch to burn through the tow cable. Another heaved lines to the men in the water.

"We picked them up out of the suds one-by-one as they were washed off the freighter," Miller later said.

Recounting the rescue, one of the four rescued men, Hollywood star Joe Kirkwood Jr. of *Joe Palooka* movie-series fame, told reporters, "None of us would have made it if it hadn't been for him. I never believed the sea could be like that. I read about it but never believed it."

Miller was happy to have survived too.

"The sea had been building up rapidly and all of a sudden they were breaking right onto the freighter," he said. "We were still hooked up to the tow cable when the waves started breaking over us. I think we got to within 50 feet of the reef at times."

The violent seas subsided the next day and Miller followed Coast Guard orders to tow *Jalisco* off the Cortes Bank. The freighter, now leaking and badly listing, was temporarily anchored to await a tow into San Diego Harbor.

Sometime that night the anchor line snapped and the next morning the tug chased down the drifting *Jalisco*. At that point, the freighter was so close to sinking that Captain Miller made a command decision; to nudge *Jalisco* right up next to the highest point on Cortes Bank and allow her to sink there rather than create a new hazard to navigation.

This time the seas remained calm and *Jalisco* unceremoniously sank on the Cortes Bank. However, owing to the 45-degree angle at which the ship sank, only a few feet of hull protruded above the surface of the sea. Before the end of winter, storm waves washed the entire vessel off the top of the bank and *Jalisco* disappeared forever.

And so too the flag of Abalonia sank beneath the waves, and along with it their dreams of a utopian nation one hundred miles west of the Eden we call San Diego.

Taluga

Island/Nation on a Half Shell

The odds are good that nobody ever had their passport stamped "Taluga."

But if one group of Pacific Northwest businessmen had its way, a micro-country off the coast of San Diego would have joined the roster of existing island nations that include Japan, United Kingdom, Singapore, and Bahrain.

Shortly after violent waves foiled two southern California men's attempt at growing an island/nation 100 miles west of San Diego (see previous chapter), a Seattle-based group announced fresh plans to build a new nation atop the Cortes Bank.

The Cortes Bank has been likened to an island that never grew all the way to the ocean's surface. The underwater mountain rises out of the depth to become a 35-mile-long by 12-mile-wide plateau that reaches to within 30 feet of the surface. Despite the recent small-scale attempt to form a new island/nation on Cortes Bank by sinking a derelict WWII-era freighter, the Puget Sound-based potential potentates planned to plunk down $8.8 million to create a 967-acre island atop the bank. Little is known about the O.S.D. Company other than they had a very elaborate plan, a few investors, a constitution, and a flag.

Rather than trying to sink a ship atop the Cortes Bank to first establish sovereignty, the group announced on November 23, 1966, they intended to dive right in by ferrying hundreds of barge loads of boulders from a Mexican quarry. When the rock pile reached a specified distance above the sea surface, marine dredges would scoop up soil from the seabed outside the rock pile and keep heaping dirt until an island was created.

Once the first island, Aurora, was built, the group felt it would have little trouble finding additional investors for a $5 million infrastructure that included water, sewers, power system, government headquarters, and other buildings. Afterward with additional funding, three additional islands would be built to comprise the island/nation Taluga.

While Aurora would serve as the main island, Trianna would become an island resort, Bona Ventura would act as a duty-free port, and Villa de Pace would host the palatial estates of Taluga's ruling elite. Construction crews would build bridges to connect all four islands.

Taluga's sovereignty would extend 12 miles in all directions and any interference with its construction would constitute an act of piracy, the group claimed.

Over the course of history, dreamers, schemers, and prospective island/nation-builders have put a lot of thought into how such islands might float financially. One such thinker believed that when fully developed to 100 square miles, such an island/nation could support about 100,000 people by harvesting and producing seafood and mining various sea minerals for use and export.

Energy requirements would be met by solar power and thermal generators that take advantage of the ocean water temperature differential between the surface and the abyss. Such generators would pump cold water from the sea floor and mix it with warmer surface water. The resultant steam produced, at least theoretically, would spin turbines to produce electric current. The anticipated net power production of several of these generators could exceed the entire island's energy needs.

In addition, the wishful island builders claimed, cold water pumped to the surface by generators could create an angler's paradise. The cold water would be loaded with nitrogen so any water discharged near the surface would attract algae, which would attract small algae-eating fish, which would attract large fish that could be caught and sold.

The group also believed they could use surplus power generated to grow the island. This elaborate plan required placing reinforced wire mesh into the water around the edge of the island. An electrical current would be fed into the wires which would draw calcium and other minerals from the sea water. These minerals would accrue on the wire mesh to create a hard structure not unlike concrete. Over years, the ongoing process would ultimately grow the baby island to full size. Once the island reached maturity, the minerals would no longer be needed so they could be sold in such abundance that they would become one of the island's chief exports.

Self-growing, self-sufficient, and self-sustaining, such a man-made island would certainly serve as the basis for a utopian existence.

But this island/nation on a half-shell never evolved past the planning stages.

Taluga lawyers filed a Notice of Intent to the Los Angeles office of the Coast and Geodetic Survey. The Notice of Intent contained 23 pages of charts, sketches, and diagrams describing how Taluga would be built.

But a letter of response from the Army Corps of Engineers informed the O.S.D. Company that the Cortes Bank was considered part of the U.S. Continental Shelf and that any unauthorized construction thereupon would be considered unlawful.

Faced with an uphill battle against the world's most powerful nation, Taluga's founding fathers bowed out and allowed the concept to sink into obscurity.

Some may ask why would anyone go to such lengths to try and create an Eden one hundred miles west of Eden? What makes otherwise clear-headed individuals dream of owning their own country?

We may never know. But it's worth bearing in mind that there are those among us who would literally go to the ends of the earth in their pursuit of life, liberty, and happiness—and maybe legalized gambling and offshore banking.

Once developers created a new island/nation by filling in an offshore undersea bank with boulders, they aimed to make "Taluga" self-sustaining by catching and selling seafood, just like the fishermen in Gloucester, Massachusetts, seen here. Unfortunately, building a new island 100 miles off San Diego was deemed illegal and authorities torpedoed the plan. *Photo courtesy Library of Congress.*

CHAPTER 48

Wald's World

A Seagoing Society

If San Diego County inventor Leonard H. Wald has his way, millions of human beings would live aboard futuristic, self-sufficient houseboats. The boats would anchor offshore, yet be able to pick up and sail the seven seas whenever wanderlust struck their owners. Boat owners could cluster together to form colonies or sail off into the world's more forsaken corners.

In addition to affordable housing, Wald's vessels might someday help solve problems that have long perplexed mankind, including the energy shortage, overpopulation, overuse of the world's raw materials, and political problems.

Since 1989, the retired nuclear engineer has spent much of his spare time in a huge metal shed in Ramona striving to design such a boat. He believes he has done so with the Aquater 2050.

"The Aquater 2050 is a concept for a new way of life based on the ocean," says Wald. "It includes a life-sustaining, energy producing (ship) that gathers energy from wind, waves, and sun by its special equipment and then stores the energy for sale to people on the land. It also has a unique design that keeps the craft from rolling in the waves, making travel more pleasant and energy harvesting on the sea possible. It has hydroponic components that can grow food on the sea, and reverse osmosis components to create potable water."

The Aquater 2050 consists of three major components. The ship itself is called SEMAN (Seagoing Energy Module with Automatic Navigation-Stabilization). The 85-foot-long by 20-foot-wide SEMAN has the appearance of a Spanish galleon hull mated to a pair of pontoons, which provide stability in heavy seas. According to Wald's equations, a SEMAN could accommodate a family of four in comfort.

The second component, a fiberglass folding-wing seaplane, is designed to dock inside SEMAN. This aircraft will give those who live on board, called Aquaters, access to land for occasional provisioning or social trips. The final component is a shore boat that berths in a storage compartment inside SEMAN.

Aquaters could grow vegetables in hydroponic gardens on deck and raise seafood in huge tanks housed in the pontoons. Reverse osmosis filters would turn salt water into fresh. Thirty- foot-diameter turbines would tap wind power, solar arrays would harness sunlight, and wave turbines would make energy by using the up and down motion of ocean swells. In lieu of conventional batteries, energy would be stockpiled by breaking down raw water into its two major components, hydrogen and oxygen, and storing those gasses in specially designed tanks. Aquaters could earn more than $20,000 per year by selling surplus energy to roving tankers, according to Wald's calculations.

Aquaters could live alone, hermit style, or cluster together in fleets to create communities. Either way, they could keep connected with the rest of the world via satellite television, radio, and broadband wireless internet access.

"The Aquater 2050 is also an idea for a new civilization based on the sea, with communities made of groups of SEMAN so that there would be social interaction on the sea," Wald says. "This civilization is called the Aquater Alliance."

If Wald's ideas take hold, the waters just off San Diego's coastline may someday host a fleet of Aquater 2050s, anchored apart from the hubbub of humanity — somewhere west of Eden.

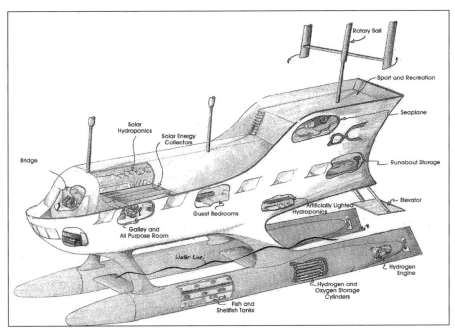

An armada of self-sufficient floating vessels would sway at anchor in San Diego's near-shore waters if inventor Leonard H. Wald's solution to the housing shortage became reality. *Image courtesy Leonard H. Wald.*

Lost Mines and Buried Treasure

"There comes a time in every rightly constructed boy's life when he has a raging desire to go somewhere and dig for hidden treasure."

— *Mark Twain*

If ancient tales of buried treasure and lost mines are revered by modern-day fortune hunters, then San Diego may well become the next Mecca for treasure seekers.

Although "official" history rarely touches upon it, San Diego's lore speaks of millions of dollars in lost gold, silver, and precious gems. This legacy from the past manifests itself in many forms. Spanish treasure galleons reputedly rest in area waters. Unimaginable fortunes have supposedly been buried and forgotten. Gold fields and silver mines are said to have been discovered and lost.

Some regard these particular legends as fanciful bedtime stories. Yet others spend weekends scouring the county for hidden riches. We may never know the outcome of those searches. To maintain secrecy (and avoid paying taxes) fortune hunters are notoriously tight lipped!

The Captain Arroa Treasure

In 1682, the Spanish galleon *Isabella Catolica* wrecked off the coast of San Diego. According to local lore, the captain and crew survived. With no hope of a quick return to Spain, they decided to try their luck at mining. Apparently very adept at finding gold, these Spanish sailors reportedly found and began to mine a rich deposit near the Superstition Mountains in the Anza-Borrego Desert.

The Spaniards were attacked by Indians and all hands were killed. But among their belongings, recovered later, was a letter left by the *Isabella Catolica's* Captain Jesus Arroa. According to the legend, the letter describes the location of the mine and a nearby gold cache. Although valued at more than a million dollars, the treasure has never been found.

Captain Arroa's galleon itself is thought to have been loaded with treasure when it sank. Aboard the few Manila galleons discovered off the California coast to date, divers have found Ming porcelain, carved ivories, and priceless objects of silver and gold; all originally bound for the homes of the wealthy in Spain and the New World.

Although supposedly wrecked off San Diego, few if any fortune hunters have tried their luck at locating the *Isabella Catolica*. Who would not feel fortunate to be standing on the shore when part of that treasure washes up?

The California coastline is a graveyard for sunken ships such as the 16th century galleon shown in this drawing. Perhaps the most important and sought after wreck in the San Diego vicinity is that of the *Isabella Catolica* in 1682. *Image courtesy Library of Congress.*

CHAPTER 50

The San Diego Mission Treasure

Overlooking Old Town, the Presidio, often erroneously referred to as San Diego's Mission de Alcalá, is actually more of a museum than a mission. In fact, it is but a fairly recent replica of a building that once stood there.

There are actually two sites where treasure hunters have searched for the Mission San Diego de Alcalá treasure. The first site is where the Presidio (Spanish for fort) now stands. It commemorates the spot upon which Father Junípero Serra held the first Catholic Mass in San Diego on July 1, 1769.

A crude building was erected there, but in 1771 the mission was moved about six miles east to its present location after it was determined

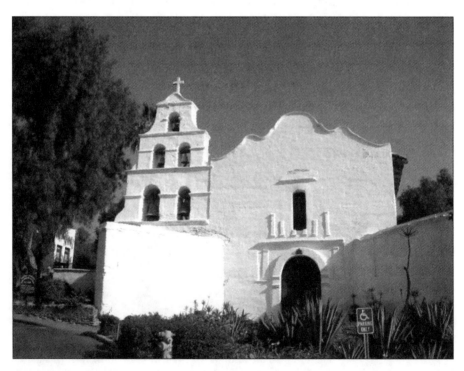

Fortune hunters on the trail of the Mission San Diego de Alcalá treasure have searched near the mission and at the Presidio, where the mission once stood. *Author photo.*

that its proximity to the garrison was not conducive to winning converts, according to information on the mission's Web site.

A few short years after that move, the mission was burned in an Indian uprising and was temporarily moved back to the garrison. In 1813, the mission was rebuilt and dedicated at its present location.

The legend of the Mission San Diego de Alcalá treasure has it that after the mission had been moved back to the Presidio, the King of Spain ordered the friars back to their homelands. Rather than bringing the wealth of the mission back to Spain, the priests buried it somewhere on the hilly Presidio grounds.

According to the legend, the priests buried their treasure in a secret tunnel that leads to a spring at the bottom of the canyon. The tunnel was originally created so that in the event of an Indian uprising, water could be obtained. Several treasure hunters have made stabs at locating the treasure, but mining activities among the ruins and unmarked graves at the Presidio are frowned upon.

Some treasure hunters believe the priests might have buried the treasure six miles east of the Presidio at Mission San Diego de Alcalá. In 1822, when San Diego was part of Mexico, the Mexican federal government ordered secularization of all the mission's land holdings. Thousands of acres were deeded to private individuals and some believe that the priests chose to bury the mission's wealth rather than have it confiscated. Forty years later, the United States returned 22 acres of land to the church. Some treasure seekers believe it is only a matter of time until someone stumbles upon the priest's trove of riches, either on, or near, the mission grounds.

The Vallecitos Stagecoach Treasure

In the late 1800s, a pair of brazen — but not too bright — bandits are said to have held up a stagecoach of the famous Butterfield Overland Mail a few miles from the Vallecitos station, on the southwest fringes of modern-day Anza-Borrego Desert State Park.

Luck was with the robbers, and it is said their take was an estimated $60,000 in gold, worth more than $1 million today.

According to legend, the pair of pistoleros (gunmen) decided to bury the booty, hightail it to the Vallecitos stage station, and have a quick shot of whiskey before the slow-moving stage could catch up.

Unfortunately for the robbers, one drink led to another, then another, and then another. And then the stage showed up.

Both bandits were shot dead during the ensuing gunfight. When the authorities checked their mounts, they found the gold was not in their saddlebags. Unable to pick up the pair's tracks, stage officials were only able to deduce that the loot must have been buried within a 15-minute horseback ride of the station.

Supposedly, the cache has never been located, but some starry-eyed treasure seekers believe it to be out there somewhere, waiting to be discovered. It might be a long wait. Official Butterfield records do not report such a robbery near Vallecitos.

Fortune hunters still seek buried treasure, worth more than one million dollars in today's currency, from a bungled stagecoach robbery at Vallecitos stage station in Anza-Borrego Desert State Park. *Photo courtesy Library of Congress.*

The Lost Treasure of San Felipe Creek

Another desert legend, probably not based in fact, intrigues treasure seekers nonetheless. As the story goes, in 1812 a small band of Spanish soldiers based in Santa Barbara marched southward, through San Diego and into northern Mexico, looting several missions and pueblos of gold, silver, jewels, and gem-encrusted statues along the way.

According to several sources, including a film documentary that aired in the early 1970s, the treasures these brigands collected were far too numerous to be carried back to Santa Barbara on horseback.

To transport such massive amounts of treasure — one solid-gold cross reportedly stood five feet high and took a dozen men to handle — the raiding party commandeered several two-wheeled ox carts. But the slow pace of the ox carts helped in their undoing.

In addition to absconding with gold and treasure, the band of soldiers also kidnapped several young Indian women. Marching north at an ox-pace, the slow-moving troops were soon overtaken by a posse of tribal warriors.

Just after sunset, the warriors surrounded the soldiers in the vicinity of the junction of San Felipe Creek and Carrizo Wash in the Anza-Borrego Desert, about 50 miles east of San Diego. The small army apparently knew an attack would likely occur the next morning, so in addition to arming and fortifying themselves, they buried their treasure in the sandy ravine bottom.

When dawn broke, the Indians attacked. All but three soldiers were slain in the ravine and the survivors were hunted down and killed before they could reach civilization. The treasure has never been recovered, although treasure hunters occasionally find pieces of ancient wagons in sandy washes near San Felipe Creek and Carrizo Wash, not far from California's Southern Emigrant Trail.

It is not easy to say how much additional sand might have been washed on top of the cache over a century-and-a-half, but the desert does average about five inches of rainfall per year, some of it in the shape of flash floods.

The Hidden Loot of Bandit Joaquin Murietta

There are several stories about buried treasure associated with an honest-to-goodness bandit, Joaquin Murietta. According to early newspaper accounts, the Mexican-born Murietta and his gang of outlaws roamed California, including the San Diego countryside in the early 1850s, raiding and robbing ranchos, businesses, and citizens.

As quickly as Murietta and his men would appear to do their deeds, they would disappear into the rugged canyons and rocky hillsides of San Diego's backcountry. According to one newspaper account, "No man dare travel a step unless armed to the teeth, or sleep without having a firearm already in his grasp."

Murietta and several of his men were killed in a gunfight in July 1853. Despite an extensive career as a successful bandito in the greater San Diego area, Murietta's treasure, thought to be substantial, has never been recovered.

While some historians doubt that Murietta operated out of San Diego County and remind us that it is possible robberies attributed to Murietta were committed by others, treasure hunters believe Murietta's local hideout — and several likely sites for his buried loot — reside on what is now the Barona Indian Reservation. Several significant attempts at finding Murietta's treasure have failed, including one that used scuba gear and underwater metal detectors to scour the bottom of Devil's Punchbowl, a pool at the base of a small waterfall.

Murietta was so notorious that after he and his side-kick Three-fingered Jack, were shot by bounty hunters in 1853, their heads were placed in jars of alcohol and paraded throughout the state.

CHAPTER 54

The Lost Gold of Pegleg Smith

Thomas "Pegleg" Smith was a real live trader, trapper, and hunter who often traveled through the Southwest. One trading trip took the one-legged man through San Diego's Anza-Borrego Desert, where he purportedly discovered — then lost — a desert knoll speckled with gold nuggets.

Legend has it that in 1829, Pegleg and his partner had been hunting and trapping beaver, bear, and deer in Utah. The men then loaded the furs and set off down the Colorado River on a raft. According to accounts, Pegleg and his partner ended their river journey near Yuma and set out with a mule team for Los Angeles.

The route, not a bona fide trail at the time, ran more or less west through what is now the Anza-Borrego Desert, then dog-legged north at the eastern slope of the Peninsular Range and meandered into Los Angeles.

Only two days out of Yuma, Pegleg and his partner supposedly ran out of water crossing the desert. In desperation, they began leading the pack animals not so much west, but in any direction they thought would lead them to water.

As they wandered through the desert, sand-storms arose. According to the story, the men probably veered northwest, but their exact route is unknown.

Pegleg supposedly made his find when he climbed one of three distinctive buttes in order to survey the land ahead for signs of water. Seeing nothing in the way of an oasis, Pegleg plopped down to rest and noticed that the small rocks there were unusual — black in color, egg-shaped, and about the size of a walnut.

He picked up one of the unusual rocks and hit it against a stone. The dark coating chipped off to reveal what looked to him a lot like copper. Smith tucked several rocks in his pockets and said nothing to his partner. Luckily, the men found water at the base of a mountain the next day.

After traveling across the mountains for several more days, the men arrived in Los Angeles and sold their furs. Later, Pegleg had his "copper" assayed, and it turned out to be gold, 88 percent pure.

In later years, Pegleg searched in vain for the original three buttes marking the black nugget site. He spent his final years in San Francisco telling stories about his find to anyone who would listen, usually for a shot or two of whiskey. Some call the story an outright lie, yet the old geezer stuck to his story until his death in 1866.

Today, the lost gold of Pegleg Smith remains the source of speculation and inspiration for many a weekend prospector. Much of the interest in Pegleg's gold seems to center around an area west of the Salton Sea, near Anza-Borrego's Coyote Mountain southeast to Carrizo Creek and the Fish Creek and Superstition mountains — areas that have proven to be rich in other minerals.

A California historical landmark in the Anza-Borrego calls Smith, "a spinner of tall tales," but admits his find might be within a few miles of the marker. A sign nearby asks all those who have looked for the lost gold of Pegleg Smith to toss 10 rocks on a nearby pile. Needless to say, that rock pile has grown quite substantial over the decades.

Of note is the annual Pegleg Smith Liars' Contest, which has been held in the Anza-Borrego Desert for more than 50 years on the first Saturday night in April.

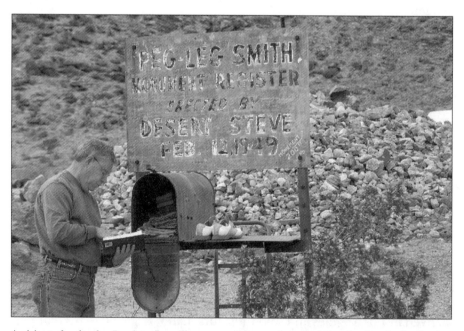

A visitor checks the "registry" mailbox near the massive pile of rocks that is the Pegleg Monument in Borrego Springs, home of the annual Pegleg Smith Liars Contest. *Photo courtesy Katalin Stark.*

The Lost Frenchman Mine

California treasure hunters and others intimate with San Diego's back-country claim there are dozens of abandoned Spanish gold mines in the area. Most of these forgotten mines caved in long ago. Those that have not are extremely dangerous, as they may collapse without warning.

According to local lore, the mother of all California lost mines contains not gold, but extremely high-grade silver and is not of Spanish origin, but French. And it is located in San Diego.

The Lost Frenchman Mine is believed to be somewhere at the base of El Capitan Mountain, east of San Diego near the city of El Cajon. The mine was excavated by a fellow named Pierre Hausenberger in the mid-1800s, according to accounts.

But if discovering a rich deposit of silver ore was a high point for Hausenberger, a low point was soon to follow. To have his ore assayed, Hausenberger was forced to leave his mine and travel to northern California. The Frenchman left San Diego on the steam side-wheeler *Senator* with five sacks of ore bound for the assayer's office in San Francisco. But along the way, Hausenberger became ill and died.

When the *Senator* tied up in San Francisco, the ship's purser found that one of the dead man's five ore sacks had torn open. Seeing nothing but seemingly worthless dirt and rocks, the purser gave the torn sack to an unidentified passenger. He then unceremoniously dumped the remaining four sacks off the pier and into the water.

Samples of the first sack ultimately made their way to the assaying office, and results showed the ore worth an incredible $20,000 per ton. But with Hausenberger dead, there was no way to connect the silver with any particular source.

Several years later, the mystery of the silver sparked the interest of San Diego pioneer Ephraim W. Morse. On a trip to San Francisco, Morse interviewed several sources and ultimately learned about the four sacks that had been dumped off the pier.

When Morse arrived at the pier, he discovered that the site had been covered over with fill-dirt. The stubborn treasure seeker embarked upon an all-out excavation of the area and — as luck seems to reward hard work — found the four sacks. The ore in those sacks assayed out as did the first.

Having verified at least part of the story, Morse gleefully returned to San Diego and gave a speech at the San Diego Lyceum in December 1879, requesting information from anyone who had known the Frenchman.

One notable San Diegan, Don Luís Estudillo, said he remembered the man well, and even recalled him showing up in town, San Francisco-bound, with five bags of ore. Estudillo introduced Morse to a local Indian who said he knew of the mine. The local scout led a small expedition around the back country for several weeks, but could not pin-point the mine.

Morse, suspecting the Indian was making the most of his per-day expense arrangement, dropped his quest and gave up on the Lost Frenchman Mine.

But a few years later, a story circulated in the press that a man who lived on the slopes of El Capitan Mountain showed up in Los Angeles with a huge chunk of nearly pure silver, which he sold for a hefty sum before going on a drinking binge.

About a month later, the man returned to Los Angeles with several bags of the nearly pure silver, sold them all, and set out drinking again. Unfortunately, the man was stabbed to death in a bar fight, and what is believed to be the secret location of the Lost Frenchman Mine was buried with him.

Unfortunately for modern-day treasure hunters, uncertainty exists as to which mountain was called El Capitan in the early days. According to most, the El Capitan of yore is now called El Cajon Peak. But others insist that El Capitan is a shortened version of El Capitan Grande de Cullamac, a mountain named after Francisco, grand chief of the Cuyamaca Indians. If El Capitan was actually present day Mount Cuyamaca, those who search for the Lost Frenchman Mine near El Cajon would be a few dozen miles south of the real find.

San Diego's Gold Rush

Few non-history buffs are aware that San Diego County was home to a bona fide gold rush. While not as grand of scale as that of northern California, the Julian Gold Rush contributed millions of dollars of gold to the San Diego economy.

The Julian Gold Rush began in 1870 when African-American rancher Fred Coleman discovered gold in a creek in the Cuyamaca Mountains. When word of Coleman's discovery leaked out, many in San Diego remained skeptical, but scores of would-be prospectors raced to the hills in search of gold.

While some found small amounts of gold by panning in creeks, others found larger quantities by mining placer deposits. Simply put, placer deposits are those found in ancient stream beds abandoned when the water way changed course, which is not unusual over centuries and millennia. Such abandoned stream beds were dug out by pick and shovel with miners concentrating on crevices and pockets in which gold would likely collect as it washed down stream.

Almost immediately, the prospectors formed a mining district and a town of tents emerged called Emily City.

Back in San Diego, skeptics were stunned when the first load of 1,500 pounds of gold-bearing quartz arrived in town. That arrival whipped the city into a gold frenzy and soon the population of Emily City reached an estimated 600, according to reports published at the time. The town of Julian was named by early settler Drury Bailey in honor of his cousin Mike Julian. Although Bailey was an important businessman, he declined to name the town "Bailey," opining that Julian was a better-sounding name.

Julian gold fever began to spread throughout the state and miners poured into San Diego by steamship or overland from Los Angeles.

Full production mines were dug into several hillside areas. Veins of gold, called "mother lodes" were found and mines with names such as George Washington, Mount Vernon, The Monroe, and U.S. Grant were established. Other significant operations went by novel names such as the "Shoo Fly," "April Fool," "You Bet," and "Don't Bother Me" mines.

Within two years, the population of Julian swelled to an estimated 2,000, nearly the size of San Diego. There were hotels, cafes, stores, blacksmith shops, livery stables, a school, a racetrack, numerous saloons, and dance halls. Julian hosted the San Diego-area United States centennial celebration in 1876.

The gold rush lasted less than a decade, and when the mines began to close, the population of Julian fell to less than 100 permanent residents.

Ten years later renewed interest in Julian gold led to the reopening of the Stonewall Mine south of Julian. Purchased by state Gov. Robert W. Waterman for $75,000, the mine yielded $1 million in gold between 1888 and 1891.

For those interested in knowing more about mining, the Eagle Peak Mining Company provides hour-long guided tours of their mine, and the diggings near the Cuyamaca Reservoir can be reached by Cuyamaca Rancho State Park visitors.

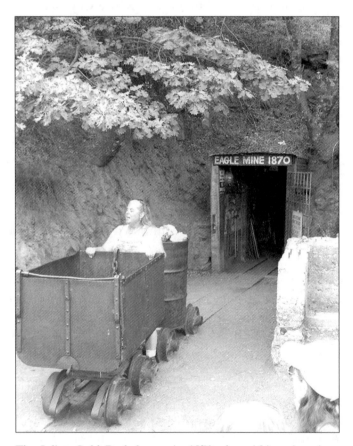

The Julian Gold Rush began in 1870 when African-American rancher Fred Coleman discovered flecks of gold in a creek. The gold rush lasted about a decade, but the Eagle Mine remains open to this day—its operators give guided tours. *Author photo.*

CHAPTER 57

The Lost Bells of Mission Santa Ysabel

One legend that has become a modern-day detective story is that regarding the lost bells of the Mission Santa Ysabel.

This true story begins in the year 1818, when the Mission San Diego de Alcalá established a sub-mission in rural Santa Ysabel to serve worshippers who had a hard time getting to San Diego. Immediately dubbed "The Church of the Desert," Mission Santa Ysabel was comprised of an adobe chapel, a granary, several houses, and a cemetery.

One of San Diego's most intriguing mysteries is that of church bells stolen from Mission Santa Ysabel in 1926. Church officials felt they were tantalizingly close to getting them back in 1965, but the anonymous source never contacted them again. *San Diego Historical Society Photograph Collection.*

In August of that year, the mission orchestrated a deal to obtain the two oldest Spanish bells in New Spain (now Mexico). The bells bore the markings, "N.S. De Loreto, 1729" and "San Pedro, 1767."

Mission authorities at the time were quite secretive about the deal that traded the bells for six burro loads of barley. But years later a records keeper coaxed a missionary into revealing the reason behind the lopsided trade. It was an era of religious persecution, the missionary said, and officials at the bells' original mission in New Spain feared zealots might confiscate and destroy them. To prevent that from happening, the friars clandestinely traded them to San Diego. (This likely occurred without the official blessings of the Catholic Church).

So it was that in the early summer of 1818, Father Francesco set out for Central Baja California on foot with six mules laden with barley. And on one particularly hot August morning, Father Francesco and his mule caravan arrived back at Mission Santa Ysabel with the bells in tow. Accounts state that Francesco's arrival was a joyous affair, and that he was accompanied by an Indian choir waving marsh reeds.

Workers at the mission quickly unpacked the mules and laid the bells on the ground while pine wood supports could be hewn and raised to form a free standing bell tower. The bells were hung by noon — in time to ring for high mass. Their golden peals were spectacular. "These are the sweetest bells in New Spain," Father Francesco announced. It is said that their initial ringing could be heard for miles and brought more than 500 Indians to the mission that day.

Thus the bells heralded the mission faithful until one dark, rainy, November morning in 1926 when the bells were stolen. There were no witnesses to the theft. A few Indians living at the mission recalled hearing a noisy truck driving up the hill in the middle of the night but thought little of it.

Come sunrise, they were surprised to find the ropes cut, the bells missing, and a set of tire tracks heading past the mission gates and fading away in the grassy fields.

One newspaper account of the theft stated, "The recent disappearance of the old bells that hung from a thick beam outside the chapel is the subject of much grievous conjecture among Indians and pioneers at Santa Ysabel, who miss their familiar clangor of a Sunday morning."

Local authorities quickly pursued — and exhausted — all leads, and the mysterious disappearance of the bells went unsolved. Although church officials and treasure hunters kept searching for the relics, all clues led to dead ends.

Then in 1965, church officials were surprised to receive an anonymous package containing a fragment of the San Pedro bell. Although precious little hard information was provided with the fragment, authorities deduced that since the fragment had been sliced at the bell's top, the thieves were hoping the bells were not brass, but solid gold covered with a thin brass layer — a legend that persists to this day.

Church officials could do nothing but wait and pray for the bells' return or at least another message. Years passed without any word about the bells.

Six years later in 1971, a mysteriously worded message about the bells came to the Rev. Dominic Passaglia. The message stated that "the bells had been stolen by four northern California Indians who had buried them in a secret location in the vicinity of Big Sur." The messengers, purported to be descendants of those now-dead Indians, wanted to return the bells, but were extremely anxious.

Church bells played a prominent role in early San Diego society. In addition to calling worshipers to service, they served as timekeepers, commemorated special occasions and events, and alerted residents to dangers such as marauding gangs and wildfires. *Photo courtesy Library of Congress.*

Rev. Passaglia told the press:

"The people who have them still are afraid they will be in some way prosecuted or blamed for the theft, even though the original culprits are dead now. We know where our bells are, and hope to have them back in 18 months or two years."

Eighteen months passed, then two years, and the anonymous messengers failed to make good on their promise to return the bells.

Treasure hunters who have tried to follow the bells' trail have come up empty handed. If the bells were recovered, they would likely fetch a heavenly price on the open market.

But the historical values of "N.S. De Loreto, 1729" and "San Pedro, 1767" to San Diego and the Catholic Church are beyond any good measure.

To this day tales persist of buried treasure on or about the Mission Santa Ysabel grounds. These tales are likely the result of confusion between San Diego County's mission and a mythical Mission Santa Ysabel in Baja California, Mexico. In the Baja mission legend, Jesuit priests supposedly buried an enormous cache of treasure.

18th Century Bell Found

A 200-year-old bell was found and recovered by a La Jolla scuba diver in 1959. The crude bell, discovered in about 20 feet of water off Fern Street, weighed about eight pounds, a fraction of the estimated weight of either one of the Santa Ysabel bells.

The discovery prompted an investigation by the Smithsonian Institution, England's National Maritime Museum, and San Diego's Serra Historical Museum. Authorities with those institutions concurred that the crude bell was probably manufactured in Mexico in the middle of the 18th century and that it may well be from the *San Jose*, one of three ships sent to San Diego to coincide with Father Junípero Serra's arrival in 1769.

The barnacle-encrusted bell first appeared to be ordinary debris to the scuba diver, Dr. Edwin A. Taylor, of La Jolla. "I was going down to spear a nice halibut when I noticed something that looked like the rim of a sewer pipe," Taylor told reporters. "I gave it a tug and up came the bell."

Curators for the Serra Museum concluded that the bell is the first relic discovered from the *San Jose*, which left Mexico in the company of two other ships and was lost, and presumed wrecked, somewhere along the way.

The Solana Beach Fighting Schooner

The discovery of the wreck of a four-masted fighting ship with cannons intact one-half mile off a North County beach was reported in August 1955 by a 22-year-old scuba diver.

Melvin Earl Scott told reporters he found the wreck while spear fishing in 60 feet of water northwest of Solana Beach. The 100-foot-long ship still had seven muzzle-loading cannons protruding out of eight gun ports.

Scott also reported finding a ring near the wreckage. A jeweler confirmed the object was at least 150 years old, foreign made, and solid gold.

The young diver told reporters that he didn't notice the wreck until he was practically on top of it. "It looked like one big ball of lettuce kelp. All four masts were snapped off. I looked for a nameplate on the stern but was unable to find one. I looked through one of the holes in the side and could see the beams were made of solid oak."

The diver described the cannons as the old type that shot balls about six inches in diameter. The barrels were about six to seven feet long and appeared to weigh about 700 pounds. They were mounted on wooden frames and hung on metal swivel bars to allow them to be tilted up and down.

Retired rear admiral Paul F. Dugan said at the time that the wreck was possibly that of the Spanish galleon *San Jose* (the same ship mentioned in the previous story), one of three galleons that sailed from La Paz, Mexico (then New Spain) to San Diego in March, 1769. Two ships arrived, but the *San Jose* was never heard from. Other authorities doubted that the wreck was a galleon, citing that the galleon design preceded that of four-masted vessels.

While Scott refused to divulge the exact location of the wreck, San Diego lifeguard Knox Harris led a team in search of the wreck a few months later. That expedition was hampered by murky water that made it impossible to see more than 10 feet. Harris told reporters that he and his partner were beginning to doubt that there was a sunken ship off Solana Beach.

According to estimates, there are more than 400 sunken ships, ranging from Spanish galleons to Chinese junks to modern freighters between Mexico and San Francisco.

The Treasure of Los Coronados Islands

Legend has it that a pirate's treasure is cached in one of the many caves that dot Islas de Los Coronados, a group of three uninhabited islands in Mexican waters, 16 miles south of Point Loma. In fact, one popular anchorage for modern-day boaters is called Smuggler's Cove.

While questions linger as to whether hidden booty exists, history tells us a real pirate, José Arvaez, used Los Coronados as a base of operations for a few years beginning in about 1830.

Arvaez arrived in San Diego shortly after Mexico began deporting convicts here in the late 1820s. After organizing a crew comprised mostly of Mexican convicts with a few veteran hands from the vanquished pirate Jean Lafitte, Arvaez stole a schooner and armed it to the teeth.

For years, and apparently without attracting too much attention, Arvaez waylaid northbound vessels headed to San Francisco from the East Coast via Cape Horn.

Since Arvaez always scuttled the plundered ships and had a firm rule never to take prisoners, most of the vessels were considered lost at sea by storm.

Arvaez thus operated as a highly profitable, low-profile buccaneer until he broke his own rule about taking captives. His undoing came about after he captured a skinny cabin boy named Tom Bolter.

Bolter was aboard the English vessel *Chelsea* bound from San Francisco to Liverpool when Arvaez and his crew attacked.

After transferring the cargo to his own ship, Arvaez ordered his men to kill everyone on aboard then scuttle *Chelsea*. But when it came to the skinny cabin boy, Bolter pleaded for his life, proclaiming it had been his lifelong ambition to become a pirate. In fact, he said, the only reason he had signed on as a cabin boy on a merchant ship was in hopes of being so captured.

Perhaps it was the boy's appeal to the pirate's vanity — but more likely that the lad knew the sailing dates of several other vessels about to depart San Francisco — that caused Arvaez to spare the cabin boy's life and bring him into his group.

Written accounts have it that the boy was sharp and cunning and participated in several raids. Then, for some reason, Arvaez grew tired of his company and made him stay on Coronado Islands during a raid.

Apparently, Arvaez told Bolter to help two of his men guard the cavern in which the pirate's treasure was stowed. But secretly, Arvaez told one of the men to keep an eye on Bolter.

Arvaez left the trio on the island and set sail with the hopes of intercepting a treasure galleon. But as soon as the pirate's schooner disappeared over the horizon, the guards leaned back, laid their weapons aside, and began enjoying the morning. A short while later, Bolter leapt to his feet and cried, "Look, Arvaez is coming back!"

When the guards raced to the water's edge to get a better look, Bolter grabbed their guns and shot them in the back.

Bolter then commandeered one of Arvaez' yawls that had been left on the beach for fishing, loaded it up with as much treasure as possible, and made for San Diego.

When the cabin boy reached San Diego Harbor, he was hailed by the crew of the New York-based trader *Grendo*. When asked what he was doing, the boy retorted that he was a pirate, and a mean one at that. The laughing crew allowed the boy to tie up and brought him to captain's cabin.

Bolter repeated his story to *Grendo's* Captain Bellue, including all details surrounding his heroic exploits. The captain seemed quite amused until young Bolter invited him to inspect the plunder from the cavern. Once the captain saw the treasure, he immediately rounded up a group of volunteers from shore and set sail for the Coronados. Following Bolter's suggestions, *Grendo* landed only long enough to discharge the boy, Captain Bellue, and the group of volunteers. They hid in the cavern while a working crew sailed *Grendo* to the leeward side of the island, out of sight from Arvaez' anticipated approach from the west.

To make the scene appear as though nothing had happened, he stationed Bolter and a pair of look-alike guards at the cave's entrance.

Arvaez and his pirates expected nothing as they climbed the cliff to their headquarters. Most of them had left their weapons back on the schooner, and after a very short skirmish, surrendered to the men from *Grendo*. Arvaez surrendered directly to Belleu.

It is said that the volunteers and crew aboard *Grendo* could not wait to reach the bay before dealing with the pirates. One by one, they were hanged from the *Grendo's* yardarms during the 16-mile sail to the port.

Bolter was allowed to keep a share of his spoils as reward and for a short while was the talk of the town at San Diego waterfront establishments.

Researchers do not agree whether or not Bolter stayed in San Diego a free man, or whether he was brought to trial and hanged for his role in the raids. Many who follow the legend believe a strong possibility exists that some of Arvaez' treasure remains hidden in caves on one of the three Los Coronados Islands.

Hunting for that treasure is made difficult, if not impossible, by the fact that the rugged Mexican islands are part of an ecological sanctuary, and aside from a few soldiers living at a lonely outpost, the area is strictly off-limits to treasure hunters and sightseers alike.

While pirates such as Captain George Lowther, shown in this 1734 etching, gained notoriety on the Eastern Seaboard and Caribbean Islands, pirate José Arvaez plundered ships off the San Diego coast in 1830. He used Coronado Islands as a base of operations and many believe his treasure still awaits discovery. *Image courtesy Library of Congress.*

CHAPTER 60

The Oceanside Treasure Galleon

In September 1968, Oceanside city and California state officials received simultaneous requests from treasure seekers to search for the wreck of the legendary treasure ship *Trinidad*.

Trinidad supposedly sank in shallow water off Oceanside in the mid-16th century. The ship's cargo may have included from $2 to $12 million in gold coins and bullion.

Legend holds that Spanish explorer Francisco de Ulloa explored the southern California coastline before the time of Juan Cabrillo, who is generally credited with discovering California and first sailing into San Diego Bay in 1542.

Although Ulloa's logbook has never been found, treasure hunters began searching the waters off Oceanside after the publication of a controversial theory by Dr. Joseph Markey, an archaeologist who claims a Spanish ship visited the Oceanside area in 1540.

Newspaper reports show that in the summer of 1969, Oceanside resident Daniel Gray spearheaded a dive team that recovered a 15-foot section of wooden hull thought to be part of *Trinidad*. The team's efforts that summer ended when a key piece of equipment failed. The team returned the following summer with a 64-foot dive boat and 110-foot barge but did not report finding the treasure galleon.

Armed with new research and more modern equipment, a new team of explorers allegedly located *Trinidad* in 1973. Diver Michael P. Carson told reporters that newly discovered historical information showed *Trinidad* was a flimsily constructed scout ship built in Mexico rather than the sturdy treasure galleon previously reported.

Their information indicated that *Trinidad* was anchored off Oceanside in 1540 when a series of storms sank the vessel. Carson and his Los Angeles-based team employed sonar and found what they claimed was the wreck, in 24 feet of water, under 18 feet of sand, about one half mile off Oceanside. Sonar readouts indicated the buried wreck was approximately 88 feet long and 25 feet wide. The team did not report recovering anything from the *Trinidad* wreck site, but it's important to note that most treasure hunters remain tightlipped about discoveries—both to thwart competition and avoid sharing bounty with the I.R.S.

SECTION VI

San Diego Underground

What you see is just the tip of the iceberg. The people, the cars, the restaurants and bars: nearly everything we know exists atop terra firma. Yet San Diego's past is chock full of fanciful legends and true narratives of underground activities that range from explorations to excavations to subterranean inhabitations.

Many find these belowground stories oddly captivating. Perhaps all this burrowing, tunneling, and underground hewing represents escape from our mainstream lives. Or maybe it's Freudian psychology at work: We have evolved from an era in which our ancestors lived in caves. Our egos strive to distance ourselves from those roots. Our ids fight to connect.

CHAPTER 61

The Cavern and the Phallus

According to the writings of early San Diego resident Helen Gohres, a massive cave with some rather odd contents was discovered in East San Diego County in 1894. Gohres personally visited the cave on at least one occasion but furnished no precise details from which others might have located the cave's entrance.

In an incredibly detailed unpublished manuscript dated 1956, Gohres described exploring a cave beneath Cajon Peak on October 11, 1894. Gohres was brought to the cavern by a man known as Captain Freeman after he had discovered it the week before. Freeman, Gohres, and four unnamed men climbed Cajon Peak from the northeast and worked their way about halfway to the top of the mountain.

From there they traversed a narrow and tortuous waterway apparently used by Indians who "were doubtless at one time acquainted with the marvelous wonders of this freak of nature, running through thick and entangled underbrush, over and around precipitous cliffs and boulders as large as the county courthouse," Gohres wrote.

The party accessed the cave through a natural vertical shaft descending at least 20 feet into a 12- by 15-foot chamber. From there, lateral passages branched out in several directions — some ending within a few feet, others extending hundreds of feet.

The cave's grand cavern was found by climbing through a 50-foot, upward-sloping crawl space that led to a large room lit by a small opening from above. "The roof, brilliant with stalactites and the floor obstructed with numerous boulders and stalagmites, reflected the rays of lights in thousands of different directions," claimed Gohres.

The group discovered a low burrow heading south for a distance of 100 feet until they came upon a drop-off of about 25 feet. After carefully navigating the drop-off, the party discovered a huge circular chamber approximately 100 feet in diameter. The chamber walls were composed of massive boulders worn smooth by water. In the center of the chamber stood a massive rock that at first appeared to have been shaped by human hand.

"A description of this is simply impossible, but if one can imagine an egg of granite set upon its largest end and about the size of an ordinary

176

horse car, some definite idea of its appearance may be had," she said, possibly not knowing she was describing a phallic symbol.

By shinnying up the huge, granite egg, she discovered a large vertical hole in the tip. The hole was about five feet deep, several feet across, and contained water that appeared to be strongly impregnated with iron and other minerals. Two perfectly round rocks, "about the size of ordinary baseballs" rested in the bottom. She conjectured that a single stream of steady drips through the cave's ceiling over the millennia had formed the hole on top of the massive rock, and had subsequently filled the tip.

After filling a small vial with water for future analysis, the group explored several other passages. They discovered more wonderful caverns and a mineral spring, "which appears to have some medicinal effect and value."

After returning to San Diego, Captain Freeman left for Los Angeles in an effort to secure the land from the government with the idea of opening the mysterious Cajon Peak Cave to the public. Captain Freeman never made good on those efforts.

Whether the Cajon Peak Caves actually exist or whether Helen Gohres fabricated them may never be known. Modern-day explorers literally hit a dead end before beginning. Since the names of some mountains, peaks, and promontories have changed over time, explorers are uncertain whether "Cajon Peak" referenced in the account is the present-day El Cajon Mountain. To complicate matters, in San Diego's very early days, El Cajon Mountain was sometimes called El Capitan Grande.

We will likely never know whether Doctor Sigmund Freud heard about Helen Gohres reported discovery of a massive phallic symbol inside a cave at Cajon Peak. Nor will we likely find out whether he thought the entire city of San Diego had a case of "cave envy," as described in the following story. *Photo courtesy Library of Congress.*

A Case of Cave Envy

Dr. Sigmund Freud was alive and well in Vienna in 1895 when word of another cave discovery echoed throughout San Diego. But if the citizens of San Diego were jealous of Kentucky's Mammoth Caves, which at the time drew tens of thousands of visitors per year, the following legend could be chalked up to a big case of "Cave Envy."

"A big cave was discovered Monday on the ocean side of Point Loma," reported the *San Diego Union* on December 4th of that year. "So far as explored, it does seem quite as large as the Mammoth Caves of Kentucky, but it is quite as interesting, and will furnish another point of interest to visitors."

Dr. Freud likely never heard of the Point Loma discovery. But then again, maybe he did. The intellectual leap from Cave Envy to Penis Envy is not all that great.

The *San Diego Union* account related the findings of two Point Loma men, Horace Metcalf and Vernon G. Mathews, who set out early one morning to do a bit of low-tide exploring around the tip of the peninsula. The duo clambered over rocks and crossed tide pools until they were about a mile and a half north of the lighthouse on the ocean side of the promontory.

There, they discovered what appeared to be the entrance to a cave just above the surface of the water at low tide. Sheer cliffs prevented them from climbing down to enter, so the men trekked north and found a spot where they could lower themselves with a rope.

"Near the place of descent they ran across a smaller hole, which they entered, finding that it connected with the larger one, and leading into the bowels of the earth," the newspaper reported.

Metcalf and Mathews worked their way into the cave until they reached a point about 250 feet from the entrance. There, the passageway widened out to form a grand chamber "big enough to hold the largest building in San Diego."

Since the entrance was only open at low tide, the men did not explore long, but noted that by appearances even a high tide would not flood the grand chamber, the newspaper noted.

Possibly playing up to potential tourists, the newspaper story also mentioned that the cave's interior was "grand and weird, and well worth a trip of hundreds of miles to see."

Although Metcalf and Mathews vowed to return to the cave and share more of their discovery with the public, they did not immediately do so.

But four months later a party of four young men reentered the cave for further exploration. This time the newspaper's front page waxed eloquent: "Perilous Journey Around the Foot of Point Loma — Entrance at Low Tide — A Big Chamber Paneled as if by Design — Extent Not Yet Known."

The March 4, 1896, story described the adventures of five young members of the San Diego Rowing Club who rowed the club's barge, *Governor Perkins*, from inside the bay to a landfall near the tip of Point Loma. H.H. Palmer, E. Perkins, V.E. Matthews, D. Seaman, and H.B. Clark left their rowing barge high and dry and walked north.

"In spite of the warnings that it was dangerous to attempt the rounding of the point on foot except at the very lowest tide, the young men found the way easy until they reached a small canyon half a mile north of the new lighthouse, on the ocean side." (The lighthouse high atop Point Loma, now a feature at Cabrillo National Monument, was discontinued in 1891 in favor of the lower lighthouse mentioned in this story. It sits about 90 feet above the waterline due west of the old lighthouse).

Rough going forced the foursome to climb the cliff at this point. They followed a rabbit trail path back down toward the water. The trail was "so steep and tortuous that although they were at no times more than 15 feet from each other, none of them could be seen by any of the others."

The path dumped the adventurers onto a small bluff about 10 feet above the beach. The men fashioned a towel into an ersatz rope to climb down. From the beach they crept along a narrow shelf above the surf, stumbling over round boulders slick with seaweed, for a distance of about 200 yards. Suddenly they came upon the entrance to the cavern. More than 20 feet high, the grotto was about 10 feet wide and positioned so that sunlight shone deep inside.

A large pool of water more than five feet deep prevented the men from entering the cave, but reflected enough light that the men were able to make out red, blue, and yellow rocks on the walls and ceiling. The men retreated and spotted a second entrance to the cavern about 100 feet north of the main entrance. Although it appeared at first glance to be too narrow for access, it widened appreciably as it led the men deeper into the cave.

After slipping over slimy boulders for about 50 yards, the men came to a passageway that connected to the main entrance. At that junction, the passage widened to a magnificent chamber more than 80 feet high. They were at that juncture about 100 yards from the ocean.

This main cavern was lit enough by reflected light so the men could admire the beauty of the ceiling, which had been "carved by the action of the sea into curious panelings of such regularity that it seemed incredible that Father Neptune could have planned his architecture without pattern or design."

The floor of the cave was described as slightly higher than the waterline at low tide. The back portion of the cave sloped upward and acted as a repository for seaweed and large cobblestones driven by the force of the waves.

A shelf that hinted of interesting developments was discovered about 20 feet off the floor of the cave but lack of available light prevented further investigation.

As the afternoon tide rose, the four young men headed back across Point Loma to the rowing barge. On the way back, they paused to take note of a smaller cave about 200 yards away from the first. A quick inspection revealed that this 15-foot-high grotto was but 50 yards deep and accessible only at very low tide.

News of the young men's discovery elicited vows of more vigorous exploration by the citizenry of San Diego but subsequent written accounts do not mention additional expeditions to that particular underworld.

Thus the Point Loma caves never furnished "another point of interest" for tens of thousands of visitors. That's why some regard this story as a big case of cave envy.

Real Caves Under Point Loma

It is not surprising residents have long debated the existence of caves and tunnels beneath Point Loma. Longtime residents familiar with the beach area south of Point Loma Nazarene University swear that at least a tunnel once led from the beach to the crest of Catalina Boulevard, which traverses the peninsula's backbone at about 400 feet above sea level. The entrance to that tunnel was closed decades ago, they claim.

Legend also has it that Cabrillo National Monument, at the tip of Point Loma, is riddled with miles of tunnels dug over the years in support of military gun batteries and that those tunnels connect to massive, natural caves that serve as ammunition and fuel-oil depots.

Officials at Cabrillo National Monument acknowledge that between 1918 and 1943, the Army constructed searchlight bunkers, fire control stations, and gun batteries. Many of those were connected by concrete-lined tunnels with massive blast-reinforced doors so that ammunition could be transferred belowground—safe from potential enemy aircraft bombardment or shipboard artillery fire. These short tunnels also housed battery crewmen, but little else, officials contend.

But a peek at declassified confidential schematics of 16-inch gun battery 134 shows an underground network of tunnels and spaces beneath the emplacement. The network includes several 25-foot by 50-foot powder magazines, shell magazines, storage rooms, equipment rooms, and personnel spaces—all connected by a 500-foot tunnel. No schematic has been declassified to show how various gun batteries might interconnect or link to possible central magazines that could resupply batteries.

Today, considerable above-ground remnants from the batteries at Point Loma exist, but the true scope of the Point Loma tunnels may never be known to the public — they are on Navy property and are strictly off limits to civilians.

Despite officials' denial that a huge network of manmade tunnels connects to natural caves under Cabrillo National Monument, those who argue that natural caves exist in Point Loma appear to have facts on their sides. In 1961, construction workers grading a 40-acre site for the Point Loma Waste Water Treatment Plant unearthed a series of caves below the plant's site.

Former city operations director Paul Beermann told reporters at the time that six caves were discovered 170 feet beneath the treatment plant site. The caves were between 15 and 20 feet high and ran from the water's edge to directly underneath the treatment plant construction site — a distance of 500 feet. City budget records show that an additional $19,791 was spent to dump rocks into the cave's entrances to prevent the ocean from undermining the earth beneath the treatment plant site.

Cabrillo National Monument at the tip of Point Loma is riddled with miles of tunnels dug over the years in support of military gun batteries. The image above shows a rare glimpse of an underground casemate, a fortified enclosure underneath Fort Rosecrans. Note the vertical tunnel and mound of dirt, indicating more burrowing. *Photo courtesy Historic American Buildings Survey (LOC).*

Prohibition Smuggler's Cave

Somewhere along San Diego County's 35 miles of shoreline, an ancient and intricately excavated smugglers' tunnel was hewn by combining natural caves and manmade tunnels. This cave and tunnel system was shown to this author only after receiving an oath never to reveal its exact location.

The underground complex is a masterpiece of determined sandstone carving. The main passageways are square cut, more than six feet high and four feet wide, with concrete lined floors, a sloping ramp, and an area used for hoisting booze or contraband from inside the grotto at water level to the passageways. Upon thorough exploration, the cave system's function is immediately understandable. During the prohibition era, and perhaps much earlier, smugglers would anchor ships offshore and under the cover of darkness use rowboats to ferry liquor or other contraband up to the base of the cliff. When low tide came, smugglers would row the boats into the grotto and use the hoist to lift barrels of liquor into the passageways. The barrels would then be rolled up a long, sloping ramp that terminated atop the sea cliff. The contraband would then be loaded into a waiting automobile — and the authorities would be none the wiser.

Nowadays, the ramp opening at the top of the cliff is permanently closed due to a cave-in and the only way to enter the system is by climbing down a steep bluff. The cliff in this area is quite sheer, and only the slightest indentations serve as hand and foot holds. The grainy nature of the sandstone seems to invite slipping, and micro-avalanches of sand and small pebbles rain down without notice.

At extremely low tides that occur only a few times per year, one must slug across slippery knee-deep rocks, climb a large pile of boulders that conceals the cave, and locate the grotto's entrance. One must enter the 40-foot-deep grotto and locate a set of concrete steps that curves up to the entrance to a square-cut tunnel, approximately 15 feet above the waterline. Decades of erosion have eaten away the sandstone at the head of the stairs, leaving a dangerous gap one must leap across to access the tunnel. Misjudging that leap would result in falling onto jagged rocks below.

The main tunnel is equally dangerous, and each step along the way brings potential danger. The tunnel floor is irregular and slippery. Several sections of the tunnel have been eaten away from below, leaving wide-open pitfalls through which unwary explorers could fall — to end up wedged or trapped, all with the constant threat of rising tides.

The tunnel is inky black and the air is stale, clammy, and evil smelling. The sounds of sloshing water echo through the halls from somewhere, and in the darkness pigeons coo and cluck in a most unsettling manner. No doubt rats and black widow spiders call this cave system home.

After a short distance the tunnel branches into two. To the left is a ramp that once terminated at the top of the bluff, but now dead-ends. To the right, the tunnel leads to the hoisting area. It is not difficult to imagine a rumrunner's ship lying at anchor off Point Loma on a moonless night. A small tender packed with booze stealthily rows toward shore and beaches at one of the many coves that dot the shoreline. A couple of men from land join the rumrunners to form a work party to help hoist the barrels and lift them into the back of a waiting car. Miles away, customs officers dutifully check the holds of each ship that pulls into San Diego Harbor.

Beyond the hoisting area, the tunnel leads to several dead ends that terminate in drop offs. One passage leads to another set of concrete

Somewhere along San Diego County's 50 miles of shoreline, an honest-to-goodness smuggler's tunnel exists. The network of hand-hewn tunnels and natural grottos dates back to at least the Prohibition Era. *Author photo.*

steps that make their way down to another grotto. It's easy to envision that due to erosion over the decades, or centuries, various parts of the tunnel system have collapsed and that the smugglers have responded by digging new tunnels.

From the foot of the steps that lead down to the second cove, the entrance to another grotto may be seen — this one smaller and more hazardous than the first. This chamber's entrance is normally almost completely filled with water and is accessible only at extreme low tides. In addition, the grotto floor is covered with fine silt that acts like quicksand that was at least thigh deep to this explorer. One can imagine getting mired in waist-deep water, ever conscious of the fast rising tide and the possibility of drowning before rescue could be affected.

In the back of this sea cave, a tunnel-like fissure branches off to the left. This naturally occurring fissure runs about one hundred feet, narrowing and tightening as it gains elevation, until it reaches a small opening that leads outside. After crawling through the opening, this author found himself standing on a small ledge about halfway up the sea cliff. The cliff's sheer face made it impossible to climb up or down so the only possible way to return was to squeeze through the fissure and wade through the quicksand grotto again. The author explored this grotto with the hope of discovering the entrance to a smuggler's tunnel rumored to lead to a trap door underneath a house. No such tunnel was found.

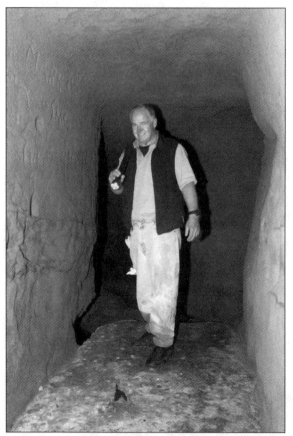

Concrete lines many of the tunnel floors but cave-ins and erosion have created numerous pitfalls. The Smuggler's Cave is so dangerous the author has vowed to never reveal its exact location. *Author photo.*

Desert Beekeeper's Cave House

Not all caves in San Diego were dug for nefarious purposes. One Anza-Borrego recluse, called the Beekeeper of Mason Valley, lived in a cliff-side cave from the early 1900s until his death in 1942.

William Hull earned a meager living by keeping bees, doing a little prospecting, and by looking after the property of a Mason Valley rancher. Few knew the Spanish-American war veteran and fewer still had any idea where he lived.

It was only after his death of a heart attack that a county coroner received information so he could check up on the man's personal property. Following a dirt trail to a scrub-covered hillside, the coroner discovered the beekeeper resided in a one-room cave carved out of solid rock.

From the outside, the cave had been boarded over for an attractive — albeit rustic — appearance. On the inside, the living room-sized quarters contained the man's bed, table, chairs, cook-stove, and other conveniences. A small room the size of a clothes closet was chiseled out of solid rock to serve as a food pantry.

Authorities acknowledged that Hull's cave was ideally suited for the harsh desert climate, since the stone walls would stay cool during summer days and warm during winter nights. Amazingly, in the harshness of the desert lived a man of balance.

Today, the exact location of the beekeeper's cave seems lost to antiquity—nobody seems to even know where to begin looking!

Wizard of Oz Creator Gave La Jolla Cave Its Name

Those wishing to walk in the underworld need not risk life and limb.

Since 1903, the La Jolla Cave has offered adventurers a safe and sane opportunity to explore the dank and musty recesses of San Diego's underground.

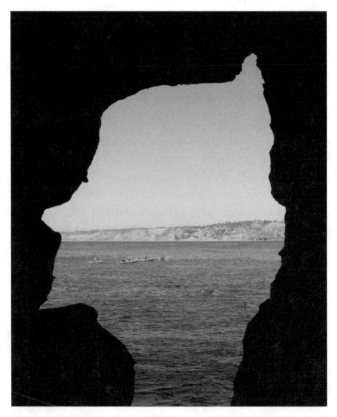

Wizard of Oz creator Frank Baum is credited with giving the "Sunny Jim" moniker to La Jolla Cave. Visitors taking the 145 wooden steps from the cliff-side entrance find themselves on a platform inside a snug little grotto. The outline of the sea cave forms Sunny Jim's silhouette. *Author photo.*

The cave entrance is a few blocks east of La Jolla Cove and for a modest fee ($5 adults, $3 children) those walking down a flight of 145 wooden stairs get to breathe dank and earthy netherworld air and hear dark waters slosh in the blackness below. Those who make it to the platform at the bottom of the steps find themselves inside a snug little grotto, squinting into a bright seascape outside. And silhouetted against this seascape is the shape of the head of a man called "Sunny Jim."

Cave operators claim the silhouette was named by Frank Baum, creator of the Wizard of Oz, after a visit in which he noticed the outline resembled a cartoon character called "Sunny Jim," who was a mascot for Force Cereal Products in the 1920's.

The catchy name likely helped propel the La Jolla Cave into prominence, since Force Cereal ran lighthearted radio ads featuring Sunny Jim jingles and pasted billboards on sides of trolley cars.

Like the Smuggler's Cave (see page 182) this cave is the result of man and nature's handiwork combined. Geologists believe the grotto part of the cave at sea level was created by wave action about 200,000 years ago. Beginning in 1902, workers hired by then-cave owner Gustav Shultz hewed a tunnel connecting the grotto to the top of the cliff. Using picks and shovels, the men carved the tunnel in about two years. Today, 145 steps lead down into the grotto where visitors enjoy gently lapping waters and view the silhouette of Sunny Jim.

Young's Cave a Haven for Hoodlums

While some caves are prone to sudden collapse, one in Mission Valley stubbornly resisted numerous attempts to dynamite its entrance shut.

W. R. Young began construction of a massive cave system for a very strange reason. He had moved to San Diego County in the 1920s with hopes of improving his poor health and somehow came up with the idea that digging would promote wellness.

It is not known why he chose a site about a half-mile east of Fairmount Avenue for his elaborate system of tunnels and caves, but for years Young could be seen shoveling and hauling dirt from the mouth of his cave, Young's Cave.

Records don't show when Young abandoned his diggings, but in the late 1920's the cave became a popular attraction for San Diego youth. The cave apparently stayed off parents' radars until 1931 when it was searched as part of a high-profile murder investigation. Although Young's Cave had nothing to do with the murder, searchers alerted city authorities to the existence of the underground chambers. Signs were immediately posted but little else was done to bar youth from entering and improving upon Young's Cave. In fact, no one knows just how far Young personally tunneled — not all burrowing was attributed to him — but accounts over the years describe a wandering maze of tunnels and rooms stretching thousands of feet.

In 1934 part of Young's cave collapsed and a child was buried alive. After successfully rescuing the lad, authorities dynamited the entrance and erected several well-placed "Keep Out" signs. It didn't take long for area youth to burrow a new entrance adjacent to the old.

Authorities pretty much ignored activities at Young's Cave until 1938 when word of a thriving underground community, comprised mainly of juveniles, reached the outside world.

Investigations led to discussions at city hall, and while most favored blasting the entrance again, one wag quipped, "Why not put up a sign saying 'Dump No Rubbish' and let the pubic fill them up?"

A few weeks later the county road department dynamited the entrance to Young's Cave. This action simply seemed to strengthen the youths' resolve, and the cave quickly reopened.

Over the next decade the cave maintained its popularity as a secret youth gathering spot. Then in 1950, authorities entered the cave in search of a runaway 12-year-old girl.

This led to the discovery that Young's Cave served as headquarters for a rather large gang.

San Diego's Sons of Satan comprised more than one hundred 14- to 20-year-old kids. Perhaps they were drawn together by the burgeoning 1950s counterculture that romanticized street-fighting gangs such as the Latin Kings and Vice Lords from Chicago. Or perhaps admission to the cave required admission to the gang. Either way, it's doubtful that Sons of Satan was a bona fide street gang with switch-blades and zip guns. More likely it was a rough-and-tumble social club for marginalized kids.

Nevertheless, the cave's role as headquarters was a highly guarded secret, possibly since members were forced to take a blood oath not to reveal the cave's location or other information to authorities or parents. The gang also kept the entrance to the cave system very small to discourage adult visitors. When police squeezed inside, they found picks, shovels, crowbars, blankets, canned food, candles, and lanterns. According to one detective involved in the case of the 12-year-old runaway, the cave system comprised nearly a mile of tunnels and vaults.

As part of the investigation into the missing girl's whereabouts during her absence, detectives apprehended several gang members. One of them had a map in his possession that traced the major tunnels and showed the location of several large halls. The names given them were intriguing: Bat Room, Kool Room, Dining Room, Spider's Room, Devil's Hallway, The Den, Queen's Room, and the Boxing Arena.

After evicting the gang, police sought to dynamite the entire cave complex to crush any dreams of reopening its chambers. But it took city hall three years to fully debate the issue. Finally, the city decided to blast the entrance and capped it off with a thick concrete plug.

Six years later, a group of teenagers dug a vertical hole above the plug and lowered themselves down with 15 feet of rope. Hoping to improve upon the blood oath of non-divulgence used by their gangster predecessors, this group required a written pledge not to tell parents or authorities. But before long, one youth blabbed to his parents. Juvenile officers rounded up the subterranean offenders and ten boys, ages 10 to 13, were evicted from the cave.

When a reporter asked one juvenile officer why he didn't lower himself into the cave personally, he responded, "I used to play in those caves when I was a kid, so I know what I'm talking about. The danger is always present of a cave-in."

The city dynamited the entrance to Young's Cave again, but it reopened within a few years, mainly as a hideout for truants.

Young's Cave kept out of the news until 1968 when a cave-in occurred, trapping three youngsters. Firefighters rescued all three. Shortly thereafter, authorities surveyed the entire system in advance of a more rigorous closing. Firefighters crawled through hundreds of yards of tunnels to inspect the cave's numerous rooms. They found no sleeping bags, bedding, canned food, or other signs of habitation: only a few cigarette butts and burned matches.

A few months later, the city poured several truckloads of wet cement into the cave's mouth to create a 20-foot-thick concrete plug.

Young's Cave was permanently closed — as far as anyone knows.

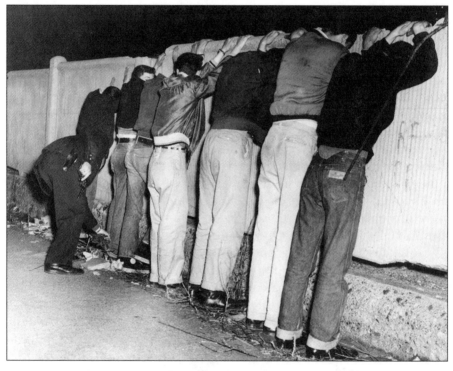

1950s teen street gangs, such as those that prowled Chicago and New York (pictured) at night, served as role models for teens in San Diego who appropriated an abandoned sprawling cave complex in Mission Valley for their headquarters. *Photo courtesy New York World-Telegram and the Sun Newspaper Photograph Collection.*

Talmadge Park House Cave

The most famous residential excavation in San Diego is no doubt the nine-room playhouse dug by a physicist and family beneath their Talmadge Park home.

Between 1949 and 1960, Dr. Glen Havens and his family dug a spiral stair-step tunnel that descended 70 feet beneath their hillside house. The stairs led to two recreation rooms — one 12 by 25 feet, the other 10 by 18 feet — and a small kitchen.

From that elevation, a horizontal tunnel led to a large room and a bevy of smaller rooms. The tunnel branched away from the house and opened up on the hillside. The mouth of that tunnel overlooked — where else? — Fairmount Avenue of Young's Cave fame!

Dr. Havens started the project innocently enough when he decided to convert an abandoned backyard barbecue pit into something a little larger that the kids could play in.

After excavating 20 feet, Havens decided he had found a new hobby. Using his five children and plenty of neighborhood kids' muscle, Havens began engineering in earnest.

Eleven years later the shoveling finally stopped. In March 1960, Havens held an "open cave" in which he escorted media and a few curious neighbors through his underground lair.

During the tour through nearly 700 feet of tunnels, Havens gave outsiders a glimpse of the structural concrete that supported the tunnels, the cave's fully functioning electrical system, and a display case full of seashells and bones he discovered while digging.

To highlight the media tour, simultaneous ping pong tournaments were held in each of the two recreational rooms.

Although the Havens family has long since moved, the house still stands and has changed ownership several times over the decades. Like that weird uncle we don't like to talk about, the Cave Houses' precise location is a somewhat-guarded neighborhood secret.

CHAPTER 69

Ocean Beach Death Cave

Not all sandstone is created equal. In San Diego County, geologists have identified several distinct sandstone formations. The type best for tunneling comprises tightly packed, angular grains of sand. Angular grains tend to lock into one another to help create a dense, cement-like material that might support a cave. Other sandstones contain more loosely packed, round grains that slide against one another. Sadly, a little more than a half century ago, a group of five teenage Ocean Beach boys discovered just how much undercutting such cliffs could withstand.

It was raining Monday, February 12, 1962, and the cave-in on the sea cliffs in south Ocean Beach likely would have occurred with no one inside—had it not been President Abraham Lincoln's birthday. With no school that day, five Collier Junior High School students aged 13 to 15 walked down to Sunset Cliffs early in the morning with the intention of removing belongings from a cave they intended to abandon.

It seems that with all the rain, the hideout's ceiling had started sloughing off clumps of dirt. In fact, local authorities had previously dropped by to warn the lads the three-room cave was dangerous.

But the lads made a final trek to the cave to retrieve a few posses-sions: most likely a few pieces of junky furniture, a few candles, and other insignificant items. Recognizing the cave's instability, the boys stationed one of their youngest at the entrance. Three of the boys were working in the dark recesses of the underground chamber and another had just entered when their world began to collapse around them.

"I was nearest the door and heard a rumbling noise over us," the youngest told reporters. "'The whole hill's coming down. Hey you guys. Get out!' I yelled."

All four boys in the cave were in the act of sprinting toward the light at the cave's mouth when tons of dirt and darkness enveloped them.

One who had just entered the cave almost made it out unscathed. The avalanche completely buried his torso up to his shoulders. After minutes of frantic scratching, clawing, and digging, he managed to move five feet of wet sand to free himself.

The first patrol officer to respond to the alarm began digging with his bare hands to try to reach the three boys still trapped. He yelled for onlookers to find shovels, volunteers, and more shovels. Within minutes, fifty neighbors were hauling away dirt.

Ten to fifteen minutes later, likely about 20-25 minutes after the cave-in, the rescuers reached the boys' bodies. Despite resuscitation efforts and a last-ditch rush to a nearby hospital, two 14-year-olds and a 15-year-old were dead.

News of the disaster quickly reverberated throughout the Ocean Beach community. Details were scant and rumors flew. Word of a possible sixth boy surfaced. Parents rushed to the hospital fearing their children were among the dead.

One mother raced to the hospital, consumed by maternal dread that her son was the mysterious sixth boy. The other five were his friends. He had mentioned the cave. She hadn't seen or heard from him since the cave-in.

"Can you tell me anything that would help identify your boy?" hospital authorities asked her in the waiting room.

"His name is George," she replied.

"One of the boys had a set of keys in his pocket. The key tag says George."

The mother rushed into the temporary morgue. She came out sobbing, "Lord! That's not my boy. That's my boy's best buddy."

Several minutes later, a haggard, bare-footed George raced into the waiting room. The two hugged.

"What about the others?" he asked.

"They're dead, son."

That same day, city construction crews fashioned a six- by 10-foot barrier of chain link fencing to seal off the Ocean Beach death cave. They also sealed off a smaller cave nearby and erected more than 100 feet of wooden fencing on the edge of the bluff to keep curiosity seekers away from the crumbling cliff edge.

Even without manmade caves and tunnels, cliffs along San Diego County beach bluffs are prone to sudden collapse. From Point Loma to Solana Beach, signs warn of such dangers, yet every few years it seems someone is trapped beneath a deadly avalanche.

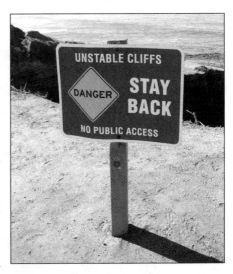

Unstable sandstone cliffs may collapse at any time. Those thinking of tunneling into them, beware! Collapses can be deadly. *Author photo.*

CHAPTER 70

Torrey Pines Hermit Cave

For nearly two decades beginning in the 1970s, a religious cave artist hermit lived in a two-room, hand-hewn cave in a hidden canyon at Torrey Pines State Natural Reserve.

Those who knew Nick Connell described him as a fitness fanatic who once earned the title of Mr. New Hampshire in 1948. He was a deeply spiritual man, a man absolutely taken in with all the world's religions, and a man absolutely given over to following his dreams.

Accounts of the era describe Connell as a Renaissance man, a recluse, a philosopher, and a high-school dropout too stubborn to conform to classroom environments. Lacking a career, Connell held an assortment of odd jobs throughout his life including a circus high-wire artist, a railroad worker, a vaudeville performer, and auxiliary policeman.

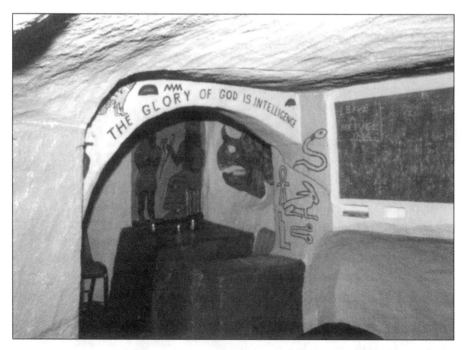

It took hermit and religious artist Nick Connell two years to hand carve this two-room cave in the desolate eastern side of Torrey Pines State Natural Reserve. *Photo courtesy Torrey Pines State Natural Reserve.*

In the early 1970s following a divorce in Salt Lake City, Connell surreptitiously began camping in the eastern portion of the Torrey Pines State Natural Reserve. One day, after a very vivid dream in which he met a wizened old man called, "the owner," Connell literally tumbled off a 10-foot cliff into a small gully and found the ideal site of his future home. It was far off the beaten path so he could come and go without attracting attention. More importantly, it afforded complete solitude.

That same day Connell began hewing with screwdriver and Bowie knife. Within a few weeks, he had carved a recess large enough to crawl out of the rain. Within a few months, he carved out a room large enough to stand in. Within a few years, he carved a two-room cave.

For decades, Connell lived totally off the grid, occasionally taking the city bus into Pacific Beach to work out at a friend's gym and get supplies. When not writing, Connell took to decorating the inside of his sanctuary with religious and spiritual figures inspired by his readings.

One entire cave wall was consumed by Connell's version of the Mayan tree of life supported by a giant turtle. A massive carving of Neptune decorated the ceiling. A Syrian winged bull stood silent sentinel just outside the entrance. Near the cave, in the ravine outside, Connell carved a sandstone throne.

Nick stayed under the park ranger's radar partly by summering with relatives in his hometown, Hudson, New Hampshire. But in the mid-1980s, Connell began writing weekly columns in the *Nassau Telegraph*. The title of his column was "View from a Cave."

Before long, word about his cave spread to San Diego and visitors began arriving en masse. In April, 1989, nearly 300 visitors scrawled their names in a guest book Connell left in his absence.

On January 8, 1991, after allowing Connell a few days to clear out his possessions and to try to save his cave paintings, park rangers used a truckload of cement to fill the cave's entrance.

Connell, devastated, returned to Hudson with the idea of recreating the cave as a tourist attraction. That never happened. Connell also snuck back into the reserve and carved out part of another cave, but that effort was quashed before he could reestablish residency.

Years later, Connell admitted he had taken things too far by altering the park's pristine environment and encouraging visitors to trek to his off-limits haunt.

Note from the author: Except for a narrow footpath that traces the valley floor, the entire east side of Torrey Pines State Natural Reserve is strictly off limits to hikers. Please do not disturb the flora or fauna within this pristine area. State rangers issue citations to anyone venturing off the path.

SECTION VII

Ancient Indian Legends and Tales

San Diego-area Indian legends and tales are among the least-known stories in San Diego history, yet they add greatly to the fabric of modern day life.

Despite possessing character polished by the hand of time, many of these ancient stories attributed to San Diego-area Indians existed only in the oral tradition until committed to writing about 100 years ago.

These Native American stories — some thought to be thousands of years old — were discovered in various archives, scattered amongst decade-old newspapers, magazines, books, and in the keep of tribes, bands, and families.

Amazingly, the legends translated herein have never before been compiled in a single resource — and some have not been made public for more than 60 years.

CHAPTER 71

The Kumeyaay Creation Legend

Native American creation stories typically vary greatly from nation to nation, tribe to tribe, and band to band. In general, creation stories explain the origin of the world and help establish how people are to live and worship. To modern readers, such legends offer up images of a different world view, one in which animals, elements, the solar system, and natural phenomena are all very highly revered.

The following Kumeyaay Creation Legend was unearthed in an obscure book dated 1910 titled, The Religious Practices of the Diegueño Indians *by T.T. Waterman. The legend also appears on the Kumeyaay Nation Web site, www. kumeyaay.com.*

In the beginning, there was no land, only salt water. In the water lived two brothers who kept their eyes closed, so that the salt would not blind them.

On one occasion, the older brother swam to the surface and looked around. He saw nothing except the vastness of the water. But while swimming to the surface to join him, the younger brother opened his eyes. When the younger brother finally got to the surface, his blind eyes saw nothing at all, so he returned to the depths of the sea.

The older brother remained at the surface and pondered the vastness of the water, then decided to create ants. Little red ants sprang from the depths and were so numerous that they filled up portions of the water with their bodies and made land.

The older brother also created certain black birds. But since there was no light to show the way, the birds became lost and could not find anywhere to roost. So the older brother kneaded together three colors of clay: red, yellow, and black to form a flat round disk. This he tossed up into the sky. It stuck to the sky and began to emit a dim light. Today we call this object, Halay, the moon.

The moon's light was too dim to be very useful, so he took another piece of clay and tossed it skyward across from the moon. It was very bright and lit up everything. We call that Inyau, the sun.

But the older brother was still not satisfied, so he decided to create people. Working with light-colored clay, he split one piece in two. First he made man, then he took a rib from the man and made woman. The children of this man and woman were called Ipai, people.

The people lived in a great mountain far to the east called Wikami, the spot where everything was created. Those who travel there today may hear singing in all sorts of languages. If you put your ear to the ground there, you will hear the sounds of dancing. These sounds are caused by the spirits of the dead who go there and sing and dance.

After the older brother had created people, a big snake arose from the ocean in the West. Now, the snake was fundamentally the same as the younger brother, but had taken a different form. When he reached the civilization, he devoured all learning and slithered to a place called Wicuwul, possibly the Coronado Islands. Thus all the arts, including singing, dancing, basket making, and speaking resided inside his body far away.

Now, the people wished to have a great ceremony, and built a ceremonial hut. But since they did not know how to dance or sing or make baskets, they did not know what else to do beyond building the hut.

One old man suggested that there was more to do than just build a ceremonial hut, but he too was at a loss to describe what it was they should do. Someone suggested they ask the snake to give them back their dances. But word soon spread that another serpent was set to devour anyone who ventured out onto the ocean in search of the knowledge-eating snake.

A medicine man heard about the problem and decided to try to reach the serpent. But before setting foot in the water, he changed himself into a bubble. The second serpent devoured him anyway. But the medicine man did not die. Deep down inside the serpent the medicine man ventured north but could find no exit.

He also tried south, west, and east but could not find his way out. Finally he went north again until he found a piece of blue flint. Breaking the flint to create a sharp edge, the medicine man slashed a hole in the top of the snake and escaped.

Once atop the snake, the medicine man noticed a circular hut with a door on top. When he went inside, he heard the knowledge-eating serpent call out, "Who is there?" The medicine man called back, "It is I, uncle. We are trying to hold a ceremony but can't remember how to sing or dance."

"I will teach the people. You go and I will follow." So the medicine man returned to his people and waited. After a while, the snake appeared, so big he stretched from mountaintop to mountaintop.

Seeing the snake was so big, the people made a large clearing around the ceremonial hut. The snake entered the hut head first, then started coiling his body around and around inside the hut. But the snake had no end, and soon the people became fearful of his size. They threw hot embers on the hut and the serpent caught fire.

When the flames became hot enough, the serpent burst, and all the knowledge within him scattered throughout the lands. Each tribe received different knowledge. That is why one tribe may be good at dancing, another good at basket making, and still a third tribe at singing.

A few individuals were struck by certain things, they became witches and medicine men.

The serpent's head burned to ashes and his entire body was flung westward from Wikami, the mountain where all was created, to what we now call the Colorado River. At a certain spot along the river, there is a great white ridge made of stone. That is where his body came to rest. People go there and make spearheads out of that stone. Nearby, there is a black mountain. That is where his head came to rest.

After the serpent had burned and scattered, the people were still uneasy, so they spread out in all directions. Wherever these early people stepped, they left footprints in the ground. Wherever they rested and set down their loads, they left hollows in the rocks.

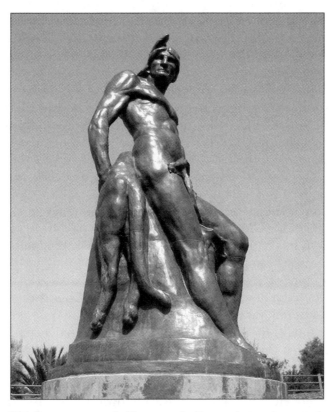

This bronze statue of a Kumeyaay Indian resting against a rock with mountain lion was sculpted by La Mesa resident Arthur Putnam and placed on loan at Presidio Park in 1933. *Author photo.*

The Kumeyaay Indians

Many anthropologists believe Kumeyaay are direct descendants of the first humans to set foot on the North American continent about 50,000 years ago during the Pleistocene ice age.

These ancient wanderers migrated southward, ultimately reaching Tierra del Fuego, land's end at the tip of South America, about 3,000 years ago.

Best current estimates place Native Americans in the San Diego County area anywhere between 12,000 and 5,000 B.C.

When the Spaniards first arrived to occupy the greater San Diego area in 1769, they encountered a well-established population of 25,000 to 30,000 Native Americans including Kumeyaay, Luiseño, Cahuilla, and Cupeño.

The Spaniards conscripted many Native Americans to build and operate San Diego's Mission de Alcalá, Mission San Luis Rey, and several out-posts. The Spanish called these natives Diegueños and Luiseños, meaning "those of (San) Diego" and "those of (San) Luis (Rey)," respectively.

Subjugation, murder, and enslavement of the Indians in San Diego continued through the Mexican and American periods. At one point in the early 1800s the Diegueño population dwindled to less than 2,000.

It was not until the late 1800s that reservations were established for several Diegueño bands including Santa Ysabel, Pala, Sycuan, La Jolla, Rincon, and Capitan Grande.

The term Diegueños was changed to Kumeyaay in the 1970s to more closely reflect the Native American language, although some within this native population prefer to be called Ipai, Tipai, or Kamia because of linguistic differences.

The Kumeyaay population is currently estimated at 20,000, about 10 percent of whom live on 17 San Diego County reservations (An 18th reservation is unoccupied.)

Additionally, there are five Kumeyaay indigenous communities living south of the Mexican/American border established by the Treaty of Guadalupe Hidalgo in 1848.

Linguistically, the Kumeyaay Indians include the Yuman language family Hokan stock and are sub-divided into the Ipai (the northern dialectical form), the Tipai (the southern dialectical form), and the Kamia (the eastern dialectical form).

CHAPTER 72

Old Woman's Whip Helped Name the Animals

This ancient legend comes from a quaint book written in 1914 by Mary Elizabeth Johnson called Indian Legends of the Cuyamaca Mountains. *This story and several others recounted here were attributed to Maria Alto, a Kumeyaay of Laguna Mountains. "Old Woman's Whip" describes how all the various animals came to possess their markings. The word Hum-poo translates loosely to the English word whip.*

Seen-u-how was an old woman who lived in ancient, magical times, when rocks and trees took on fantastic shapes. The earth was so young that all the different types of animals we know now were nearly identical, so a person living back then could hardly tell a coyote from a rabbit, or a snake from a bird.

Seen-u-how lived with her twin sons in a half-moon shaped cave in the mountains of East San Diego County. One of the twins was light-hearted and happy, spending his days singing in the mountain woods. The other was sullen and dark-spirited, spending his days in the shadowy cave, absorbed in self-pity.

Throughout his days, the carefree son roamed the land, talking with all the birds and animals, learning their wisdom, and loving and

In an ancient tale set in the Laguna Mountains, an old woman wielded a whip to give animals distinguishing features. The unnamed wizened woman shown here lived in Santa Ysabel. Her photo appeared in 1924 in the book, *The North American Indian, by Edward S. Curtis.*

understanding their ways. The animals, in turn, became devoted to him and would even help guard Seen-u-how's cave when the lad was away on long journeys.

In fact, so many animals would wait for the carefree son to return to the ancient woman's cave that it became quite crowded at times.

Strangely, Seen-u-how and her sullen son never said a word to the kind animals. Nevertheless, the animals watched over the old woman, and listened to the mournful wailing of her sorrowful son.

The animals noted that Seen-u-how possessed a great deal of magic, for more than once they had seen the old woman change into a beautiful maiden, garbed in beautiful buckskin and adorned with the finest beads. In this form, the maiden would leave the cave and her wailing son and embark upon long journeys. Somehow, despite the great distances she traveled, she'd return in a very short amount of time, and only slightly out of breath, as though she had only sprinted a short distance.

The animals also knew Seen-u-how was very adept with the Hum-poo (whip).

One day, when a crowd of animals gathered in the cave with the woman and her sad child, coyote felt a drop of water on his face. "It must be raining outside," he whispered to the other animals. He did not know it, but because the shadows in the cave were so deep that he could not see, the water he felt on his face actually came from the weeping son, who was sitting very close by.

Other animals sitting nearby quietly disagreed. But coyote persisted and whispered. "Be quiet and listen, you can hear the sound of the raindrops falling." Indeed, when the animals really concentrated they could hear the sound of water steadily dripping to the ground.

Gleeful that rain had begun, the animals all dashed toward the mouth of the cave. Seen-u-how, not knowing why all the animals were rushing away so suddenly, became angry at the mass departure, picked up her Hum-poo, and began lashing at the animals as they passed by the mouth of the cave. She did not kill them, but greatly changed their appearances and left marks by which all future generations could identify them.

She lashed out three times and made three marks down the back of badger. One lash shredded coyote's tail, making it fluffy for evermore. Just one of her lashes lopped off deer's long tail, leaving the short stubby one we see today. A flick to the face of owl hurt his eyes. Now he can only see at night.

Even the tiniest of birds felt Seen-u-how's whip.

Bright red marks adorn the throat and wings of many birds, even today.

Not one animal in the kingdom escaped the Hum-poo that day, and that is how we can tell one animal from another.

Fisherman Brings Home Fleas, Wins Heart of Princess

This legend appeared in the December 1951 edition of The Southern California Rancher. *The article was written by Elizabeth Judson Roberts of San Pasqual who interviewed an unnamed, but very old Indian at the Mesa Grande Reservation. The Indian spoke through an interpreter and attributed the story to the Kumeyaay.*

In the beginning, Ahmyyaha, the all-spirit, who lives in the east in the land of the rising sun, created the original Indians. Under the leadership of a wise Indian called Quissei, they set out west and crossed the desert, the Cuyamaca Mountains, and beheld the sea, which they called Weelamee.

As time went on, the original Indians split off into tribes. The Kumeyaay established themselves in the hills near what is now San Diego and lived in huts or caves dug in the side of cliffs.

The Kumeyaay lived a peaceful existence by the bay and subsisted by eating nuts and berries they gathered and deer and bear taken with bow and arrow. Boys hunted squirrels and rabbits while girls dug in tide flats for clams. Younger women ventured onto nearby mesas to bring back seeds, roots, cactus fruit, and acorns for meal. Near the village, older women sat at the mouth of their caves and wove baskets, made clay jugs, or twisted the strong milkweed fibers into strings and ropes to be used for fishing nets and lines.

Kumeyaay men also liked to fish from reed canoes. Fishing canoes were made by cutting long tules (freshwater reeds) that were woven into large, tight braids. These tule braids were then twisted together and tied into very strong bundles, which were pointed at both ends and flat and wide in the middle. Fishermen straddled these canoes and ventured into the bays and nearby kelp forests using paddles fashioned from tree branches. The fishermen used hooks carved from seashells, nets and lines woven from milkweed fiber, and stone-tipped spears.

In the evenings, cooking fires appeared outside the huts and hillside caves and the Kumeyaay would sometimes gather around large bonfires near the bay to listen to tribal legends and sing songs to spirits that brought peace and protection to the village.

The leader of the Kumeyaay was Katong, a tall and handsome widower with a daughter Epaclune. Epaclune was Katong's pride and joy, and she did everything in her power to earn and keep Katong's pride. Quiet and busy with her work, Epaclune grew into a very beautiful young woman. Her glossy black hair fell to her knees, and she usually wore it tied about her head with a strand of seashells. From the headband protruded a single eagle feather, signifying her father's rank.

Often the glances of the young men in the Kumeyaay tribe would be cast upon the slender figure of Epaclune as she worked near the opening of her father's cave or while she stopped to mop her brow and stare at the faint outlines of the Coronado Islands in the distant haze.

The most skillful fisherman in the village was a tall young man named Matiweel. He often found fish when others failed, and sometimes paddled his boat out to the great underwater kelp forests in the morning. Many evenings his net was so full of fish it had to be dragged up onto the beach. At those times the village would feast on Matiweel's catch. But Matiweel always saved the largest and best fish for the princess Epaclune. One small smile from Epaclune was payment enough for Matiweel.

Now one late afternoon, a group of young men had gathered around the mouth of chief Katong's cave and were talking with Epaclune. The girl shaded her eyes with her hand and gazed toward the islands barely visible in the distance. "If I were a man," she said with great conviction, "I would never rest until I reached those islands."

The young men smiled at her words, but they had no craving for adventure and were happy to live their lives with the least amount of effort. But the comment alerted Matiweel, who was standing off from the others. To him, her words were inspiration itself, as he had always wondered what might be found on the distant islands. With a quick, understated glance, Matiweel turned and headed down the steep trail. Soon, the other young men headed down to their home fires, now glowing in the early evening's light.

Early the next morning, before dawn, Matiweel set out on his tule canoe. Only a few other fishermen saw him glide through the calm and glassy bay, and they supposed the young man was merely going fishing. Nobody but Matiweel knew of his intended journey as he headed out to sea.

As soon as he reached the open ocean, the sun came up and Matiweel began paddling vigorously toward the islands, far off on the horizon. Although he paddled hard all morning, the islands still seemed very far away. Yet when he turned around, his homeland also seemed to be far off in the distance. By noon, a heavy fog settled over the sea, blocking out the sun and forcing Matiweel to guide himself by sensing the direction of the ocean swells as they passed beneath his canoe.

At nightfall, the fog covered those familiar stars that the older fishermen had taught Matiweel to use to find his direction. Still Matiweel pushed on, reckoning his direction the best he could, singing to the spirits to guide his canoe to the islands.

With the following morning, the fog lifted and there, not far away, Matiweel saw the islands. As he paddled nearer he could see people scurrying about the shoreline in anticipation of his landing. "Good," Matiweel said to himself, "where there are people there is food, and I'm hungry." As he reached the shore, he could see people running from all over racing to greet him. He felt happy that he would finally find out what Epaclune had wished to know.

But when his canoe touched the shore, Matiweel also felt a little fear. Although the people were small, a little more than half Matiweel's size, they were gathered around the beach as thick as bees. They were the most unusual people Matiweel had ever seen. Although shaped like men, their eyes were big, round, and unblinking, like the eyes of a fish. Their skin was so smooth and hard-looking that Matiweel at first thought the people were made of smooth stone or polished wood.

As they clustered around him, they talked in high, squeaky voices that Matiweel could not understand. They crowded very close and gently poked at Matiweel's body with their hands and gazed at him with their large, unblinking eyes. Matiweel spoke to them, but they clearly did not

A Kumeyaay man stands in front of his thatched kish in Eastern San Diego County about 1900. *Photo courtesy Anza-Borrego Desert State Park Archives.*

understand. Matiweel gestured to his mouth that he was hungry. At first, they signaled that they did not understand, but then one of the people produced a bowl-shaped seashell with a small bite of what appeared to be food inside. The people then gestured Matiweel to eat the substance, which was a golden liquid, a little thicker than honey.

Seeing the tiny morsel in the bottom of the shell, Matiweel was tempted to drop it to the ground to signal to them the amount of food was too small in comparison to how much hunger had built up during his trip. But Matiweel thought the better of it, and scooped up the food with one finger and swallowed it. It was delicious. Matiweel then raised the shell, hoping to scrape out whatever tiny residue that was left inside, when he noticed to his astonishment that there in the shell was another bite of the honey food.

This Matiweel ate quickly, and every time he took a bite, more food appeared in the magical shell. When he was full, Matiweel handed the shell back to the man who had given it to him, and gestured that he was very sleepy. But try as he might, the fisherman could not make the little people understand, so he started walking toward a hill, in hopes of finding a dry cave in which he could sleep. Walking was difficult, with all the little people crowding near him and reaching out at every opportunity to touch him, but he finally found a cave that the sun had made warm and dry.

Matiweel sat down and gestured that he wanted to sleep, that he wanted them to go away, but the little people crowded around him, talking noisily in their high-pitched voices. The fisherman was beginning to get the feeling that, although the little people did not appear to want to harm him, they also did not appear to want to let him be alone on their island. Angry and afraid he would become a prisoner, but quite tired, Matiweel laid his head on his arm and finally fell asleep.

Matiweel did not know how long he had slept, but the little people were still there, in the exact same position they had been in before he had gone to sleep, and they were still staring at him with those strange, unblinking eyes.

With more than a little impatience with the situation, Matiweel leapt to his feet and walked down the hill. The little people followed close behind. Upon reaching the beach, Matiweel discovered that his canoe was gone. He motioned to the little people, who Matiweel figured out called themselves Ahwicks, that he wished to return to his own land.

But the Ahwicks did not seem to understand, but instead motioned for Matiweel to follow them to a large flat rock near the edge of the sea. There they placed one of their tribe beside Matiweel and began touching, poking, and prodding both men in what appeared to be an attempt to compare them with one another.

After comparing the two closely, one of the Ahwicks walked up behind the man next to Matiweel gave him a fierce blow on the head with a stone hatchet. The man's head split wide open and he fell to the ground. The little people crowded around to look inside the fallen Ahwick's head. It was solid, with no blood or brains inside, and the little people jabbered and jabbered with one another and were soon satisfied with what they had seen.

Without further ado, they produced some twine and wrapped the man's split head back together. They stood him up on his feet but the repeated the procedure again and again, but each time the man fell down. Soon, there was an animated discussion between the Ahwicks, and Matiweel could not help but feel that this was their first experience with death and they had somehow connected this event with Matiweel's arrival on their island.

The mood of the crowd seemed to grow angrier, and Matiweel again motioned that he would like nothing better than to leave for home.

Finally, the man who had produced the magic seashell seemed to prevail in the heated discussion and took Matiweel by the hand and led him, with every Ahwick following, to a small cove where the tribe had hidden Matiweel's canoe. To a person, the Ahwick pointed out to sea, in the precise direction of his homeland, and gestured for Matiweel to go.

Matiweel was overjoyed that he was allowed to leave and climbed on board his tule canoe. But before he could arrange himself, the man who had given Matiweel the shell produced a small bundle wrapped in rags, and by sign language made it clear to the fisherman that he was not to open the bundle until he had reached his homeland.

Matiweel agreed, and began paddling home. With the wind at his back, soon the mysterious island was far, far away in the horizon and his homeland began to loom large. Matiweel approached landfall after dark and wondered to himself why there was a large bonfire burning on the beach, since such bonfires were usually only used to announce the visit of a neighboring tribe.

But as he pulled himself onto the beach, his friends all flocked around him, all questioning at once. He had been gone so long that they were afraid he was lost, they explained, so they lit a bonfire to help him find his way home.

When his friends inquired about the bundle, Matiweel answered, "I do not know. But first let me come to the fire, for I am cold. Then I will tell my strange story and open the bundle."

Matiweel stretched out by the fire with all his friends around and told them of his fantastic experiences. As Matiweel talked, he noticed Epaclune had also come near, and he also noticed that his heart seemed to swell with joy and hope.

"And now," he exclaimed after finishing his story, "I will open the bundle and truly I hope that we shall find inside the magic shell, for then our people would never more need fear the famine."

Matiweel opened the bundle only to find that it held three smaller bundles, all tightly wrapped. As he began untying the string that bound the first bundle together, the Indians all crowded around. When the bag was finally opened, a stream of tiny, hopping insects poured out. The Kumeyaay had never seen fleas before, and watched them with much interest until the hungry horde began to bite.

"Ugh, ugh, ugh," grunted the Indians in surprise and pain. Then, as the fleas bit harder, the grunts grew louder and the crowd of Indians scattered until most of the fleas had been brushed off.

Seeing that no sickness followed the flea's bites, the Indians gathered around the fire again and urged Matiweel to open the second bundle. "Open the bag with care, Matiweel," they said, "and if it contains more of these hopping creatures, close it quickly and throw it into the fire."

Matiweel opened the second bag very slowly and carefully. When he had opened only a tiny corner, a puff appeared out of the hole that looked like smoke. It was, in fact, a swarm of mosquitoes. The Kumeyaay had never seen mosquitoes before, and watched with amusement as the little insects flew from the bag.

The Indians soon found that the mosquitoes were as hungry as the fleas, and with angry grunts ran from the onslaught of the small, yet hungry critters.

As soon as they realized that no large harm came from the bites, only small swelling and an itching discomfort, the Indians returned to the fire and beseeched Matiweel to open the remaining bag, but very, very carefully.

Matiweel did not want to open the third bag. He felt that all hope of finding the magic shell was gone. He understood that the Ahwicks had used him to revenge the death of the little man whose head they had split apart. He knew he had lost all hope of impressing Epaclune.

But as his friend urged him on, Matiweel knew he must finish what he started. Very carefully, Matiweel began tugging at the string that held the mouth of the third bag closed. Matiweel paused, then asked a nearby man to hold the bag in his hand while he untied the string, the better to throw it into the fire if it turned out to be another type of pest.

Even as Matiweel tugged very slightly at the strings, the man jerked his hand away and dropped the bundle. He pulled several large, biting red ants from his hand and threw them to the ground. The rest of the ants ran quickly out of the bag and scattered into the darkness, and occasionally a loud grunt could be heard as they found a toe or ankle of an Indian to munch on.

Far worse than the stinging of the red ants was the stinging in Matiweel's heart that he had failed to gain the favor of Epaclune. The fisherman had risked his life, and instead of bringing great things from the far away islands, had brought biting, stinging pests, which would be with the Kumeyaay the rest of the days.

Mattiweel hung his head in shame. All hope was gone. He gathered up the three empty bags and tossed them into the fire. He turned to leave, but before him stood Epaclune and her father. Epaclune was smiling.

"Aeee," sighed Matiweel with his head bowed to his chest. "After the pests I brought, I thought you would not care to see me again."

Standing at the side of her father, Epaclune spoke. "It is the heart we look at, Matiweel; the pests sent in revenge by the Ahwicks are bad, but each time they bite us we will remember that you risked much to bring us a good gift, and the failure to do so was no fault of yours."

Matiweel raised his eyes to Epaclune and was grateful to see the look in her eyes he had long hoped to see. He was searching for something to say when Katong spoke. "It is a woman's way to see the good, especially in someone she loves."

Matiweel and Epaclune married and lived happily ever after. Fleas, mosquitoes, and red ants are with us to this day.

CHAPTER 74

Water Spirit Blinded Babies

This legend, also attributed to friends of Mary Elizabeth Johnson living in the Laguna Mountains, regards an evil spirit living by a particular spring located in Descanso in present-day east San Diego County.

Those who dwelt near the spring named No Eyes in Water would sometimes awaken to hear the eerie screams of Kwin Mari, the blind baby, who lived in the spring.

The baby's screams were so mournful, so penetrating through the night air that brave men would gasp and young mothers would draw their sleeping infants near and shiver in fear.

Everyone in the village knew that the screams meant that the blind baby was seeking a victim, hoping to cast a spell over a mother before her baby could enter the world. Babies born under the spell of Kwin Mari would arrive in this world blind.

An evil spirit lurking in a spring such as this one in Pine Valley could blind an unborn baby if the mother so much as touched the water. Indians called the spring, No Eyes in Water. *Author photo.*

One morning after the cries of Kwin Mari had faded away, a strange woman crawled into the village in need of help. She was large with child and near death. After the villagers revived her, she told them how all those in her village had been killed during a raid, and that she alone had escaped.

She related how she had traveled many days and nights, and that how, on the previous night, she had heard the screams of a baby crying. Despite her waning strength, the woman stumbled toward the sounds, tripping over rocks and tearing her clothes on bushes. She finally found the source of the crying, a small spring. Standing on the bank, she could see a baby crying under the water. Startled, she reached down to pick up the baby, but her hands came up empty. Although the baby had disappeared, the crying sounds persisted from between her feet. Frozen with terror, she was unable to move until the following morning.

The villagers knew what fate had come to the woman, but decided not to tell her. Instead, they took her in and cared for her as one of their own.

Only after her baby was born, with tightly closed eyes that refused to open, did the villagers tell the woman about Kwin Mari, the spring named No Eyes in Water, and how the spirit could blind an unborn babe by merely touching the mother.

Stinkbug Outfoxes Coyote

This story's central character is Stinkbug, a large, black, flightless beetle that inhabits San Diego trails from the ocean to the desert. Rather than run away when threatened, the stinkbug will point its rear end skyward and exude a noxious odor to ward off predators.

The Coyote and the Stinkbug story seems to have roots in various Southwestern Native American cultures and has been recounted by Benito Peralta, Kumeyaay elder and storyteller. Peralta lived in northern Baja California where his people (Pai Pai) have a long history of interaction with San Diego-area Indians.

Hungry Coyote ambled down a mountain trail one morning, nose to ground, sniffing for something to eat, when he came upon an old Stinkbug crossing the trail. "Ah, just my luck. The first tidbit of food I find turns out to be a stinkbug!"

Coyote had heard about stinkbugs but had never eaten one, so he wasn't surprised when instead of running away, Stinkbug aimed his rear skyward and emitted his odor.

Coyote came closer and sniffed. "Hey, you don't smell as bad as I thought. I think I'll gobble you up."

"Shhhh!" said Stinkbug, thinking fast.

"What are you doing?" asked Coyote.

"I've got my ear to the ground, listening to people talking underneath the earth. These trails belong to them and they're very angry."

"Angry about what?"

Stinkbug put his ear back to the ground and pretended to listen. "Many travelers have used this trail and most have left it clean. But the people are angry because three travelers have been leaving messes along the way. The people are so angry that they already caught two of the messy travelers and burned them alive. They are looking for the third one right now!"

Upon hearing this, Coyote remembered that he too, had been leaving messes along the trail.

"Could the third traveler they are looking for be me?" he said.

Stinkbug shrugged.

"Wait right here," Coyote told Stinkbug. "I'm going back and clean up all my messes before the people can figure out it was me. You keep listening and find out as much as you can."

Coyote dashed off and ran far up the trail and cleaned up everything, even messes he didn't make. When the trails were spotless, Coyote used a branch to cover his footprints, and even walked downstream in a creek so the people could not follow his tracks.

It was late afternoon when he came back to the spot where he had left the old beetle, but Stinkbug was long gone.

"Stinkbug must have given up on me and left," Coyote said to himself. Now very hungry, Coyote ambled down the trail, nose to ground, looking for something else to eat.

"Oh well," he said to himself. "At least I know now what all the people under the earth have been talking about."

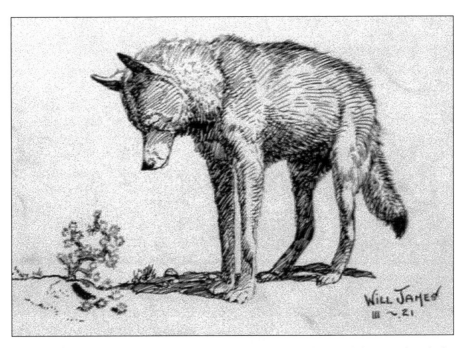

In the tale, "Coyote and the Stinkbug", the stinkbug uses the coyote's natural curiosity and skittishness to his advantage. This sketch by Enos A. Mills appeared in a 1922 periodical called Watched by Wild Animals. *Photo courtesy Doubleday, New York (Library of Congress)*.

Coyote Blood Created Red War Paint

This story, another from Johnson's quaint book on stories by Indians living on the Laguna Mountains, describes how a particular red war paint, Ah Kwir, gained its power.

Ah Kwir is the name of a powerful red war paint made from a particular patch of soil hidden in the desert. Ah Kwir was highly sought after, and the desert Indians would often trade it for things made by the tribes living in the Cuyamaca Mountain area.

The legend of how that particular patch of desert soil became red began long, long ago, when the distinction between man and animal was not so great, and there roamed Hatapaa (coyote), the meanest man who ever lived.

Hatapaa had been waiting and carefully watching his father, who was about to die. When people asked why he was watching his father so closely, Hatapaa told them that he wanted to make sure that his father's body was placed upon a funeral pyre and accorded a proper ceremony. But the people knew that Hatapaa was not only a cruel man, but a liar too, and feared that he wanted nothing more than to make a meal out of his father when he died.

So Bear told Hatapaa, "You look hungry. Why don't you go off and hunt something to eat? The rest of the people will watch over your sick father."

When Coyote heard that, he felt defeated, at least temporarily, and sulked off with his bushy tail between his legs. But after a very short while, he returned and announced that he could find nothing to eat.

The people were quick to realize that Hatapaa had not gone to hunt, but had merely circled around and watched from the bushes, so they again sent him to hunt.

Again Hatapaa returned after only a short while, and repeated his lies. Losing patience, Bear told Coyote in strong language, "Go far away and hunt. Do not dare to return before the sun has set, or we'll kill you."

Now despite the Coyote being very mean, he was also very cowardly, so he ran far away and hid. While he was gone, his father died. The people built a funeral pyre and started a fire as quick as they could. They placed Coyote's father atop the pyre in hopes that he would be consumed by the flames before Coyote could return.

But smoke from the pyre wafted up through the trees and was carried a great distance by the breeze. Off on a faraway hill, Hatapaa's long nose perked up and he raced back at full speed.

Bear and others, upon hearing Hatapaa's approach, formed a circle around the blazing pyre to keep Coyote away. Hatapaa shrieked and wailed, "I must see my poor father one last time before the flames consume him." But the people knew the nature of Coyote and refused to let him inside the circle.

However, Coyote soon noticed that one of the members of the circle, Wildcat, was quite a bit shorter than the rest. Coyote feigned disinterest and ambled toward a far off bush. Suddenly, he turned and ran and jumped over wildcat, landing right next to the funeral pyre.

Hatapaa quickly snatched his father's heart from the glowing embers, jumped back over Wildcat, and ran as fast as he could. He did not stop until he reached a small hill in the desert. There he gobbled up the heart of his father. And there, red drops of blood fell from his jaws to the ground. To this day the ground near that hill bears a red stain from the blood of Hatapaa's father.

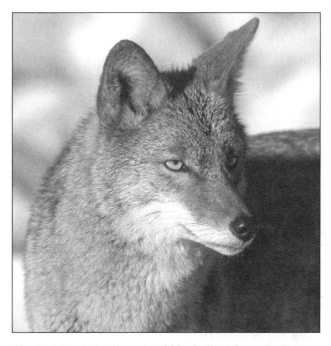

The Red War Paint legend, told by Indians from the Laguna Mountains, describes how a coyote named Hatapaa snatched his father's heart from a funeral pyre and ate it. Blood spilled in the desert gave special powers to red war paint called Ah Kwir. *Image courtesy, Illinois Department of Natural Resources, Doug Herr.*

The Three Deaths of Chief Captain Moro

According to a story written by well-known newspaper columnist Herbert Lockwood, an Indian chief in the Agua Caliente Springs area, Chief Captain Moro, died not once, not twice, but three times.

Lockwood's Feb. 5, 1970, article in The Independent *related an incident that reportedly occurred in the year 1885.*

Although records do not show whether Chief Moro's title of captain was self-bestowed, history has it that he was more than a 100 years old when he first died.

After death called in April 1885, the venerated Chief Captain Moro's body was laid out in a coffin. A great number of Indians came to pay their respects to the 100-year-old chief. Rites were given and ceremonial dance — to precede his burial — began. All of a sudden, Chief Captain Moro sat straight up in his coffin and demanded to know what the commotion was all about.

The wake was canceled and word of Moro's resurrection spread around the San Diego area.

Some say that since Moro apparently enjoyed the attention brought to him by his resurrection, it was with a bit of predetermination that the chief died again six weeks later.

Captain Moro's body was again laid out at the tribe's grand council lodge. But before the burial ceremonies could begin, a white man visiting the grand council lodge told those present that he thought he could detect the chief breathing. He suggested the tribesmen offer the chief something to eat.

They did, and the chief slowly stirred to life once more.

Now the legend has it that following the July 24, 1885, death of Ulysses S. Grant, Chief Captain Moro became jealous of the nation-wide attention being lavished on the fallen president.

Moro is said to have been further urged into the great beyond when the same white man who had noticed him breathing at his second "death" came to show the chief a local newspaper. In it, many gushing eulogies had been written and all the columns concerning Grant's death were framed in black.

Jealous, old Captain Moro promptly died again.

This time, his tribesmen quickly dug a grave, hammered the coffin lid tight, and buried old Captain Moro "quite a bit more" than the traditional six feet under, according to the tale.

The tribesmen then stomped on Captain Moro's grave to make sure the dirt was packed down nice and firm.

Two other such tales made it into print in San Diego newspapers:

Santiago Segundo's Second Chance

While some Indian tribes in San Diego County buried their dead, others cremated theirs. Another story involves an old medicine man, Santiago Segundo, from the Los Coyotes tribe in the county's northeast area.

While a boy, Segundo and his friend had been hunting near a creek when Segundo was bitten on the leg by a rattlesnake. Although his friend carried him all the way home, Segundo's leg swelled, his throat constricted, and his eyes swelled shut and he lost consciousness.

After lying motionless and presumably dead all night, his relatives prepared his body for cremation. After binding his legs and arms together and readying the funeral pyre, Segundo came to life.

He said he was brought back to the land of living by a woman in a dream. The woman was in a house, and when Segundo tried to enter the house, she motioned him away. When he turned away from the woman, the medicine-man-to-be awoke, and found himself in the arms of three large tribesmen, ready to carry him to the burning funeral pyre.

Dead Man Leaps, is Clubbed to Death

Another Indian in San Diego history was not quite so lucky. According to printed accounts, in the 1870s, an old Indian died and his body was placed on a funeral pyre. When the flames reached his body, the old man leapt into consciousness. Those in the funeral procession were so startled that they instantly attacked "dead man" with clubs and beat him all the way back into the afterlife.

The mourners then set the now-really-dead Indian back on the funeral pyre and finished the cremation, certain they had vanquished a supernatural specter.

Spinning White Basket Foretold Death

This story illustrates the importance of adherence to tradition. It was told to an unidentified journalist by John Felisho, an Indian who lived on the Baron Long Reservation east of Alpine sometime before his death in 1957 when he was in his 60s. While telling this story as a first-person narrative, Felisho displayed a closely woven, shallow white basket: the object of the legend.

"You wouldn't think to look at this basket that it was worth three lives. It used to belong to a man in our tribe.

"While walking home alone one night, he saw this white basket just ahead of him, spinning on edge and moving magically from side to side on the road. He scooped up the basket and carried it to his cave where he lived with his three daughters.

"If he had paid attention to the message the spinning basket was trying to foretell, that his girls were in danger, he could have offered tobacco and sung, he would have been spared sorrow. But he did not heed the basket warning him about the girls. One by one the girls got sick and died; the oldest girl died first.

"Then he gave me the basket.

"I filled the basket full of tobacco and offered it three times to the sky. After all the dead ones in the sky smoked, then I smoked from the tobacco in the white basket.

"Our people use it to this day. When we do certain things and sing certain songs, we have to offer the white basket filled with tobacco to the dead ones for three nights in a row. Then we have to smoke the tobacco for three nights in a row and sing to the dead ones if we don't want to get sick.

"After I tell you this story and sing some songs for you, I have to offer the white basket to the dead ones for three nights and smoke and sing for three nights unless I want to get very sick."

Legends like these can evoke strong feelings. Since most of these accounts were taken from literature written by non-natives, the names by which people, places and things are or were known may not correlate with those used by the people themselves. It is also possible that details in the stories — and in some instances even the act of retelling the stories themselves — may not be viewed as correct or appropriate from the point of view of all San Diego-area natives, depending on their particular tribe, band, or family affiliation.

SECTION VIII

When Nature Calls!

San Diego's natural beauty is the stuff poems are made of (see pages 259 – 260). Living within this beautiful dreamscape, one seldom hears complaints. Indeed, few have the heart to grouse when the thermometer hovers between 65 and 75 degrees; when on a clear spring morning the view from the mountains opens up sixty miles or more; or when on a mild winter day one is tempted to spend the morning at the beach, the afternoon in the snow at Mount Laguna, and the evening in the desert.

But our appreciation of this area's beauty should be tempered with the knowledge that San Diego's nature can turn against us, sometimes with deadly results.

Shake, Rattle and Roll
The Real Story Behind San Diego Earthquakes

Cross your fingers!

That's the advice many longtime San Diego residents give newcomers worried about earthquakes. And it might pay to knock on wood too.

Although several major faults paralleling the notorious San Andreas fault traverse the region, San Diego County has not experienced a building-busting earthquake since the year 1800. And that begs the question, are we immune or merely overdue?

When most folks think of the San Andreas fault, two major earthquakes come to mind: the 1906 San Francisco earthquake (3,000 deaths and $524 million in property damage) and the 1989 Loma Prieta earthquake (63 deaths and $6 billion in property damage).

San Diego is situated about 100 miles west of the southern tip of the San Andreas fault, much closer are the five parallel faults that are all capable of causing seismic devastation, cross the county. From west to east we have:

About 25 miles offshore, 100-mile-long San Diego Trough remains relatively dormant.

About 15 miles offshore, the 112-mile-long Coronado Bank fault is essentially continuous with Los Angeles' Palos Verdes fault. It's capable of producing a 6.0 to 7.0 magnitude quake or greater, geologists say.

The 25-mile-long Rose Canyon fault connects with the 50-mile-long Newport-Inglewood fault and peters out at the northeast corner of Pacific Beach in the canyon that bears its name. It's capable of producing a probable 6.0 - 7.4 magnitude earthquake.

The 112-mile-long Elsinore fault parallels North San Diego County about 10 miles east of Oceanside near Julian and has the potential to unleash a 6.5 - 7.5 shaker.

The 50-mile-long San Jacinto fault runs 10 miles east of, and parallel to, the Elsinore fault near Borrego Springs and Ocotillo Wells and is also capable of dishing up a 6.5 - 7.5 temblor.

But to the east of all these lies the granddaddy of all faults. Just outside the San Diego border in Imperial County, the 750-mile-long San

Andreas is more than capable of delivering an upheaval in excess of 8.0 on the Richter scale. Such an earthquake would likely have a devastating effect on San Diego.

By way of example, a modern study of the 1857 Fort Tejon 8.0 earthquake (about 130 miles north of San Diego) documented an amazing surface-rupture scar more than 220 miles long that bore ground ruptures ranging from 15 to 30 feet high. According to written accounts from that era, the current of the Kern River (more than 70 miles from the epicenter) reversed direction for a while. The waters of Lake Tulare, more than 100 miles distant, were shaken out of the lakebed. Because the area was sparsely populated in 1857, the Fort Tejon quake caused only two deaths. But were such an earthquake to strike in or near San Diego, losses would likely be catastrophic.

The only building-busting earthquake in San Diego's recorded history occurred on November 22, 1800. That quake leveled much of San Diego Mission de Alcalá and part of the Mission San Juan Capistrano some 90 miles to the north. Although magnitude detection equipment obviously did not exist in that era, modern estimates based on structural damage and the large distance the quake covered peg the magnitude at about 6.5 on the Richter scale.

You won't find evidence of earthquake damaged buildings (such as those in San Francisco shown here) in San Diego history unless you dig back to November 22, 1800. *Photo courtesy USGS.*

More recently on Easter Day 2010, a 7.2 magnitude event struck about 150 miles southeast of San Diego near a small Mexican town 60 miles south of Calexico. Centered near Guadalupe Victoria, the quake killed two, injured hundreds, and shot cracks across paved roads all the way up to the border. The earthquake was felt throughout southern California, Arizona, Nevada, and northern Baja California, Mexico. In San Diego, the shaking swayed high rise buildings and had residents rounding up children and scrambling for safety. The shaking lasted nearly a minute but caused no significant damage.

So is San Diego, due to some strange confluence of underground faults, really immune to the big one? Or are we just overdue? Either way, here's some earthshaking information about earthquakes and Richter scale equivalents:

A 1.0 on the Richter scale is equivalent to about 30 pounds of TNT, the same as a large blast at a construction site.

A 2.0 is equivalent to about one ton of TNT, the same as a large quarry or mine blast.

A 4.0 equals about one thousand tons of TNT, the same as a small nuclear weapon.

A 4.5 packs the same energy as an average size tornado.

A 6.0 is equivalent to one million tons of TNT. Such a quake hit San Diego in 1951.

A 7.0 is about the size of the largest thermonuclear weapon.

An 8.0 is equivalent to about 1 billion tons of TNT. Such a quake hit San Francisco in 1906.

A 9.0 is equivalent to about 32 billion tons of TNT. Such a quake hit Chili in 1960.

A 10.0 may be powerful enough to create a single fault line that circles the earth.

A 12.0 earthquake? Some think it might cleave the earth in two!

So cross your fingers. (And knock on wood too)!

San Diego Weather Extremes
Hurricanes!

Think hurricanes don't hit San Diego? Most Eastern Pacific hurricanes form off the coast of Mexico or Central America, but their paths are hard to predict. Many head west or northwest and peter out in the open ocean. In 1992, Hurricane Iniki traveled all the way to the Hawaiian Islands where it struck with sustained winds of 130 mph and created more than $2.3 billion in property damage on Kauai. Other Eastern Pacific hurricanes veer north, inside the Sea of Cortez, and make land-fall or otherwise die out.

Although most don't typically associate San Diego with hurricanes, a search of historic meteorological records shows two typhoons have smashed our shoreline.

The Hurricane of 1858

According to a newspaper accounts published in the *San Diego Herald* and *Daily Alta California* newspapers, a hurricane slammed San Diego on October 13, 1858. An intense heat wave had camped over the San Diego area for several days and the wind was calm in the morning until about eleven o'clock when a terrific gale rose out of the south-south east. Several houses were blown down and others had roofs blown off. Trees were uprooted, fences destroyed, and several ships in the harbor dragged anchor and ended up on the beach. At about noon, winds roared so fiercely that Point Loma Lighthouse keeper Captain James Keating abandoned his post, fearful that the tower, just built the year before, would topple.

An eyewitness reported in the *Daily Alta California*:

> "Roofs of houses, trees, fences, &c., &c., filled the air in all directions, doing a large amount of damage, in and about the city and its immediate vicinity. From this time until dark a continuance of the above was experienced, interspersed now and then by a crash of some house, tree, fence, or something of the kind. With the sun the

wind went down; during the night we had considerable fall of rain, which made a very pleasant change."

Based on the complete destruction of homes and the blowing down of trees, meteorologists have pegged this hurricane as a category F1 or F2, with wind speeds in excess of 75 mph. Thankfully, no deaths were reported.

The "Lash of St. Francis"

In September 1939, no fewer than five hurricanes moved northwest, bent around the tip of the Baja Peninsula, and worked north along the coastline. Two veered east and made landfall near the center of the Baja Peninsula, about five hundred miles south of the border. Two turned east and came ashore about two hundred miles below the border. But on September 21, the fifth hurricane churned all the way to the 32nd parallel before slamming the shoreline between San Diego and Los Angeles.

That hurricane caused $2 million in damage and resulted in the loss of 45 lives, mostly mariners in the Newport Beach area. The media labeled the hurricane, "The Lash of Saint Francis" in homage to St. Francis of Assisi's October 4 feast day. The term now refers to any late-season hurricane that parallels the Mexican coastline.

One common factor in both hurricanes is that the weather beforehand was insufferably hot — more than 100 degrees for several days running. So if you happen to find yourself on the beach during a long-running, late-September or early-October heat wave, keep one eye peeled for dark clouds on the horizon!

Santa Ana Winds

Considering these winds strike every year without fail, Santa Ana winds may qualify as the most severe meteorological event residents and tourists are apt to encounter.

Santa Anas are hot, dry, and sometimes fierce winds that blow from the eastern deserts and mountains, opposite the prevailing onshore breezes. At their greatest strength these airstreams top 100 miles per hour on mountain tops. More typically, stiff Santa Anas range from 30 to 40 mph with gusts to 70 mph. But that's more than enough to topple trucks and recreational vehicles and to blow shingles off roofs.

But even gentle Santa Ana conditions bring about dry, dusty conditions that cause discomfort.

Author Raymond Chandler in his story *Red Wind* referred to them as, "those hot dry [winds] that come down through the mountain passes and curl your hair and make your nerves jump and your skin itch."

These bone dry conditions also create a perfect environment for the buildup of static electricity. Simply walking across a carpeted floor will result in an irritating shock when a metal doorknob or faucet is touched. Lovers fear kissing lest they zap the tips of their noses.

Santa Ana winds are caused by massive high pressure domes that camp out in the mountains to the east, mostly in spring and fall. Since high pressure air moves toward low, the winds move west where they sink, heat, and dry out as they flow toward the coast. Santa Ana season is prime wildfire season in southern California.

Meteorologists agree on what causes Santa Anas, but historians have little success convincing one another how the winds got their name. The most widely held theory is that they were named after the blustery Mexican general and president, Antonio de Santa Anna. Those who support that theory liken the wind's strength to the way the general in the early- to mid-19th century might have charged down canyons to attack those below. Critics of this theory seek to establish that the term Santa Ana wind appeared in local literature long before the general ever stepped onto the battlefield.

Heat Wave!

The month of September hosts about one-third of all days in which the temperature in San Diego tops 90 degrees. It should come as no surprise then, that the hottest day on record was 111 degrees at Lindbergh Field on September 26, 1963, according to published reports. On the first week of September in 1988, the city thermometers hit 100 degrees for three days running. That heat wave included a run to 107 degrees at Lindberg Field.

Snow Way!

Although 25 degrees may not send chills down the spine of Midwesterners, it sure seems cold to San Diegans acclimatized to a mean high temperature of about 70 degrees.

The Horton Plaza fountain froze over on January 7, 1913—at 25 degrees, the coldest day on record. Snow also fell in downtown San Diego in 1932, 1949, and 1967 prompting the *Union Tribune* headline, "B-R-R-R-R! A Mini-Blizzard Chills San Diegans." The front-page photo showed a San Diego State College co-ed wearing a mini skirt despite the chilly conditions.

Aurora Borealis

Heat wave and hurricane, 1939 was a weird weather year, right? Things got even weirder when a handful of East County residents were treated to an atmospheric phenomenon normally reserved for denizens of the earth's north polar regions: northern lights.

The strange glowing, shifting aurora borealis first appeared at about 1:30 a.m. and lasted until almost dawn. At first, the red hued sky was initially thought to be a far-away fire until the red hues morphed into vertical rays of purple and gold, according to an East County forest ranger who witnessed the phenomenon. The northern lights disrupted radio communications in the area, causing radio station *XEMO* of Tijuana to fade in and out of sound.

Those sightings marked the first time in nearly 50 years that the lights had been visible in the area. According to the weather bureau, which began keeping records in San Diego in 1850, the aurora borealis had been seen only twice before, in November, 1882 and February, 1888.

Green Flash

While not solely a San Diego phenomenon, the search for the elusive "green flash" — a brief burst of greenish light occasionally witnessed just above the horizon moments after sunset — keeps the shoreline packed with tourists and locals alike just before nightfall on many evenings. The flash is small and visible only for a brief moment immediately after the sun completely dips below the horizon. The green flash occurs very infrequently and oddly, when one does appear, not everyone witnesses it! Some longtime sunset watchers have never seen one.

Critics claim the flash is merely an illusion from having stared at the fading orange sun too long. When the orange light source disappears, all that's left is the illusion of a contrasting hue, green, they say. But others believe the flash is produced by refraction, which explains its appearance just after sunset and its color. They also like to point out that numerous photographs of the green flash prove the phenomenon is no illusion.

The best way to catch for the flash is to wait for a cloudless, haze-free day and find a place to watch the ocean's horizon. Chances are you'll have plenty of company. To avoid eye damage, don't look directly at the sun.

These Insects Do the Chomp!
Nothing But Sand and Fleas

Long before this fair city became a popular tourist destination, many travelers avoided San Diego County due to an infestation of fleas. The infestation lasted more than a century!

By way of example, in 1865 the City of San Diego built a new schoolhouse on Mason Street in present-day Old Town. The school's first teacher, Mary Chase Walker, was fresh off a schooner from New England when she chronicled her first impression:

"I arrived in the bay of San Diego on the morning of July 5, 1865. Of all the dilapidated, miserable looking places I had ever seen, this was the worst. The fleas were plentiful and hungry."

As it turns out, fleas inhabited San Diego long before Miss Walker arrived. Father Antonio Peyri, founder of Oceanside's Mission San Luis Rey, penned a report in 1827 stating that corn, wheat, and barley grew and cattle roamed at nearby "Las Pulgas," Spanish for fleas!

A few months after Peyri's report, mountain man and fur trapper James Pattie languished in San Diego's jail. Of his lengthy stay beginning March 26, 1828 (for the crime of being an undocumented alien), Pattie writes:

"We forgot our past troubles, opened our bosom to hope, and resigned ourselves to profound sleep. It is true, innumerable droves of fleas performed their evolutions, and bit all their pleasures upon our bodies. In the morning my body was as spotted as though I had measles, and my shirt specked with innumerable stains of blood, let by the ingenious lancets of these same Spanish fleas."

Ultimately, San Diego's massive flea infestation was eradicated, notwithstanding modern-day sporadic outbreaks typically confined to household pets, by use of pesticides. But not all early flea treatments worked. One idea was to wrap a piece of raw meat in fly paper in hopes of trapping carnivorous fleas. Another, culled from a turn of the century newspaper account, might have chased off fleas strictly by its foul smell:

"The Hindoos (sic) use a crude oil emulsion consisting of eighty per cent of crude petroleum mixed with twenty per cent of whale oil soap. This combination forms a jelly which mixes freely with water. A three per cent solution is used. At ten per cent it kills fleas with perfect certainty. Any animal washed with it will be relieved of the insects. It can be applied to walls, ceilings, and floors by means of a garden sprayer."

Today, San Diego still bears a reminder of a flea invasion that lasted more than a century. Motorists traveling Interstate 5 north of Oceanside pass a freeway exit named Las Pulgas — The Fleas!

Do the Chomp!

Most insect invaders prefer to dine on flora, and infestations culled from county records include outbreaks of caterpillars, gypsy moths, Oriental fruit flies, Mediterranean fruit flies, bark beetles, Mexican fruit flies, eucalyptus beetles, whiteflies, and Argentinian ants.

But aside from fleas, a handful of other insects like to do the chomp on humans—sometimes, directly or indirectly, with deadly results.

Africanized honey bees are close relatives to the more mellow European honey bees that once solely inhabited San Diego County. Africanized honey bees were first introduced into Brazil in 1956 and have moved steadily northward since.

These highly temperamental insects, also called "killer bees," defend their colonies much more aggressively and with far less provocation than other varieties. In 2010, a 54-year-old Encinitas man died after he was stung more than 500 times by a swarm of angry bees he inadvertently disturbed while clearing brush on a tractor.

The San Diego Department of Agriculture now estimates that 80 percent of all bees found in the county are Africanized. They advise against disturbing bees in any way and urge caution when hiking or doing yard work. Avoid approaching a nest by accident, listen for steady buzzing, and especially do not block the colony's entrance or flight path.

Fire ants came to San Diego in the late 1990s. You definitely don't want these critters as picnic guests, they can kill. Although their venomous bites typically cause only blisters and burning, approximately 20 deaths per year in the United States are attributed to fire ants, mostly in Florida and Texas.

Mosquitoes have always been around. Father Junipero Serra arrived in San Diego in 1769 riddled with mosquito bites from his journey. The robes he wore made his legs especially vulnerable and complications from mosquito bites plagued and debilitated him throughout much of his life. While mosquitos don't kill directly, their bites may transmit deadly diseases including malaria, Dengue fever, encephalitis, Yellow fever, and West Nile virus. In 1988, an especially bad year, 23 documented cases of malaria were attributed to mosquito bites. Most victims were migrant workers who camped in canyons near streams. The Navy helped the county spray and fog hot spots that year.

Other insects in San Diego County worth avoiding include tarantula wasps, ticks, scorpions, black widows, brown widows, and desert recluse spiders. (According to the county's Vector Control, there are no brown recluse spiders in the county).

With all these critters ready to chomp, some San Diegan may be tempted to eschew the great outdoors completely, stay in bed, and hide under the covers all day.

To them we say, "Fine! Don't let the bed bugs bite!"

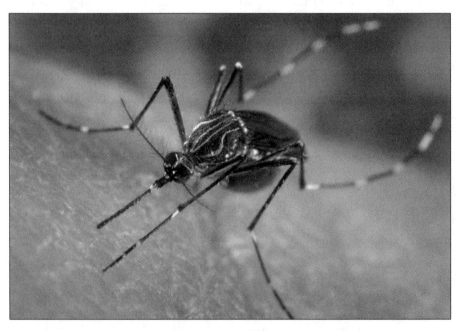

Father Junipero Serra arrived in San Diego in 1769 so riddled with mosquito bites on his legs that he could barely walk. Mosquitos spread deadly diseases including malaria, Dengue fever, encephalitis, Yellow fever, and West Nile virus. *Photo courtesy U.S. Center for Disease Control and Prevention.*

Tsunamis

Something Else to Worry About!

San Diegans don't spend much time worrying about tsunamis, but maybe they should!

History shows these so-called "tidal waves" struck our shores in the past, and scientists believe they will again. Although San Diego has avoided catastrophic damage in the past, were a certain type of large tsunami to strike, giant waves could wreak havoc on our shores with little or no warning.

San Diego's first encounter with a major tsunami came more than 50 years ago.

On May 22, 1960, the largest earthquake in recorded history struck Valdivia, Chile. The 9.5 quake spawned a tsunami that spread throughout the Pacific and killed more than 3,000 people. Seventy-foot waves inundated much of the Chilean coastline. Thirty-five-foot waves devastated Hilo, Hawaii.

More than 5,500 miles from the epicenter, San Diego also stood in the tsunami's path. Seismic sea waves in the three-foot range surged into San Diego Harbor. Although often small in height, tsunami waves may be more than a mile thick and can strike like 50-footers! Waves from this tsunami generated powerful surges of water that rushed in and out of the harbor. The surge obliterated the 140-foot Harbor Police dock at the western tip of Shelter Island. It ripped docks from their pylons and yachts from slips, sending several into a vortex that swirled in the middle of the channel.

"I've never seen anything like it in my life," San Diego Harbormaster James Murtha told reporters on scene. "It was very, very turbulent and at times the rush of water coming into the yacht harbor was judged between 20 to 25 knots (26 to 29 mph)!"

But the tsunami was not done. The surge swept deep into the bay, near the present-day site of Seaport Village, and shoved the San Diego-Coronado ferry *North Island* more than a mile off course. Captain Frank White battled the current until the car and passenger ferry came to rest alongside a group of Navy destroyers anchored in South Bay.

At about the same time the inbound Japanese freighter *Yaki Maru* steamed past Shelter Island toward the 10th Avenue Marine Terminal. The rush of water spun the 10,000-ton freighter sideways in the narrow channel and sent it toward shore at such speed that there was no hope it would stop on its own. Luckily the freighter's harbor escort tugs had just arrived to help guide the ship to the dock. They stopped the massive ship's momentum and repositioned it in the center of the channel. The tugs then raced to save a large lumber barge being forced aground by the incredible surge.

In Mission Bay, a 100-ton dredge rammed the Mission Bay Bridge and tore out a 50-foot section. A bait barge in the sport fishing basin tore from its moorings, smashed several docks, broke in half, and sank.

Four years later an even larger tsunami struck the San Diego shoreline. On March 27, 1964, the largest recorded earthquake in North America rumbled through Prince William Sound in southeastern Alaska. The 9.2 temblor generated a tsunami that ravaged parts of Alaska and British Columbia before heading down the western United States coastline. Due to the orientation of the earthquake, the tsunami waves hit

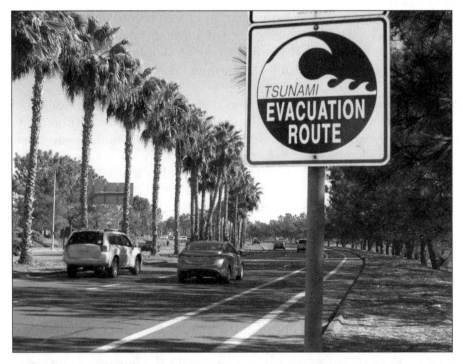

Authorities warn that tsunamis could produce 98-foot-high waves that could force San Diegans to follow evacuation routes (such as the one posted on this sign near Sea World) to seek higher ground. *Author photo.*

California at an angle so that the highest waves struck in the northern part of the state. Twenty-one-foot waves killed 10 in Crescent City. Due to its south-facing orientation, the waves that hit San Diego were only seven feet—relatively small—and damage was minimal.

From the earliest recorded tsunami in San Diego history (1854) to a 2010 tsunami (again from Valdivia, Chile) that brought four-foot waves into the harbor, San Diego has been spared mammoth waves such as the 50-footers that claimed more than 150,000 lives in the Indian Ocean in 2004 or that killed more than 10,000 in Japan in 2011.

But according to the USGS, California coastal communities are highly vulnerable to tsunamis. Hundreds of thousands of people live within what's called maximum tsunami-inundation zones. In addition to permanent residents, on any given day millions of visitors flock to public places within these impact zones such as beaches (more than 20 million visitors per year), amusement parks, marinas, hotels, fairgrounds, public piers, waterfront parks, restaurants, bars, retail shops, military installations, museums, sports stadiums, and recreation centers.

So far, loss of life within these maximum tsunami-inundation zones has been relatively low because most distant earthquake-triggered tsunamis lose energy as they travel across the ocean to reach this area. The great distances also allow earthquake and tsunami centers to provide alerts that give the public ample notice.

But scientists warn that huge tsunami waves generated by local geological events could strike with little or no warning.

"Evidence of past events and modeling of potential events suggest that tsunamis are significant threats to low-lying communities on the California coast," states a USGS report titled, "Community Exposure to Tsunami Hazards in California."

"The tragic loss of life and property damage associated with recent catastrophic tsunamis (for example, 2004 Indian Ocean, 2009 Samoa, 2010 Chile, 2010 Sumatra, and 2011 Japan) has raised global awareness of tsunami hazards," the report states. "Historical and geologic evidence indicate that the California coast has experienced similar large-magnitude tsunamis and is likely to experience more."

There are two types of locally generated tsunamis that San Diegans might want to spend a bit of time worrying about. A large local earthquake could cause a sudden vertical displacement of the seafloor, which may create a tremendous tsunami capable of striking with little or no warning. A local offshore undersea landslide may also produce massive waves that could strike before authorities could issue alerts.

And these local earthquake or local underwater landslide tsunamis could reach terrifying heights.

According to a report by NOAA's West Coast and Alaska Tsunami Warning Center, "Tsunamis may reach a maximum vertical height onshore above sea level, called a run-up height, of 30 meters (98 feet). A notable exception is the landslide-generated tsunami in Lituya Bay, Alaska, in 1958 that produced a 525-meter (1,722-foot) wave."

So what to do in event of a tsunami? Beyond building an ark in case the big one strikes, NOAA's advice includes:

> A strong earthquake in a low-lying coastal area may mean immediate danger. Move quickly away from the coast and to higher ground.
>
> A tsunami is a series of waves that may last 36 hours or more, not a single wave. Keep to high ground until advised by official sources. Do not rely on unofficial reports that the danger has passed.
>
> Approaching tsunamis are sometimes heralded by a noticeable rise or fall of coastal waters. Heed this warning and vacate low lying ground.
>
> Tsunamis move faster than a person can run! Gain elevation as quickly as possible.
>
> Never go to the beach to watch a tsunami! If you can see one, chances are you will not be able to escape it.

So if you live, work, or play in San Diego's low-lying areas, you don't necessarily need to worry about tsunamis, just have a plan in case one strikes.

SECTION IX

❧

San Diego Lore: an Assortment of Things Past

The dusty annals of San Diego's past are filled with legends and strange events that defy categorization. From early laws that shaped our present-day city, to the famous individuals who once called San Diego home, these stories are odd but important parts of San Diego's cultural history that simply must be told.

CHAPTER 83

Juan Cabrillo
Not San Diego Discoverer?

Although Juan Rodríquez Cabrillo is credited with being the first European to discover San Diego, Native Americans living here at the time insisted he was number two.

When Cabrillo's party of explorers dropped anchor in San Diego Bay on September 28, 1542, a crowd of Native Americans stood on the shore watching. As soon as the explorers began rowing ashore all the Indians fled, except three.

Those three were given gifts and questioned by way of sign language. When asked why the crowd on the beach ran away, the three Indians indicated that people resembling Spaniards had previously arrived further inland. These men had caused considerable harm to the villagers.

Puzzled, the sailors returned to the vessel and reported their findings. Cabrillo ordered his men to stay aboard ship until nightfall, when he sent a few men to shore to fish with a net.

The Indians shot arrows at the fishing party. Three were wounded.

On the third day in port, Cabrillo's party began to get a clearer picture. According to the Cabrillo National Monument Foundation's translation from the original log of Bartolomé Ferrer, Cabrillo's chief pilot, the Indians were familiar with Europeans and had previously engaged them in battle:

> They showed that they (the bearded men) had crossbows and made gestures with their right arm as if they were spearing. They went running as if they were on a horse, and for that reason they were afraid.

Among plausible explanations is that one or more expeditions beat Cabrillo to the area we now call San Diego. Written accounts refer to a 1539-40 expedition led by explorer Melchior Díaz that explored the Colorado River delta area around Yuma. He purportedly sent scouts across the river well into what would later become San Diego County.

Others believe that Hernando de Alarcón sailed up the Colorado River at about the same time Díaz and men from his expedition crossed the river to the now-California state side.

Still others believe that a side party from Francisco Vázquez de Coronado's 1540 expedition crossed the Colorado River. Any of these other possible early excursions into the greater San Diego area would explain why the Indians at San Diego Bay seemed already familiar with the Europeans.

While Juan Rodríquez Cabrillo is generally credited with being the first European to discover San Diego, Indians present when he landed in 1542 made signs that they had previously engaged bearded white men in battle. *Image courtesy National Park Service.*

Cabrillo Festival Erupts Into International Spat

Was he Spanish explorer Juan Cabrillo, or Portuguese explorer Joao Cabrilho? We may never know. But a debate over the explorer's nationality erupted in San Diego at the Cabrillo Festival in the mid-1980s, ruffling diplomatic feathers and threatening the festival's future.

While history shows Cabrillo sailed for the Spanish government, a dispute exits whether the explorer was of Spanish or Portuguese origin. The inscription on Cabrillo's statue at Cabrillo National Monument is decidedly Portuguese, no doubt because the statue was carved by Portuguese sculptor Alvaro de Bree. Note the archaic spelling. *Author photo.*

Most historians agree that European explorer Juan Cabrillo entered San Diego Bay on Sept. 28, 1542, and anchored his two vessels, *San Salvador* and *Victoria,* for six days.

There seems little dispute that Cabrillo sailed for the Spanish government when he made his discovery.

What lives on is a long-standing dispute between the Portuguese and Spanish communities whether Cabrillo was Portuguese or a Spaniard.

Divided chiefly along lines of nationalities, many Portuguese are adamant that Joao Cabrilho was Portuguese and that history was rewritten during Spain's rule of California. They claim Joao Cabrilho was changed to the Spanish version of Juan Cabrillo to reflect that Spain, not Portugal, was behind the discovery of what is now California.

That dispute boiled over in earnest during the 1985 Cabrillo Festival. During the Sept. 28 ceremony — attended by high embassy officials of Spain and Portugal — a priest blessed Portuguese explorers and sailors and entirely omitted reference to Spain.

Feeling slighted, the Spanish consul general in Los Angeles protested and threatened to boycott all future Cabrillo Festivals. Spanish residents of San Diego further protested that the festival itself was weighted in favor of Portugal.

So festival organizers, most of whom were Portuguese, began asking historians for opinions and interpretations on Cabrillo's nationality. They didn't like what they heard.

An official from the Los Angeles County Museum of Natural History replied, "The preponderance of the evidence shows he was born in Spain…(Cabrillo's) family thought he was born in Spain, his friends thought he was born in Spain, none of his contemporaries said he was born in Portugal."

Although no direct proof exists in the form of birth certificates or baptismal records, Cabrillo was most certainly a Spaniard, he said.

Portuguese festival organizers scoffed at the idea of a "Spanish Cabrilho," and threatened to boycott the festival.

Emotions ran high until the 1986 festival president diffused the situation by pointing out that the Iberian Peninsula, which contains both Spain and Portugal, was mainly under religious, not national rule during the 1500s.

"The idea of nation-states was just evolving. National identity is more important to us now than it was for him," he said. Cabrillo, or Cabrilho's, nationality is just not that important, he concluded. His explanation smoothed ruffled feathers and the festival was not interrupted.

There are those who still argue the issue. But despite the fact that the accepted spelling of the explorer's name is the Spanish Cabrillo, the festival itself has a decidedly Portuguese flair.

The nationality of explorer Juan Cabrillo has long been the subject of dispute between San Diego's Portuguese and Spanish communities. One historian, when pressed, dodged the question entirely by saying Cabrillo was a native of the Iberian Peninsula. The Cabrillo National Monument houses a life-size waxwork of the explorer. *Author photo.*

Cabrillo Statue History

In 1935, the Portuguese government came up with the idea of creating a statue to commemorate the explorer Joao Cabrilho. The statue was to be displayed at the 1939 World's Fair in New York, then given to the state of California.

The work of creating the limestone edifice was assigned to noted Portuguese sculptor Alvaro de Bree. But de Bree was unable to finish the project in time for the fair, so authorities decided to retain the statue and deed it directly to the state of California at the 1940 International Exposition.

The statue was delivered in time for the exposition, but upon un-crating in San Francisco, organizers discovered the statue had been damaged in transit — so much that it could not be displayed. A white elephant among California state belongings, the statue was re-crated and stored in a private citizen's garage until 1940 when state Senator Ed Fletcher and Lawrence Oliver had it moved to San Diego. At some point in time during that period, a crude and highly visible repair was made to the statue.

From 1940 through 1948, the statue of Cabrilho was displayed at the Navy Sonar School on Point Loma. In 1949 it was moved to the Cabrillo National Monument and exhibited near the old Point Loma lighthouse. In 1966, the park service moved the statue to a site near the park's visitor center.

But decades of exposure to wind, rain, and sunlight severely eroded the limestone statue, and by 1983 it became apparent the edifice was deteriorated beyond repair.

A fundraising campaign began in 1983 to pay for the construction of an exact replica. A large donation by Mrs. Marion Reupsch in 1985 made the replacement possible.

In October, 1985, the Cabrillo Historical Society commissioned Joao Charters Almeida, a Portuguese sculptor with an international reputation, to supervise the carving of the statue.

The new Cabrillo sculpture was shipped to San Diego aboard a Portuguese navy frigate and dedicated in 1988.

The original statue was placed in museum storage at Cabrillo National Monument.

Coronado Bridge, City, and Islands Named for Failed Explorer

The name *Coronado* enjoys prominence in San Diego; denoting a bridge, a city, and a group of islands visible just 16 miles offshore in Mexican waters. All share the name of an explorer who might be considered a "failure."

While many readily associate the name Coronado with Francisco Vázquez de Coronado, Spanish conquistador who searched the New

Francisco Vázquez de Coronado searched the Southland for treasure, but never set foot in San Diego. This painting by Nevin Kempthorne was commissioned for the National Park Service's Coronado National Memorial in Hereford, Arizona. *Courtesy National Park Service.*

World for treasure, few realize that the explorer failed so miserably in his real quest — to find and bring back treasure — that he was actually put on trial when he returned home.

Coronado set out from mainland Mexico in 1540 in search of the legendary Seven Golden Cities of Cíbola and another fabulously wealthy country, Quivira.

Leading an expedition, Coronado zigzagged across the southwestern United States — venturing east as far as present-day Wichita, Kansas.

The idea that these legendary sites existed were given credence when a shipwrecked sailor, Álvar Núñez Cabeza de Vaca, found the willing ear of Antonio de Mendoza, Viceroy to New Spain (now Mexico) in 1536.

Cabeza de Vaca claimed he had been shipwrecked off Florida in 1528 and had wandered throughout (now) Texas and northern Mexico before finding his way back to society.

Based on his claims, Mendoza sent an expedition in 1539 led by a black slave known as Estéban and priest, Fray Marcos de Niza.

Although the expedition failed to physically reach the fabled Seven Golden Cities of Cíbola, Fray Marcos claimed to have seen them in the distance. Some accounts state that he based his testimony on assurances by an Indian guide who claimed to have seen them.

That was enough for Mendoza, who organized a second, two-pronged attempt to reach the cities.

By sea, Mendoza sent two ships under the command of Hernando de Alarcón. By land, Mendoza sent Coronado with a party of some 300 Spaniards, hundreds of Indians and native slaves, horses, and herds of sheep, pigs, and cattle.

Coronado's expedition proceeded up the west coast of Mexico. From there, they entered what is now southern Arizona in April 1540. Moving northward, Coronado came upon a Zuni pueblo in western New Mexico but found no gold. Coronado then sent out a scouting party that made it to — and some say forded — the Colorado River somewhere between California and Arizona.

Coronado spent two more years in search of Cíbola and Quivira before returning to Mexico City in 1542.

After recounting his findings to Mendoza, Coronado was labeled a colossal failure. The explorer was put on trial for incompetence, but acquitted.

He later became a provincial governor, but in 1544 was convicted of corruption, negligence, and atrocities against Indians. Coronado returned to Mexico City, where he died the same year.

The Battle of San Diego

Unlike counterparts on the East Coast, San Diego Harbor has not been the site of numerous naval gun battles.

But in 1803, cannons blazed in the legendary "Battle of San Diego."

At the time under Spanish rule, San Diego was an unauthorized trading port for English and Russian ships. Little could be done to prevent these boats from trading at the expense of Spain, until English explorer George Vancouver visited in 1793 and drew up plans for a harbor fortification. Shortly thereafter, the Spaniards took Vancouver's advice and established Fort Guijarros on a rocky rise just inside the harbor's entrance at the narrowest point (now known as Ballast Point).

Like all good harbor fortifications, it was positioned so that ships would need to pass beneath it both upon entering and leaving the port.

During the next few years, two Yankee ships visited San Diego. The first such visit was on Aug. 25, 1800, when Captain Charles Winship's brig *Betsy* dropped anchor in the bay, asking for food and water. After *Betsy's* visit, word soon spread among seafarers that an enormous colony of sea otters inhabited the San Diego area. Highly valued for their fur, the sea-otter furs were prized by Yankee traders for sale in China. Naturally, Spain desired to keep the fur trade for itself.

In February 1803, there appeared off the San Diego coast another ship, *Alexander*. With many of the crew nearly dead from scurvy and the ship almost out of water and in dire need of repair, *Alexander* was desperately in need of safe haven. The ship was allowed in San Diego Harbor on the condition that it did not engage in otter fur trade.

But contrary to the captain's promises, in short order *Alexander's* crew managed to amass a stockpile of nearly 500 otter furs. Furious, the Spaniard confiscated the pelts and forced *Alexander* to leave port.

Alexander's sails had barely disappeared below the horizon when a new set of sails appeared. These belonged to the brig, *Lelia Byrd*, out of Portsmouth, Virginia.

Captain William Shaler asked for and received permission to drop anchor and bring firewood and water on board *Lelia Byrd*, but was under strict orders not to try to collect any otter furs.

Within a short time, the commandante of San Diego heard news that the crew of *Lelia Byrd* was actively procuring pelts. Beyond breaking trade laws, the commandante found out that the American crew had bribed one of his guards and stolen his own personal cache of pelts.

The commandante quickly seized part of *Lelia Byrd's* crew. That night, Captain Shaler led the remainder of his crew to the jail, overpowered the jailers, freed the captive crewmembers, and returned to his ship, still anchored in the harbor.

But this left the captain with only two options; try to sail past the cannons at Fort Guijarros or wait on board ship and face eventual capture.

At first light, *Lelia Byrd* hoisted sail and began to ride a very light morning breeze. Cannoneers at Fort Guijarros opened fire, but *Lelia Byrd* returned fire with cannons of her own, forcing the fort's gunners to duck for cover.

The brig slipped out of San Diego Harbor with broken rigging and some minor hull damage after the very brief, yet historic, Battle of San Diego.

Smuggling, thievery, and betrayal led to the 1803 Battle of San Diego in which the U.S. flagged Lelia Byrd was forced to run a Spanish blockade to escape capture. *Image, 'The Escape of the Hijacking of Lelia Byrd (1803)' by Jerry MacMullen, courtesy San Diego Maritime Museum.*

San Diego's Trail of Tears
The Cupa Indian Expulsion

Many people are aware of the 1838 expulsion of the Cherokee from Georgia, called the Trail of Tears. In that saga of American history, approximately 15,000 members of the Cherokee Nation and other tribes were forcibly uprooted and made to walk nearly 1,000 miles from Georgia to Oklahoma. Many did not survive.

But few know that a similar expulsion, on a much smaller scale, happened here in San Diego.

Local Cupeño Indians refer to it as "the removal."

Smaller in number than most native American tribes in southern California, countless generations of Cupeño once occupied mountain territory near the headwaters of the San Luis Rey River, about 50 miles northeast of San Diego. The area encompasses a natural hot spring, sacred to the Indians. Today that spring is known as Warner Springs.

Contact with Europeans was relatively limited until the mid-1800s when miners following the gold rush trail and an assortment of settlers began encroaching on the native lands.

But behind the scenes, a succession of land grants passed through Mexican and American hands, taking legal ownership from them even as they lived on their ancestral lands.

In the mid-1840s, the land was granted to Juan José Warner, a Connecticut-born Yankee.

A few years after California became a state, officials decided to tax the Indians. Despite decades of oppression by federal, state and local officials, the Cupans begrudgingly paid the $600 assessment.

Tensions mounted further when Cupeño clan-leader Antonio Garra attempted to unite southern Californian Indians and organize a revolt against all foreigners. Garra and his son convinced many Indian tribes in the region to join in the fight.

On November 21, 1851, a group of Indians raided Warner's Ranch. They killed four men, looted and burned buildings, and made off with livestock.

The revolt was put down. Garra, his son, and a renegade American sailor named William Marshall, who was married to Garra's daughter, were captured and executed. The village of Cupa was burned.

After the attack, Warner left his ranch to the hired help. The Cupa continued to live at the springs, using its water to irrigate farmland and for daily use.

But word spread throughout southern California of the medicinal value of Warner Springs' mineral water.

Visitors came to the springs and paid to bathe in the pools. Some Cupa rented their homes to guests while others made baskets and mats to sell to tourists.

But while they did so a lawsuit was working its way through the state court. Former Governor John Downey had acquired the land in 1880 and had filed a lawsuit demanding eviction of the Cupa from the property. That lawsuit was to trudge on past Downey's death in 1894.

In court, the Cupas argued that Mexican law, as well as the Treaty of Guadalupe Hidalgo, precluded takeover of their land. But the state court sided with Downey's heirs. In 1901 the U.S. Supreme Court ordered the Indians evicted. The Indians were declared "trespassers" on their own lands.

During a meeting with government officials at Warner Springs in 1902, Chief Cecilio Blacktooth was asked where else the Cupa would like to live. Mrs. Celsa Apapas translated his reply:

> You ask us to think what place we like next best to this place where we always live. You see that graveyard out there? There are our fathers and grandfathers. You see the Eagle Nest Mountain and that Rabbit Hole Mountain? When God made them he gave us this place. We have always been here.
>
> We do not care for any other place. It may be good but it is not ours. There is no other place for us. We do not want you to buy us any other place. If you do not buy this place, we will go into the mountains like quail and die there, the old people and the women and the children.

Nevertheless, the tribe was ordered to relocate with the Luiseño tribe on the 10,000-acre Pala Reservation.

On the morning of May 12, 1903, Indian Bureau agent James Jenkins and 44 armed teamsters arrived to carry out the eviction.

Belongings and clothing were tossed into carts. At bayonet point and under threat of cracking whips, about 100 villagers were forced to march to Pala. The 40-mile journey took three days, and has been called the Cupeño "Trail of Tears."

Today, the Cupa and the Luiseño live together in harmony and consider themselves one people — the Pala.

Many of those who trace their ancestry to Cupa take part in an annual May event called Cupa Day Celebration. Celebrants offer prayers to the sacred directions — east, south, west, and north. They pray to the earth and sky.

On the 100th anniversary of "the removal" in 2003, tribal members reserved rooms in their ancestors' cottages and enjoyed the hot springs much like their ancestors did.

The Cupeño people of northeast San Diego County were forced to march from their ancestral lands after former California Governor John Downey acquired the property and filed a lawsuit demanding eviction. *Library of Congress photo.*

San Diego Almost Became an Industrial Steel Town

San Diego may not have grown into the clean and beautiful city it is today had the visions of Dr. Charles Eames been realized. The city would have become a steel-factory town — a Pittsburgh, Pennsylvania, of the west.

In the spring of 1889, as was most of the nation, San Diego was in the midst of a severe financial downturn. It is said that even the pickpockets had left town, tired of lifting wallets full of IOUs.

It was then that a Pittsburgh steel magnate decided he needed a huge West Coast plant and commissioned a dapper, monocled Englishman named Dr. Charles Eames to find him a site.

Eames arrived by steam locomotive, settled into the best room at the Horton House Hotel, and began wining and dining the press. Within days of his arrival, Eames announced firmly that he would erect an iron and steel producing factory.

Eames purchased a large hunk of bayside land in Point Loma and built a pier to accommodate ocean-bound freighters. He then telegraphed an order to San Francisco for all the machinery needed to produce nails and wire screen.

The factory itself was immense, requiring 400,000 feet of lumber and 75 tons of corrugated roofing iron to construct. Eames brought iron ore from Baja California, Mexico, and coal from San Francisco. He hired dozens of men and soon began producing nails and screen in abundance. The Santa Fe Railroad agreed to build a switch yard to service the facility as soon as the mill was in operation.

"There's a great market on the West Coast for all sorts of steel products," he told the press. "It's a long way from Pittsburgh and freight rates from the East are far too high. We'll make money."

Eames told backers he would immediately begin construction on several steam schooners to bring in materials and added that as soon as the nail and wire project was in complete operation, he would install a full-sized steel plant capable of turning out 100 tons of high-quality steel a day. Soon, he said, shipyards would open, auxiliary factories would be built and the economy would flourish again.

Eames' numbers looked promising on paper. With its own steamers, the company could bring in coal to fire the furnaces at less than five dollars per ton. The same steamers would carry away the nails, screen, and other steel products.

But back in the real steel city, the Pittsburgh steel magnate who was Eames' main backer had a fatal heart attack. Soon after the funeral, the company's board of directors boarded the first west-bound train for San Diego.

Eames and a group of prominent citizens met the board of directors at the train station and wined and dined them before taking them on a carriage ride to tour the plant. The proud Eames pointed to the five kegs of nails recently produced at the plant.

"Good grief," one board member snapped at Eames. "You may know how to make steel but you don't know beans about locating a plant. You're 200 miles from iron ore, 600 miles from coal, and a million miles from making a red cent. Close her down."

Before returning to Pittsburgh, the board proposed to pay the city of San Diego a flat-rate $5,000 settlement for losses resulting from promises Eames had delivered.

But by this time, the movers and shakers of San Diego were bent on becoming Pittsburgh west and hotly refused the board's offer.

A small amount of money was raised for the purpose of finding new backers for the closed steel mill, but few bankers were willing to shoulder the risk and soon the plant fell into ruin. Scavengers made off with much of the machinery and the building finally caved in on itself.

Today, one short road at the north end of San Diego Bay bears the name Bessemer Street, a name given by Dr. Charles Eames himself in reference to the famous English steel engineer, Sir Henry Bessemer.

Folks living near Bessemer Street say that occasionally an old iron nail or pellet will surface in a backyard or at the beach after a hard rain.

"Impossible Railroad" Plans Derailed

Those who enjoy travel by train often wonder why San Diego is not the terminus of an east-west railroad.

Be it passengers or freight, all rail connections to this southwest-ern-most city must be routed through Los Angeles, about 90 miles to the north. San Diego is but a branch line.

In 1919, a railroad did directly connect San Diego with the nation's heartland. But the San Diego & Arizona Railway took 12 years to build, ran sporadically for 30-some-odd years, and ultimately collapsed, living up to its nickname, "The Impossible Railroad."

Soon after the Mexican War, the government and public began calling for an east-west railroad link. The U.S. Army moved most of its troops and equipment by rail and was eager to make it easy to shore up its forces in southern California. The public also wanted a pleasant

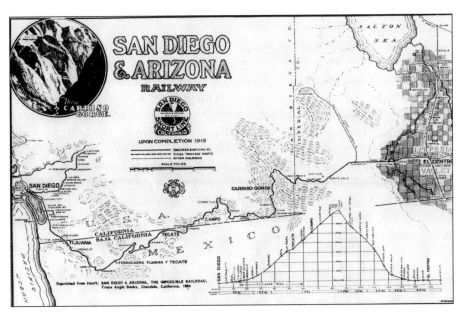

Rugged canyons east of San Diego forced builders of the San Diego & Arizona Railway to employ several hairpin turns, construct numerous tunnels and trestles, and dip into Mexico. *Photo courtesy San Diego Railway Museum.*

mode of travel to connect San Diego with the rest of the nation, a connection that ships and stagecoaches could not provide.

But early surveyors could only scratch their heads. While the majority of the connection from Arizona and beyond to San Diego could be made relatively simply across the desert, laying track over the last few dozen miles was nearly impossible.

Between the rolling foothills east of San Diego and the flat desert stood some of the steepest slopes imaginable, they reported. Carving a level bed for railroad tracks through one 11-mile stretch alone, the Carrizo Gorge, would require 17 tunnels between 200 and 2,600 feet long. The severe slopes would also require 14 side-hill trestles, where the inside rail would perch on solid ground and the outside rail would be supported by half of a bridge. To climb about 3,000 feet in such narrow confines, the grades would be so steep as to tax the locomotives' power on the incline and brakes on the decline.

The curves would be so tight as to strain the trains' ability to stay on track. To make matters more difficult, the only way to make the plan work would be to dip the railroad in and out of Mexico.

Physical construction of the line would tax the imagination. Getting water to the work camps would be a problem, especially in the summers when temperatures often exceeded 100 degrees. Carving a bypass road for the construction of nearly every tunnel and side-hill trestle would in effect double the amount of grading along the route's most severe sections.

Even with the sharpest estimating pencil, the Carrizo Gorge section alone would cost $4 million and the entire railroad would top $18 million (more than $340 million in present-day spending power).

Nevertheless, in 1906 a private consortium announced that "The Impossible Railroad" would soon become a reality. Condemnation proceedings to obtain rights-of-way and land for stations, switching yards, and other facilities were begun in San Diego and teams of surveyors were sent to map out the exact route. Amid much fanfare, a groundbreaking ceremony was performed in 1907 near the foot of 28th Street.

Contracts were awarded and a right-of-way was obtained through Mexico, but initial construction was delayed when the nation fell into a depression. In 1908, grading finally began and the first locomotive arrived from Pittsburgh, albeit via Los Angeles.

Construction stumbled when one of the consortium's partners died, but in 1910 a section of track connected San Diego to the Mexican resort Agua Caliente.

Mexico suffered a spate of revolutions in 1911 and construction was further delayed when virtually all Mexican laborers walked off the job. Months later, the revolution was quelled and the workers returned. The year 1912 marked the beginning of a four-year lawsuit when an earlier partner tried to back out and recover his $3 million investment. By 1913, railroad service from the east took passengers to Tecate, Mexico, about 50 miles from San Diego.

But the world was on edge in 1914. WWI loomed, and construction slowed to a crawl. Problems arose with the railroad's right-of-way when U.S. troops landed in Veracruz and all American citizens were ordered out of Mexico. Hopes died for the railroad's completion in time for the 1915 Panama California Exposition in Balboa Park.

Although the big connection had not been made with the east, limited service was under way in 1916 when San Diego City's notorious rainmaker, Charles Hatfield, began his rainmaking project in the foothills. The floods of that year knocked out nearly every railroad bridge in the county, including some of those on "The Impossible Railroad."

One of the new locomotives sank in the mud and flipped onto its side. Even the limited rail service was suspended while the trestles were being rebuilt.

In 1917, the U.S. entered WWI and construction was slowed by labor shortages and the high costs of materials. By 1918 the track finally reached the foot of the infamous Carrizo Gorge. But a world-wide influenza epidemic hit the construction camps. When construction began

A 1932 tunnel cave-in forced construction of this 180-foot tall 600-foot long trestle over Goat Canyon. The San Diego & Arizona Railway ultimately ran out of steam. *Photo courtesy San Diego Railway Museum.*

again, workers were stymied by one of the tunnels at Carrizo Gorge — Tunnel Number 8.

Most of Tunnel Number 8 was being carved through solid rock. But when any progress was made, whole sections of loosened rocks would slide down inside the tunnel, blocking progress. One cave-in claimed the life of a worker.

Finally, on November 15, 1919 a gold spike commemorating the completion of "The Impossible Railroad" was driven into the ground. But jubilation was short lived. An avalanche closed Tunnel Number 7 in 1920. A subsequent inspection revealed more likely landslides. The decision was made to carve out the entire hillside above Tunnel Number 7 at a cost of more than $250,000. Train service was halted for months.

Flash floods and landslides caused more interruptions in 1926 and 1927.

A series of disasters struck in 1932. A suspected arson fire broke out in Tunnel Number 3. Although the ends were sealed up to smother the flames, the fire raged for four days. Finally the tunnel's roof caved in, halting rail traffic for nearly two months.

Shortly after service resumed, a gigantic landslide blocked Tunnel Number 15. Three months and $300,000 worth of track alignment and tunnel work later, service resumed.

Later that year, Tunnel Number 7 caught fire and the railroad line was closed until a bypass could be built around it.

Floods struck again in 1939.

The railroad worked well through the WWII years, but passenger traffic never really picked up after the war. In late 1950, the San Diego & Arizona Eastern Railway filed an application with the California Public Utilities Commission to abandon its passenger service. The last passenger train on "The Impossible Railroad" left San Diego at 7:05 a.m. on January 11, 1951.

Proposals to re-establish the railroad crop up every few years. Sections of the line have been recently reworked and are currently carrying cargo in a limited capacity. Maybe someday the Impossible Railroad will run again.

Modern day train buffs can ride segments of the Impossible Railroad departing from the San Diego Railroad Museum in Campo, 60 miles east of San Diego.

The William Randolph Hearst Yacht Murder Mystery

Perhaps no other legend is shrouded in mystery and intrigue as the murder of Thomas Ince aboard William Randolph Heart's yacht, *Oenida*, in the waters off San Diego in November 1924.

Although the story has never been proved — or disproved — there has been enough written about the subject to reconstruct what many believe happened: A jealous William R. Hearst was gunning for Charlie Chaplin when he mistakenly shot and killed 43-year-old Hollywood filmmaker Thomas Ince.

The story begins in San Pedro on November 15, 1924, when Hearst invited a dozen or more celebrities aboard *Oenida* to celebrate Ince's 43rd birthday. The weekend cruise was to take the revelers to San Diego and back, but with a meandering course designed to keep the luxurious 220-foot yacht outside the 3-mile limit, and beyond the jurisdiction of Prohibition-era authorities.

Among attendees, some of whom later disavowed they were ever on board, were Hearst, Ince, Chaplin, actress and longtime Hearst mistress Marion Davies, Hearst's personal doctor Daniel C. Goodman, and an up-and-coming Hearst Newspaper gossip columnist Louella Parsons.

The story has it that in the early hours of Monday, November 17, shortly after celebrating Ince's birthday, Hearst caught Chaplin kissing Davies. Hearst shot at Chaplin, missed, and struck Ince in the head instead.

The wounded Ince was unconscious, but still breathing, so Hearst ordered *Oenida* directly into San Diego Harbor.

But instead of summoning an ambulance and taking Ince directly to a San Diego hospital, Hearst allegedly used the ship's radiotelephone to bring an ambulance from Los Angeles to meet the vessel when it tied up.

According to a recent film on the Ince murder, "Cat's Meow," Hearst also summoned cars to ferry all the yacht's passengers back to Hollywood. Among the drivers was Chaplin's personal chauffer, Toraichi Kono.

While waiting for Chaplin to debark, Kono was stunned to see the unconscious Ince, severely wounded and still bleeding from the head, being carried off *Oenida* in a stretcher and placed in a waiting ambulance.

The next morning, a Los Angeles morning newspaper — a Hearst rival — splashed the headline, "Movie Producer Shot on Hearst Yacht!" But the paper did not repeat the headline in the evening edition. Instead, the paper printed the following day that Ince had died of acute indigestion.

The same day, the Hearst organization distributed a statement that Ince had fallen ill while visiting Hearst at his upstate ranch and that Ince had been rushed home where he had died in bed. Those who had sailed aboard *Oenida* greeted this version of Ince's death with intense skepticism.

Soon, the rumors made their way back to San Diego, where the district attorney's office began an investigation. But the district attorney was able to interview only Goodman, Hearst's own doctor, who disavowed any knowledge of the events on board *Oenida*. Goodman did offer, however, that on a previous train trip Ince had confided to him that he had a history of heart problems.

After being stonewalled by Goodman, the district attorney learned that Ince's body had been cremated very shortly after his death.

Without witnesses, a body, or a coroner's inquest, the district attorney dropped his investigation and advised the Los Angeles district attorney to look into the matter. There is no record of them having done so.

The legend has it that soon after Ince's last rites were administered, the mortgage on Ince's mansion and several rental properties were paid off in their entirety.

Gossip columnist Loella Parsons — who supposedly witnessed the actual shooting — was given a lifetime contract as a syndicated columnist for $1,000 a week, three times her salary before the cruise.

Marion Davies stayed by Hearst's side — as his mistress — for years until the multimillionaire newspaperman died at age 88.

Even after Hearst's death, passengers on the 1924 *Oenida* cruise remained tight-lipped about Ince's death — certainly adding grist to the rumor mill.

Author's note: Several years after this story debuted in the first edition of San Diego Legends, dear friend and fellow Scotsman John Campbell noticed something odd while perusing an Innis clan Web site. He called immediately to let me know that Ince is listed as an alternate spelling of Innis. "It just might be that Hearst shot a distant relative of yours," Campbell remarked.

CHAPTER 91

Poets Try to Capture
San Diego's Essence

While numerous poems have been penned in San Diego's honor, city officials do not recall ever having an official verse.

Among San Diego rhymes, these two may be noted for their dissimilarity:

San Diego — Our Queen

Soft purple mantles fold the mountain range,

Opal and scarlet robes drape sky and bay;

And then the over-tonings slowly change,

Up-flung in gleaming gold and pearl, and gray.

Night lays a velvet, diamond-spangled gown—

Reveals a rising crescent moon for crown.

Dropt down from sky — ships passing in parade,

Quick-silver nets form slumber laceries;

In perfumed gardens, night-birds serenade,

Unseen, midst romance and God's mysteries.

Engilding dawn lines Cuyamaca's spire—

Each rugged peak a jewel-pointed crest—

Gowns sky and sea with raiment born of fire,

Entraps the hills, and flows into the west.

O'er-draping sun-gold softly veils our queen,

Now clad in day-dream robes of blue and green.

—Royal Hand, 1936

In stark contrast with the opulent floral quality of Hand's vision of San Diego is Sam S. Porter's poem entitled, "San Diego." This undated verse was once used by the San Diego Chamber of Commerce and may be the closest thing to an official poem.

San Diego

Where the spring comes

in the summer,

The summer comes in

the fall,

The fall comes in the

wintertime,

And winter don't

come at all.

CHAPTER 92

Strange Early City Laws

Law is the highest reason implanted in Nature, which commands what ought to be done and forbids the opposite.

—*Roman statesman Cicero (106–43 B.C.)*

While thousands of ordinances have been "implanted in Nature" over the course of San Diego's history, some earlier statutes make less sense in today's world than they did then. The following ordinances were enacted during San Diego's first few decades of citihood: (For those who are wondering, it is practically impossible to say whether or not these early laws are still on the books.)

In 1876, the city made it unlawful to keep more than 50 pounds of gunpowder within one-half-mile of any residence except in a metal-lined chest on the ground floor inside a building. Such gunpowder chests must be kept within eight feet of the front door, the ordinance stated.

An 1885 ordinance prohibited the discharge of any gun, pistol, or cannon along San Diego Bay or from wharves. But lawbreakers could not be jailed and paid no fine, only the cost of prosecution up to $50.

Six miles per hour was the speed limit imposed on any mule or horse team within San Diego's business district in 1886. The limit outside the business district was 10 mph.

No mule or horse could be left unattended in 1886 in the city unless attached to a "dray, truck, car, delivery or freight wagon" or securely hitched or held by a person.

The following games were banned in 1886: poker, stud-horse poker, tan, fan-fan, faro, monte, roulette, lasquenet, rouge-et-noire, rondo, chuck-a-luck, and props.

In 1886 it became unlawful for the keeper of any "saloon, bawdy house, house of assignation or house of ill-fame" to remain open on Sunday.

Opium dens were not outlawed until 1886.

Only with a permit from the city's President of the Board of Trustees in 1886 could one carry a concealed, "pistol, sling-shot, brass or iron knuckles, iron bars as are usually carried by Chinamen, sand-club, dirk or bowie-knife."

In 1887 it became unlawful to burn rubbish between Second and Eighth streets, south of B Street.

It became illegal in 1887 to drive any mule, horse, or cattle over the iron bridge at Old Town at a speed faster than a walk.

It became a misdemeanor in 1887 for:

> Any person or persons, without having first obtained a license therefor, to engage in selling any medicine, implement, appliance or merchandise, or to advertise any physician, quack, surgeon, dentist or other person or business calling or vocation, by crying the same, singing songs, making addresses, telling anecdotes, jokes, etc., or performing instrumental music upon any of the public streets or places of the city of San Diego.

Pay was established for the 12 members of the 1887 San Diego Police Department at $80 per month for 11 officers and $105 per month for their chief.

In 1888 an ordinance was passed that, "all prisoners sentenced by Police Court shall constitute a chain gang." The prisoners were made to work between 8 a.m. to 5 p.m. daily and were forced to walk to and from the work site.

A $10 fine awaited anyone in 1888 who allowed any chicken, duck, turkey, or other fowl to enter the enclosed premises of any other person in the city. But it was an offense only if the offended party had previously given the chicken, duck, turkey, or other fowl's owner 3 days' notice that their fowl had been trespassing.

In 1889 land owners could be compelled by the city to clean and disinfect their trees with only three days' notice.

It became unlawful in 1889 for any engineer, passenger or pedestrian to cause a streetcar to stop and block a street, crosswalk, or intersection. Doing so could net a $50 fine.

An 1890 law prohibited blasting with gunpowder or any other explosive material within 20 feet of any brick building within the city.

A law passed in 1890 made it unlawful for any person to "shoot with what is commonly known as a 'nigger shooter,' or in any manner shoot or throw or send at or toward any person, animal, bird or building any missile or other thing, within the city of San Diego."

In November 1892, the City Council repealed its November 1891 ordinance requiring the licensing of all dogs.

The following monthly water rates were set by city ordinance in 1892: saloons, $2–$5; dental rooms, $1.50; bakeries, $2 per 25 barrels of flour used; blacksmith shops, $2–$3.50; water troughs on sidewalks, $2–$5;

bath tubs in private residences, 35 cents; public bath tubs $1.25; toilets in private residences, 35 cents; public toilets, $2 (urinals, 50 cents); water for hydraulic elevators in hotels, 15 cents per 1,000 gallons.

It became unlawful in 1893 for any city worker to work more than 8 hours per day.

A 1900 ordinance prohibited the discharge of fire arms in La Jolla Park "except in cases of self-defense or for the purpose of destroying noxious animals."

It became illegal in 1900 for any person to visit any place where a lottery was being drawn, prepared, set up, or conducted.

In 1901 it became illegal to possess a lottery ticket.

It became illegal for any person in 1901, except a police officer, to enter any place for the practice of gambling.

A 1901 law prohibited any person from owning, conducting, or managing a shooting gallery within city limits. It also banned the discharge of firearms between 10 p.m. and 7 a.m.

It became illegal in 1901 to beg or solicit alms for support or to make a business of begging. However, "no provision within this section shall apply to healthy beggars."

The speed limit for bicycles in 1901 was set at 8 mph.

A 1902 ordinance prohibited placing above the ground floor of a building, "any flower pot in a window sill so situated that it could be knocked out of said window and fall on sidewalk or street."

In 1902 it became illegal to keep beehives within 600 feet of any city road, street or highway.

Beginning in 1903, a drunk and disorderly person "making a loud noise, disturbance, or using any loud, noisy, boisterous, vulgar, or indecent language" faced a $50 fine or 25 days in jail.

Every fortune teller, seer, soothsayer, astrologer, mind-reader, palmist, and hypnotist had to pay $25 quarterly for a license beginning in 1903.

Beginning in 1904, all male employees of the city were required to be U.S. citizens and reside within city limits.

A 1904 law set the limit at three the number of cows that could be kept at any residence.

In 1904 a $50 fine would be levied on any person who used an "explosive cane or stick, bomb cane or stick, torpedo cane, or stick or any other cane or stick that explodes dynamite, cartridge or powder." The ordinance also called for one day in jail for every $2 of fine that went unpaid.

A 1904 city ordinance created a "Misdemeanor Room" on the county jail's second floor. It consisted of six cells including "one padded cell for insane persons." The city paid the county $10 per month rent.

In 1904 a law was passed prohibiting minors from visiting, entering, or loitering in any pool or billiard room.

In 1905 it became unlawful for any person in La Jolla Park to allow any "horse, colt, donkey, burro, ox, bull, cow, calf, hog, pig, sheep, or goat" to run at large.

An ordinance passed in 1906 made it illegal for anyone south of the San Diego River and east of San Diego Bay to run an irrigation system "during time of fire."

Another 1906 law regulated saloons. In order to avoid leaving open loopholes, the law read:

> It shall be unlawful for any person to keep a saloon, bar, barroom, tippling house, dram shop, store or other place, where any wine, beer, ale, or any spirituous, vinous, malt or mixed liquors or any intoxicating drinks are man-ufactured, sold, dispensed, or given away without first having obtained a license.

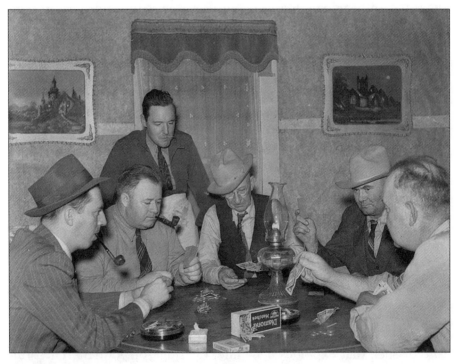

In 1886 the city banned most forms of gambling including poker, rouge-et-noire (a form of solitaire), roulette, and chuck-a-luck (a game played with three dice). Most forms of legal gambling today take place at area Indian casinos and the Del Mar Race Track. *Photo courtesy Library of Congress.*

CHAPTER 93

Movie Stars With
San Diego Connections

Robert Duval

Rather than following in the footsteps of his father, a naval rear admiral, native San Diegan Robert Duval chose to give his all to show business. After earning his degree in dramatic arts from Principia College in Illinois, Duval served a hitch in the Army during the Korean War before heading to New York where he studied at The Neighborhood Playhouse.

Sorting mail by night at the post office to pay rent and studying acting during the day, Duval suffered through his "salad days" until landing the lead role in Arthur Miller's *A View from the Bridge* in 1957.

Duval's silver screen debut came in 1963 when he starred as Boo Radley in *To Kill a Mockingbird*, which paved the way for his work in the *Godfather* films I and II, and as an unbalanced American colonel in Viet Nam in *Apocalypse Now.*

On the fifth Oscar nomination of his career, Duval finally captured the Best Actor Award for his portrayal of a down and out country western entertainer in *Tender Mercies,* partly by singing every song on the soundtrack and dancing a respectable two-step to boot.

Today, Duval lives on a Virginia ranch where he rides horses in competition and enjoys country music.

Whoopi Goldberg

In 1974, Caryn Johnson moved to San Diego and began developing skills as a comedic actor with the improvisational group, Spontaneous Combustion. During those very lean years, Johnson, better known by her stage name, Whoopi Goldberg, worked a string of odd jobs, including bricklayer, funeral-parlor cosmetician, bank teller, and dish washer at The Big Kitchen Restaurant in Golden Hill. As a single mother with a daughter, Whoopi was even forced into the welfare lines at times to help pay the bills.

But Whoopi finally caught the attention of a New York producer who offered her a show of her own, which ultimately became, Whoopi Goldberg: Direct from Broadway.

Whoopi's San Diego-based ascent to stardom found her starring in films such as *Sister Act I & II, Jumpin' Jack Flash, Ghost,* and *The Color Purple.*

Along the way, Whoopi has tirelessly worked on fundraising benefits such as Comic Relief, which has raised millions of dollars for the nation's homeless.

Regis Philbin

Among the most successful stars to ever call San Diego home, venerated television talk-show host Regis Philbin can say his TV career got started here.

Philbin is perhaps best known for the nationally syndicated, "LIVE with Regis & Kelly" and for launching "Who Wants to be a Millionaire?" in the United States.

But many longtime San Diegans best recall Philbin's talk show, "The Regis Philbin Show," which aired locally on KGTV.

Philbin got his start in the broadcasting business by bluffing his way into the office of a Los Angeles radio station manager. Telling the manager's secretary he was an old friend, Philbin succeeded in getting thrown out of the office, but not after leaving behind his resume and, apparently, the impression that he had some talent to offer. Philbin slunk back to New York and found work as a stage hand on the "Steve Allen Show." Two years later, the Los Angeles station manager called and offered him a job as a news writer.

Feeling underpaid, under-appreciated, and over worked, Philbin quit that job and moved to San Diego. In 1956 he found work as a reporter/broadcaster at KSON radio. "There, I learned to make it fun, make it different, and make it interesting," he said in his autobiography, *I'm Only One Man.*

Regis' reporting was fun, different, and interesting enough that local television executives began to take notice. Soon, he was lured away from radio by KFMB-TV, where he became a familiar face to San Diego television viewers, delivering quirky feature stories.

A year later he was hired by KOGO-TV to bring his features to the 6 o'clock news and to become anchorman for the late-night news. Part of his agreement with KOGO included the promise of his own talk show. "I finally got a late night show on Saturday nights," Philbin writes. "That was the start of it all for me."

After developing a host-chat routine that would ultimately become his trademark, Philbin left San Diego and plied his trade in Los Angeles for three years before moving back to New York and eventual super-stardom.

"My years on the West Coast were nice," he writes. "All that peace and sunshine — and tremendous local ratings. But it was an impossible place to do a live national morning show. The West Coast is the wrong coast because of the three-hour time difference."

In 1983, Philbin created, "The Morning Show" on WABC-TV. He was joined by Kathie Lee Gifford in 1985, where their vinegar/honey chemistry shot ratings through the roof. "The Morning Show" debuted before national audiences in 1988 with a new name, "LIVE with Regis & Kathie Lee."

The popular showman found co-host Kelly Ripa in 2001.

Now retired, Philbin and his wife Joy live in Manhattan with their two daughters.

Clevon Little

What would one of the most popular comedy films in history, Mel Brooks' *Blazing Saddles*, be without San Diegan Clevon Little hamming it up as a black sheriff in an all-white cow town?

Little was born in Oklahoma in 1939, moved to San Diego at age three, and discovered acting at Kearny High School. He pursued his career at San Diego City College and the Old Globe Theatre, then went on to San Diego State University but dropped out to help provide for his family of seven.

But Little returned and earned his bachelor's degree from SDSU in 1965 and won a television network competition for an American Academy of Dramatic Arts scholarship in New York.

His stage work landed him roles in *Purlie, MacBird!, Scuba Duba,* and *Jimmy Shrine,* where he worked closely with Dustin Hoffman.

Little's silver screen credits include *Once Bitten, Toy Soldiers,* and *Fletch Lives.* His television work landed him roles in, "All in the Family," "Police Story," and the made-in-San Diego series, "Simon and Simon."

Clevon Little died in October, 1992 after a struggle with cancer.

Gregory Peck

Few actors have left such a legacy to their communities as did the late Gregory Peck with the founding of the La Jolla Playhouse.

Born April 5, 1916, Eldred Gregory Peck was the son of a La Jolla pharmacist. After his parents divorced, Peck lived alternately in La Jolla and San Diego and passed through the fifth grade at La Jolla Grammar School.

At 10, Peck was sent to St. John's Military Academy in Los Angeles where he graduated ninth grade with the rank of captain. Peck moved again and attended San Diego High School in the early 1930s.

Peck's father desperately wanted young Eldred to become a doctor, so after graduating from San Diego High in 1933, Peck attended San Diego State College with hopes of transferring good science grades to the University of California at Berkeley.

During his scholarship at San Diego State, Peck discovered that being a doctor was not his calling, but he did transfer to U.C. Berkeley as an English major.

One day on campus, the drama department director approached the six-foot three-inch Peck. The professor explained he was in a pinch. He was doing a production of *Moby Dick* and had cast a short, stocky fellow as Capt. Ahab and needed a tall slender man to play Starbuck.

Peck tried out for the role, and one month later his acting career began.

Records show that Eldred Peck skipped the 1939 graduation ceremonies at Berkeley and took off for New York with a letter of introduction in his hand and $160 in his pocket. Somewhere on his transcontinental journey east he dropped the Eldred in favor of his middle name.

Gregory Peck first worked as a barker at the 1939 New York World's Fair, goading fairgoers to try various attractions and rides. After the fair's run, he began to find steady roles on stage throughout the East Coast, but he did not find significant success until being discovered by director Guthrie McClintic. Peck made his Broadway debut in 1942, received excellent reviews, and began finding regular work there until 1944 when Hollywood called.

Five years after leaving, Gregory Peck returned to California, a film star in the making.

A versatile actor, the tall, dark, and handsome Peck usually landed the role of leading man. His Hollywood career blossomed, but he never forgot his start in theater or his roots in San Diego.

Together with actors Dorothy McGuire and Mel Ferrer, Peck founded the La Jolla Playhouse Theater in 1947. La Jolla Playhouse thrives to this day as a not-for-profit, professional theatre-in-residence on campus at the University of California at San Diego.

Peck's career of 55 film titles includes John Huston's 1956 *Moby Dick*, in which he played the brooding Captain Ahab.

In 1962 he played Sam Bowden, an attorney being terrorized by a convict he helped incarcerate eight years earlier in *Cape Fear*.

But perhaps Peck's finest silver screen portrayal was that of Atticus Finch in *To Kill a Mockingbird*. His role as a Southern attorney defending a wrongfully accused black man earned him the Academy Awards Best Actor Oscar for 1962.

Gregory Peck died June 11, 2003, in his Los Angeles home. He was 87.

Kathy Najimy

Among the most outspoken homegrown San Diego stars, Kathy Najimy has performed in numerous movies including *Sister Act, Sister Act II, The Fisher King, Soap Dish,* and *Hocus Pocus.* Her role of Sister Mary Patrick in *Sister Act* earned her an American Comedy Award for funniest supporting actress.

Born in San Diego to Lebanese immigrant parents, Najimy studied drama at San Diego State University. She later appeared in more than a dozen musicals at the Old Globe Theatre, including *Godspell* and the ever-popular *Grease.*

In 2003, Kathy Najimy returned to the Old Globe Theatre for a critically acclaimed starring role in "Dirty Blonde." *Photo by Craig Schwartz, courtesy Old Globe Theatre.*

Najimy sang and danced her way through the Fox-TV special "Cinderelmo" and starred in the Emmy Award-winning TNT musical special "In Search of Dr. Suess."

She wrote and starred in the Off-Broadway hit *Kathy & Mo Show: Parallel Lives* and directed the Off-Broadway production *Back to Bacharach and David* and the Off-Off Broadway plays *Don't Get Me Started* and *I Can Put My Fist In My Mouth.*

In addition to being an actress, singer, writer, dancer and director, Najimy lends her voice and support to such causes as AIDS, Arab anti-discrimination, gay and lesbian liberation, and animal rights.

She has posed twice for People for the Ethical Treatment of Animals popular campaign, "I'd Rather Go Naked than Wear Fur," and received PETA's Humanitarian of the Year Award from Paul McCartney.

Among her influences are Marlo Thomas, star of the late 1960s-era TV series "That Girl" and daughter of Lebanese-American actor Danny Thomas.

"Marlo Thomas was Arabic and beautiful and smart and feminist, an author, actress, activist, and the first woman character on TV who was single, a career woman, not living at home and not supported by a man," she said at an American-Arab Anti-Discrimination Conference.

Najimy draws strength from her Arabic heritage. "Being Lebanese is something I have grown up being very proud of," she explained. "As a kid, I wore it like a badge. I was a different breed as far as I was concerned, the blessed breed. And I talked about it all the time."

When not lending her voice to worthwhile causes, Najimy can be heard characterizing the role of Peggy on the animated satire "King of the Hill."

Ted Giannoulas Popularized Sports Mascots

Sports fans everywhere love to watch the antics of costumed team mascots along the sidelines. Few realize that they probably should shout an extra cheer to San Diegan Ted Giannoulas, who popularized such suited stadium performances with his chicken act for KGB radio in the early 1970s.

Giannoulas graduated from Hoover High School with a focus on journalism. As a San Diego State University student, Giannoulas happened to be in the campus radio studio when a KGB executive rushed in, desperate to find someone to wear a chicken suit at the San Diego Zoo as part of an Easter promotion.

The five-foot-four inch Giannoulas met both KGB criteria; he fit into the chicken suit and he wanted to do it.

Once inside the chicken suit, Giannoulas discovered he possessed a penchant for physical comedy, and what started as a one-day stand evolved into a career as the radio station began booking him at sports events.

Giannoulas' comic relief antics made him a popular part of stadium events for the years that followed.

In 1979, Giannoulas broke away from his KGB radio ties and sued to win rights to perform free-agent style. Since then, the Famous San Diego Chicken has appeared at an average 250 events per year with pratfalls and antics that poke fun at sports teams, umpires, and audience members, almost always in the spirit of good fun.

Kelsey Grammer

While many associate Kelsey Grammer's name with the pompous, egotistical character Frasier Crane on the hit series "Frasier," few seem to recall the three-time Emmy Award winner followed his road to superstardom through San Diego.

St. Thomas in the U.S. Virgin Islands, Grammer's world was shattered when his father was shot and killed. Raised by his grandparents in New Jersey and Florida, Grammer's grandfather died before the future star reached his teens.

Perhaps finding solace in literature, Grammer began reading Shakespeare. Finding himself drawn to the stage, Grammer landed a role in his high school production of *The Little Foxes*.

Tragedy struck again when the then-20-year-old actor's sister was abducted and brutally murdered. Several years later, Grammer lost two half-brothers in a diving accident.

Grammer was accepted at the prestigious Juilliard School, but dropped out after two years.

Grammer moved to San Diego in the mid-1970s and worked at the Old Globe Theater where he played characters such as Denis, the adjutant, in Shakespeare's comedy, *As You Like It*, as well as other supporting roles in *Othello* and *Troilus and Cressida*.

After three years with the Old Globe, the bit actor moved on to appear in various productions across the nation, ultimately working his way to Broadway.

Grammer found occasional work in television and had regular roles in three soap operas including, "One Life to Live."

Then in 1984, Grammer's career took off with when he portrayed the sophisticated, charming, yet oh-so-neurotic Frasier Crane on NBC's "Cheers." Grammer's character became a regular fixture on the program until it was cancelled in 1993.

Although "Cheers" came to an end, the character Frasier Crane did not. A year after "Cheers," the man who once played bit roles at the San Diego Old Globe Theater helped steer "Fraiser" down the road to success.

San Diego fans of "The Simpsons" who recognize Grammer's vocal talents know he often provides the voice of Sideshow Bob, a brilliant criminal who often receives his come-uppance at the hands of Bart and Lisa Simpson. More recently, Grammer starred in the action flick, *Expendables 3.*

Raquel Welch

"Once you get rid of the idea that you must please other people before you please yourself, and you begin to follow your instincts — only then can you be successful," said San Diego's most well-known sex symbol, Raquel Welch.

Raquel attended San Diego's Bay Park Elementary School and graduated from La Jolla High School in 1957.

Welch won numerous beauty contests, including Miss Fairest of the Fair in 1957, before breaking into films in 1964 with bits in *A House is Not a Home*, Elvis Presley's *Roustabout*, and *A Swingin' Summer* in 1965.

Raquel worked to supplement her income as a model while landing larger and larger roles. Fantastic Voyage gave her a co-starring role which led to *One Million B.C.*, in which she displayed many of her prominent features.

Raquel auditioned for but did not land the role of "Gilligan's Island's" Mary Ann, and turned down the lead in *Barbarella*, a role that ultimately went to Jane Fonda in 1968.

Among 1960s films in which Welch interested audiences — mostly by her dazzling figure displayed in skin-tight costumes or bikinis were: *Fathom, Bedazzled, Lust, Biggest Bundle of Them All, Bandolero, Lady in Cement, Flareup, 100 Rifles*, and *The Magic Christian.*

Her starring presence faded in the 1970s, but she landed roles in *The Three Musketeers, The Four Musketeers, Bluebeard, Fuzz, The Wild Party, Mother, Jugs & Speed*, and *Crossed Swords.*

In the 1980s Raquel launched a cabaret act that made it to New York's Broadway. She also starred in several made-for-television movies including *Right to Die* and *Scandals in a Small Town.*

Even in her 40s, Welch was able to show off her figure in a series of exercise videotapes and accompanying fitness books. Raquel played herself in the 1994 comedy hit, *Naked Gun 33: The Final Insult.* She later starred in the San Diego-based television series, "American Family." More recently, Raquel landed roles on "CSI Miami" and the made-for-TV movie, *House of Versace.*

Welch once remarked about her early career, "Being a sex symbol was rather like being a convict."

Saint Didacus

One name stands out as the most famous of all people associated with San Diego. He wasn't born here. He never lived here. He didn't die here. In fact, he never heard of the city.

Yet his name — slightly altered from its Latin form — appears dozens of times throughout this book, is uttered daily throughout the world, and appears on virtually every city and county document ever produced.

Despite this popularity, few know the legend of the man behind San Diego's name, Saint Didacus.

Saint Didacus, or San Diego in Spanish, was a Franciscan lay brother born of poor parents in the early 15th century in San Nicholas del

Although the Spanish version of his name is uttered thousands of times every day, few know the legend of San Diego's namesake, Saint Didacus. *Author photo.*

Puerto, Spain. At a very early age, Didacus was sent to live under the direction of a devout hermit. He supported himself by weaving and selling mats and gathered a following for his conversations on religious matters.

Didacus lacked formal education, but he felt the calling and applied for admission to the Franciscan Order at the convent of Arizafa, where he was admitted as a lay brother.

Lay brothers are religious men occupied solely with manual labor and with the secular affairs of a monastery or friary.

Didacus entered the order with one simple goal: To serve all others. In a practice attributed to Saint Thomas Aquinas, the lay brother would undertake any task for his brethren. His only possessions were his tunic, a crucifix, a rosary, a prayer book, and a book of meditations, and these he never considered truly his own.

Historical sources cannot agree on the date, but between 1440 and 1445, Didacus was sent as a missionary to the Canary Islands to help bring Christianity to the islanders. At the time, few missionaries returned alive from such isolated and dangerous outposts, but Didacus accepted the assignment joyfully, hoping to win the crown of martyrdom. Didacus excelled at converting islanders and eventually was recalled to Spain.

Didacus was next sent to Rome for the canonization (sainthood) of St. Bernardine of Siena in 1450. There, illness overtook most of the 3,800 members of his order. Amid widespread disease and famine, Didacus found ways to nurture and comfort them, often by self-sacrifice.

One day in Rome, Didacus heard a poor woman lamenting. She had lit a fire in her large outdoor kiln, not knowing that her seven-year-old son had crawled inside to nap. Hearing her son's cries from the furnace and knowing she could not stop the flames, the mother raced to the friary.

Didacus sent her to the altar of the Blessed Virgin to pray while he and a group of people went to the oven. Despite that all the wood inside had burnt, the child was lifted from the oven without so much as a trace of burns.

The miracle was so evident that the canons of the Church dressed the lad in white in honor of the Virgin Mary.

After a long illness, Didacus died in 1463, clutching the cross he held so dear throughout his life. His body remained unburied for several months, exposed to the devotion of the faithful. In 1588, after years of urging by King Philip II of Spain, the church canonized Didacus.

King Philip had become a Didacus admirer after the king's son fell from a ladder and suffered what would have been a mortal head wound in 1562 — had he not been attended to by priests who exposed the young lad to items from Didacus' personal possessions.

San Diego Was Not the City's First Name

In its earliest iteration before Europeans first arrived in the mid-1500s, the Native American village near San Diego Bay was called Cosoy.

When Spanish explorer Juan Cabrillo first landed here on September 28, 1542, he named the bay San Miguel. This was in keeping with a long-standing Roman Catholic tradition to name important landmarks after saints — especially those with feast days celebrated on days nearest the day of discovery. Saint Michael's (San Miguel's) feast day is September 29.

Some 60 years later, using copies of Cabrillo's charts, Sebastián Vizcaíno sailed into San Miguel Harbor in November 1602. Despite orders from the Spanish admiralty not to change place names, Vizcaíno changed the charts from San Miguel to San Diego, in honor of St. Didacus' November 13 feast day and because his flagship was named San Diego.

Modern-day residents may cheer that Vizcaíno did not rename San Diego after some of the other Roman Catholic saints honored in November.

Imagine telling friends you're reading a book titled, *San Heliodorus Legends* or *Santa Wilfretrudis Legends!*

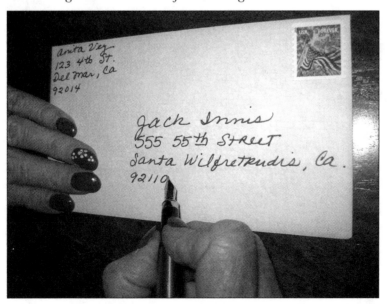

To contact the author directly, please visit www.jackinnis.com

SELECTED REFERENCES

Botts, Myrtle. *History of Julian.* Julian Historical Society, 1969.

Caughey, John and La Ree. *California Heritage.* Ward Richie Press, Los Angeles, 1966.

Fages, Pedro. *The Colorado River Campaign, 1781-1782* (edited by Herbert Ingram Priestley). University of California Press, Berkeley, 1913.

Fages, Pedro and Serra, Junipero. *Letters of Captain Don Pedro Fages & the Reverend President Fr. Junipero Serra* (introduction by Henry R. Wagner). Grabhorn Press, San Francisco, 1936.

Geiger, Maynard J. *Life and Times of Fray Junipero Serra; 1901-1977.* Academy of American Franciscan History, Berkeley, 1959.

Gerdes, Marianne. *The Impossible Railroad* (videorecording). KPBS, San Diego, 1999.

Johnson, M.E. *Indian Legends of the Cuyamaca Mountains.* M.E. Johnson, San Diego, 1914

Joyce, Barry Alan. *A Harbor Worth Defending: a Military History of Point Loma.* Cabrillo Historical Association, San Diego, 1995.

Lindsay, Diana. *Anza-Borrego A to Z.* Sunbelt Publications, San Diego, 2000.

McGroarty, John S. *California; its History and Romance.* Grafton Pub. Co., Los Angeles, 1911.

Nuttall, Donald. *Pedro Fages and the Advance of the Northern Frontier of New Spain, 1767-1782.* University Microfilms, Ann Arbor, Mich., 1964.

Pepper, Choral. *Desert Lore of Southern California.* Sunbelt Publications, San Diego, 1999.

Robinson, Alfred. *Life in California.* Peregrine Press, Santa Barbara, 1970.

Schad, Jerry. *Afoot and Afield in San Diego County.* Wilderness Press, Berkeley, 1992.

Waterman, T.T. *The Religious Practices of the Diegueño Indians.* Berkeley, The University Press. 1914.

Account of the Voyage of Juan Rodriquez Cabrillo. Cabrillo National Monument Foundation. San Diego, 1999.

National Audubon Society Field Guide to North American Weather. Alfred A. Knopf, New York, 1995.

Those wishing to learn more about San Diego's fascinating history may visit the California Reading Room at the San Diego City Library. There they will find books, magazines, and newspapers archived. The San Diego Historical Society at Balboa Park provides both text and photographic archives.

INDEX

W

Y

Z

San Diego Legends: The Events, People, and Places that Made History,
2nd edition
Jack Innis

The former editor of The San Diego Log describes many of the most fascinating characters and episodes that influenced the development of San Diego plus colorful celebrities that made headlines in past centuries.

Baja Legends: Historic Characters, Events, and Locations, **2nd edition**
Greg Niemann

A long-time Baja California journalist shares his extensive knowledge of the peninsula, its colorful past and booming present, in this easy-to-read reference book including its world-famous faces and still-famous places that keep this long finger of the continent in the international spotlight.

A Good Camp: Gold Mines of Julian and the Cuyamacas
Leland Fetzer

An informal history of the gold mines of the Cuyamacas, peopled with famous and not-so-famous Californians who made names for themselves on and in the rugged mountains and canyons of San Diego's backcountry. Includes a guide to the mines that can still be viewed today, plus those that offer guided tours.

Las Vegas Legends: What Happened in Vegas...
Greg Niemann

Tells the stories behind the headlines and history of "The Entertainment Capital of the World" aka "Sin City"— Vegas! From the first explorers and early founders to the famed entrepreneurs and entertainers who continue to shape this unique city.

Palm Springs Legends: Creation of a Desert Oasis
Greg Niemann

From the original Cahuilla inhabitants of the area, to the settlers who were drawn to the therapeutic waters of the original hot springs, you will get to know the stories that made Palm Springs famous.

San Diego County: Place Names, A to Z
Leland Fetzer

From the earliest peoples of the county to later settlers, each wave of immigration has left its mark on San Diego County in place names. From Spanish land grants, Mexican Ranchos, Indian Villages, and gold mines to family farms, tiny hamlets, and short-lived post offices - each has made a mark in history by putting a place name on a map. Here are over 1500 of these revealing portals into history.

San Diego: California's Cornerstone
Iris Engstrand

This work is a sweeping history of the region from the time of its indigenous people to the 21st century. Chapters cover the Spanish, Mexican, Victorian, World War eras, and the postwar boom, up to the founding of Petco Park. Includes a 25-page chronology of historical events, plus bibliography and index.

Strangers in a Stolen Land: History of Indians in San Diego County
Richard Carrico

This expanded 2nd edition tells the story of the Native Americans of San Diego County from 1850 through the 1930s - including the Kumeyaay (Ipai/Tipai), Luiseno, Cupeno, and Cahuilla - from their prehistoric origins through the Spanish, Mexican, and American periods. Contains previously unpublished maps and illustrations.

San Diego: An Introduction to the Region, 5th edition
Philip Pryde

This is the essential one-volume reference to the history, economics, demographics, natural features, and environmental issues of today's binational region on the Pacific borderlands, home to Native Americans for millennia with an insightful overview of "The County's First Residents."

Inspired By Nature: the San Diego Natural History Museum after 125 years
Iris Engstrand and Anne Bullard

This is a celebration of the institution's colorful past and points the way to an understanding and commitment to the future. The biodiversity of its binational region is wonderfully unique and the core of its Mission remains research, education, and conservation requiring true binational participation and leadership.

SUNBELT PUBLICATIONS

Incorporated in 1988 with roots in publishing since 1973, Sunbelt produces and distributes publications about "Adventures in Natural History and Cultural Heritage." These include natural science and outdoor guidebooks, regional histories and reference books, multi-language pictorials, maps, and stories that celebrate the land and its people.

Our publishing program focuses on the Californias which are today three states in two nations sharing one Pacific shore. Somewhere in the borderland between reality and imagination, a Spanish novelist called adventurers to this region five centuries ago: "Know ye that California lies on the right hand of the Indies, very near to the terrestrial paradise."

Sunbelt books help to discover and conserve the natural and historical heritage of unique regions on the frontiers of adventure and learning. Our books guide readers into distinctive communities and special places, both natural and man-made.

Visit us online at: www.sunbeltpub.com

ABOUT THE AUTHOR

Jack Innis, Legend Hunter

Jack Innis began freelance writing in 1990; took his bachelor's degree in Literature and Writing from California State University, San Marcos in 1994; and has since published more than 1,200 stories in national and local newspapers and magazines.

His career as San Diego's Legend Hunter began in 1999 when a magazine publisher gave him free rein — and every column inch in one entire publication — to tell history his way. Eschewing convention, Jack opted to hunt the annals of history to uncover legends, stories, and myths that were simply too fascinating to find in typical history books. That small magazine sold 10,000 copies and spawned subsequent books and articles containing stories once heard only around campfires — stories that entertain us and help us connect with our cultural heritage.

Since the first edition of San Diego Legends hit the bookstores in 2004, Jack has made more than 100 speaking appearances and is a frequent guest on XETV Channel 6 morning show, San Diego Living.

Jack loves giving multimedia presentations to clubs, groups, and organizations throughout San Diego County. For information on how to book an appearance or to contact the author, go to:

Deep in the bowels of a seacoast smuggler's cave (see story page 182), author Jack Innis uses a broken surfboard and a fiberglass panel from a wrecked canoe as ersatz snowshoes to keep him from sinking in quicksand. All in the name of research!

www.jackinnis.com